FIRE POWER

CREATED BY **ROBERT KIRKMAN**
AND **CHRIS SAMNEE**

ROBERT KIRKMAN
Creator, Writer

CHRIS SAMNEE
Creator, Artist

FIRE POWER VOLUME 1: PRELUDE
JULY 2020
ISBN: 978-1-5343-1655-3

Published by Image Comics, Inc. Office of
publication: 2701 NW Vaughn St., Ste. 780,
Portland, OR 97210. Fire Power™ (including
all prominent characters featured herein),
its logo and all character likenesses are
trademarks of Robert Kirkman, LLC and
Chris Samnee, unless otherwise noted.
Image Comics® and its logos are registered
trademarks and copyrights of Image
Comics, Inc. All rights reserved. No part
of this publication may be reproduced or
transmitted in any form or by any means
(except for short excerpts for review
purposes) without the express written
permission of Image Comics, Inc. All
names, characters, events and locales in
this publication are entirely fictional. Any
resemblance to actual persons (living or
dead), events or places, without satiric
intent, is coincidental. Printed in the U.S.A.
SKYBOUND.COM

SKYBOUND®
FOR SKYBOUND ENTERTAINMENT

ROBERT KIRKMAN Chairman
DAVID ALPERT CEO
SEAN MACKIEWICZ SVP, Editor-in-Chief
SHAWN KIRKHAM SVP, Business Development
BRIAN HUNTINGTON VP, Online Content
SHAUNA WYNNE Publicity Director
ANDRES JUAREZ Art Director
ALEX ANTONE Senior Editor
JON MOISAN Editor
ARIELLE BASICH Associate Editor
KATE CAUDILL Assistant Editor
CARINA TAYLOR Graphic Designer
PAUL SHIN Business Development Manager
JOHNNY O'DELL Social Media Manager
DAN PETERSEN Sr. Director of Operations & Events

Foreign Rights Inquiries: ag@sequentialrights.com
Licensing Inquiries: contact@skybound.com

image®

FOR IMAGE COMICS, INC.

ROBERT KIRKMAN Chief Operating Officer
ERIK LARSEN Chief Financial Officer
TODD MCFARLANE President
MARC SILVESTRI Chief Executive Officer
JIM VALENTINO Vice President
ERIC STEPHENSON Publisher / Chief Creative Officer
JEFF BOISON Director of Publishing Planning
& Book Trade Sales
CHRIS ROSS Director of Digital Services
JEFF STANG Director of Direct Market Sales
KAT SALAZAR Director of PR & Marketing
DREW GILL Cover Editor
HEATHER DOORNINK Production Director
NICOLE LAPALME Controller

IMAGECOMICS.COM

MATT WILSON
Colorist

RUS WOOTON
Letterer

KATE CAUDILL
Assistant Editor

SEAN MACKIEWICZ
Editor

ANDRES JUAREZ
Logo, Collection Design

CARINA TAYLOR
Production

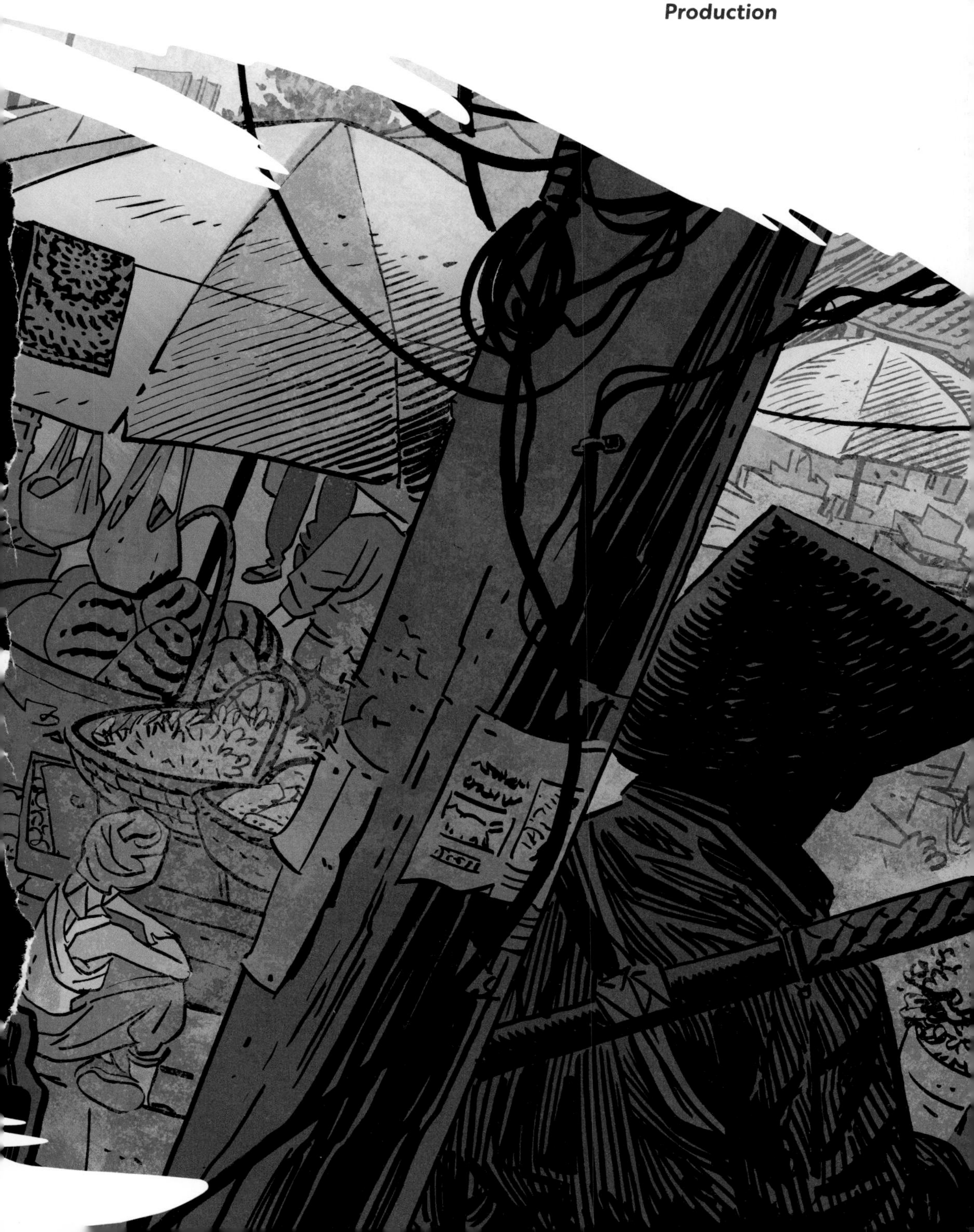

CHAPTER ONE

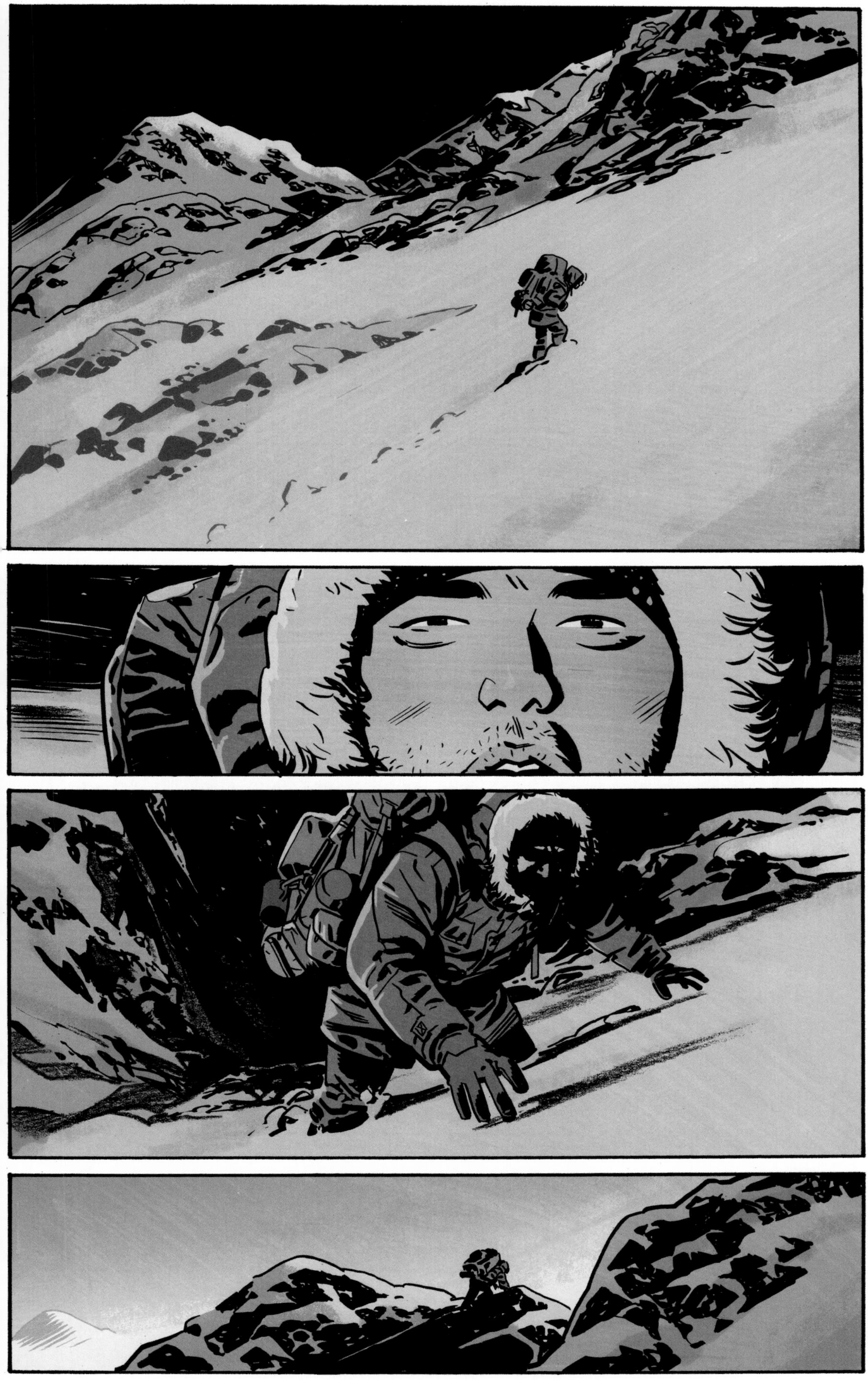

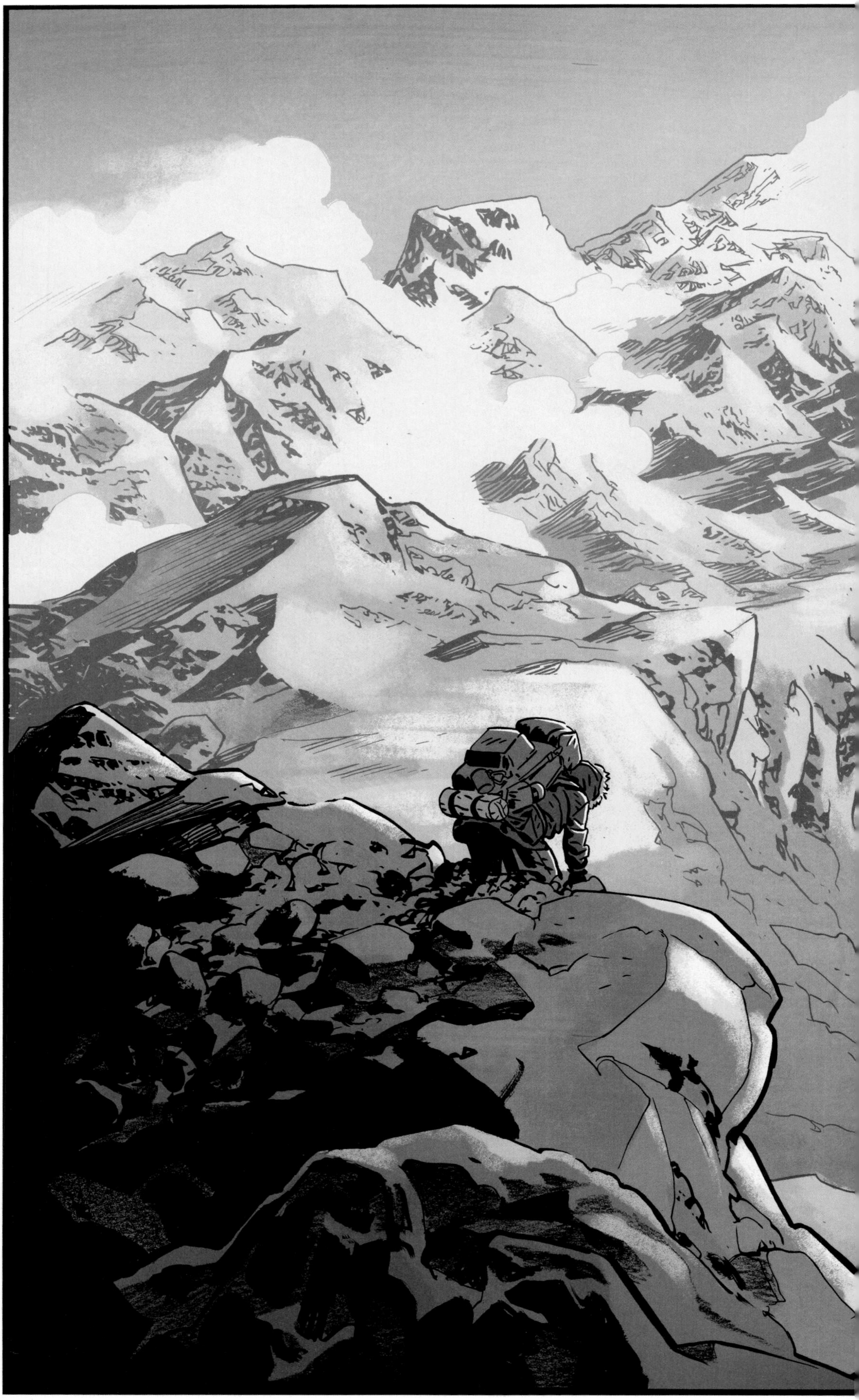

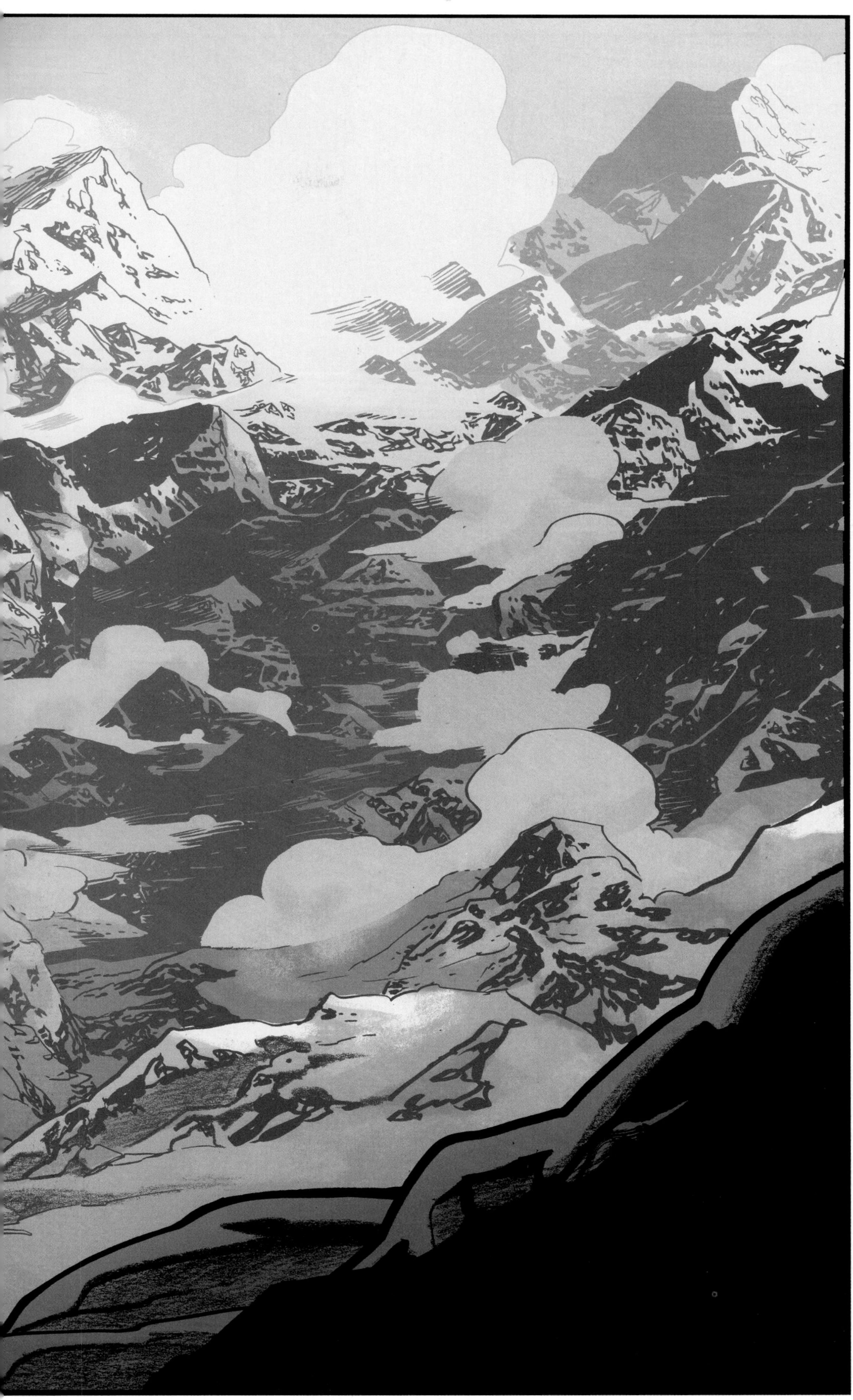

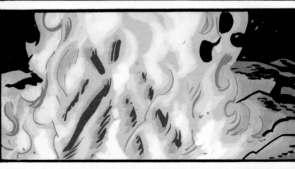

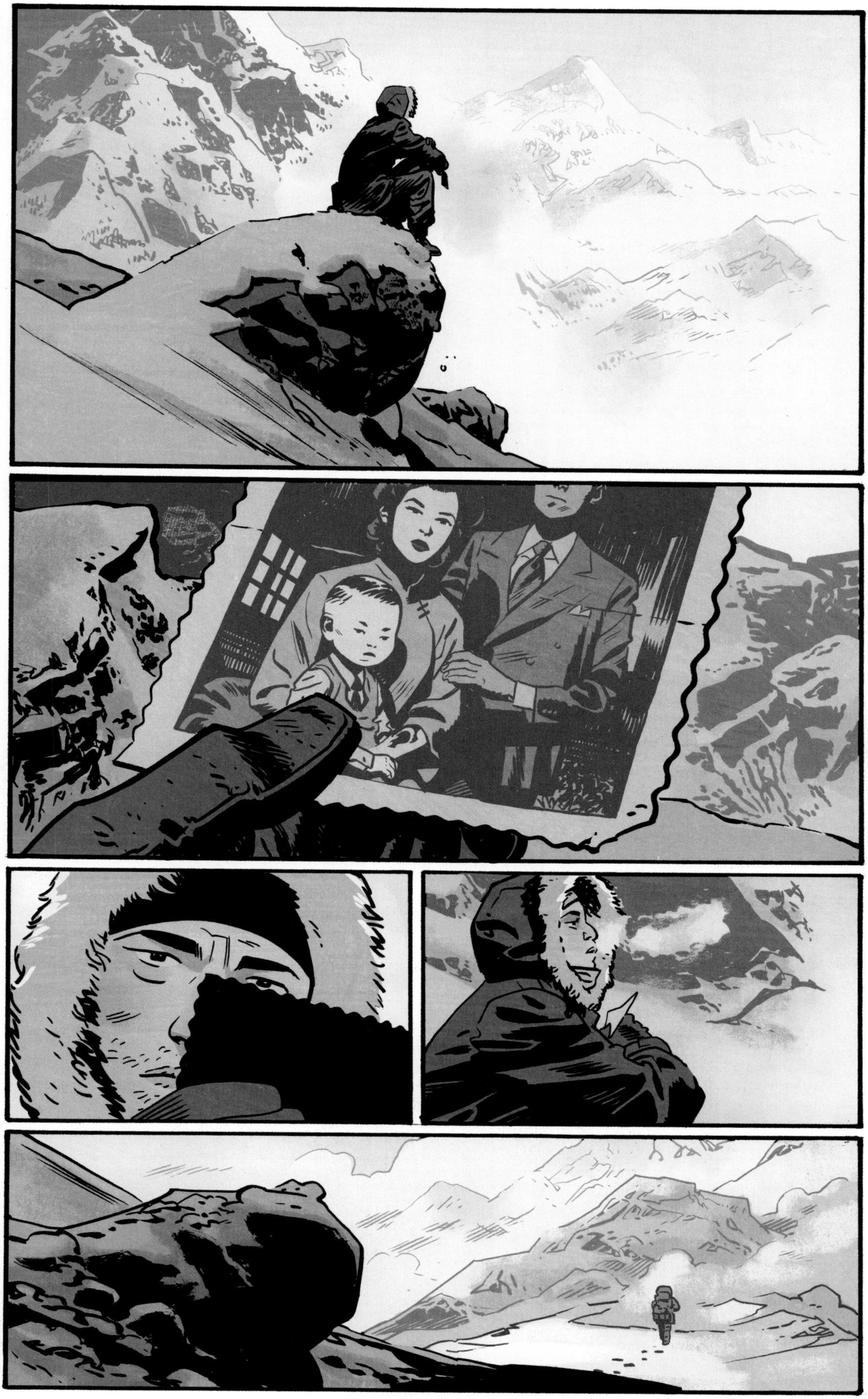

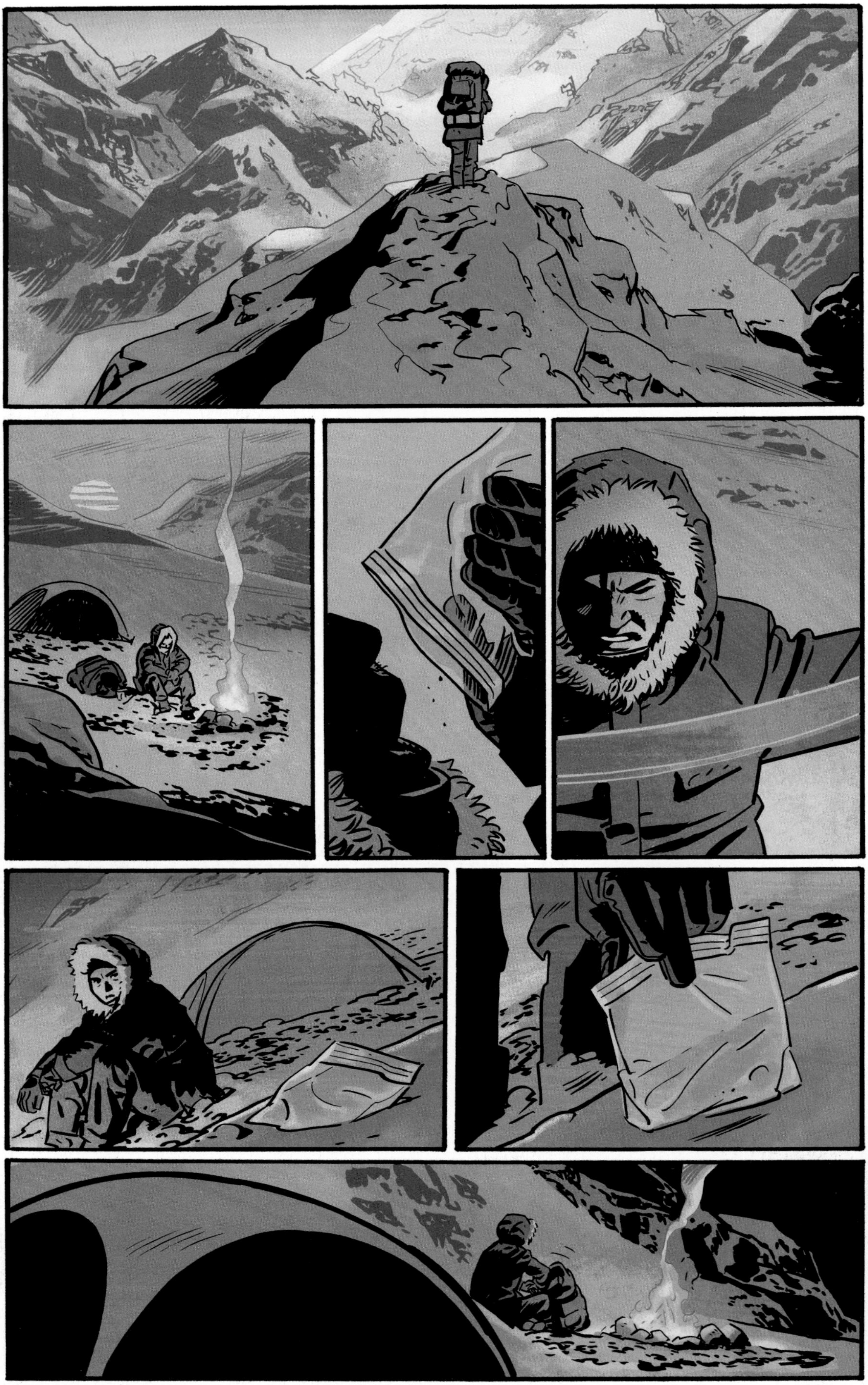

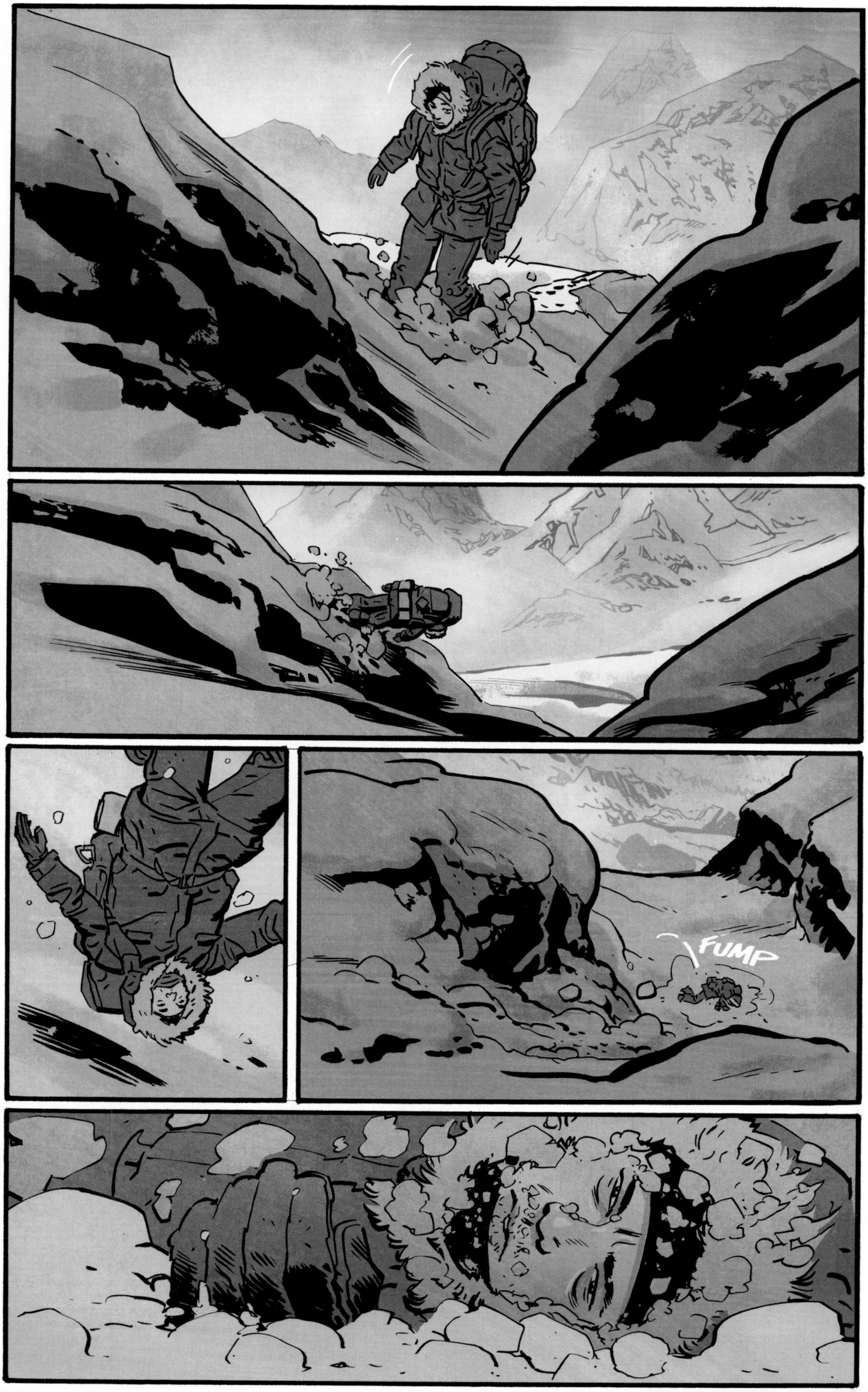
FUMP

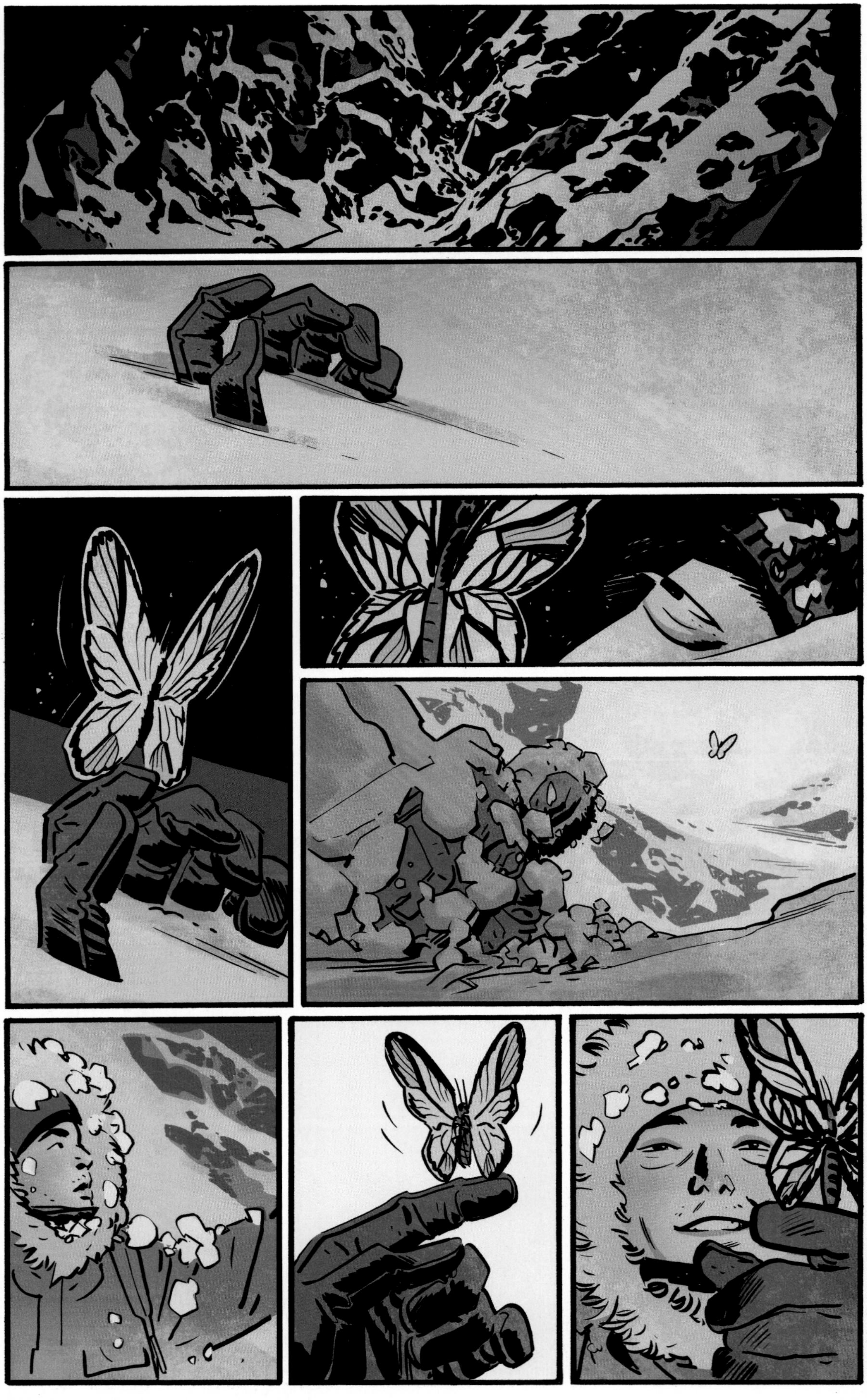

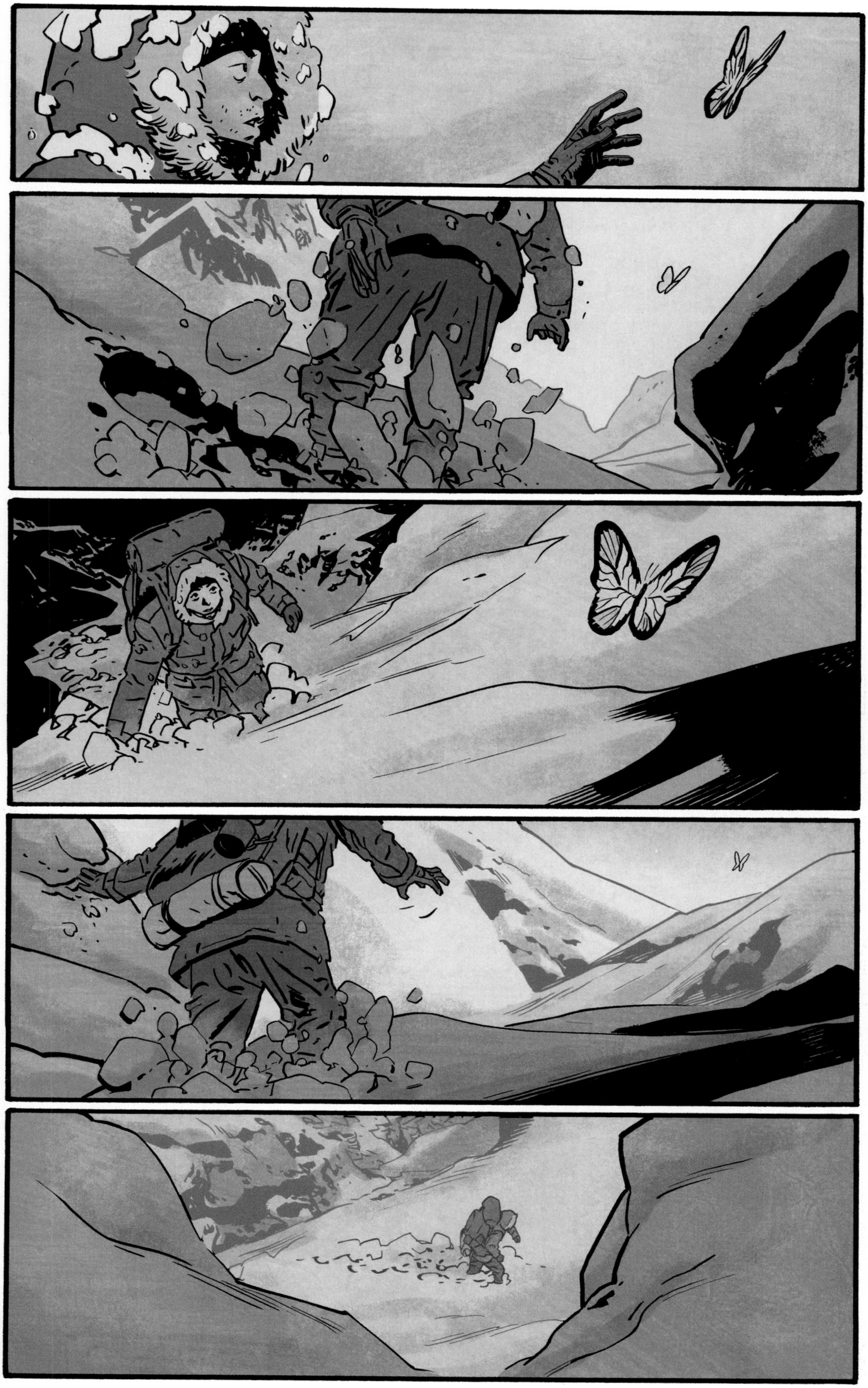

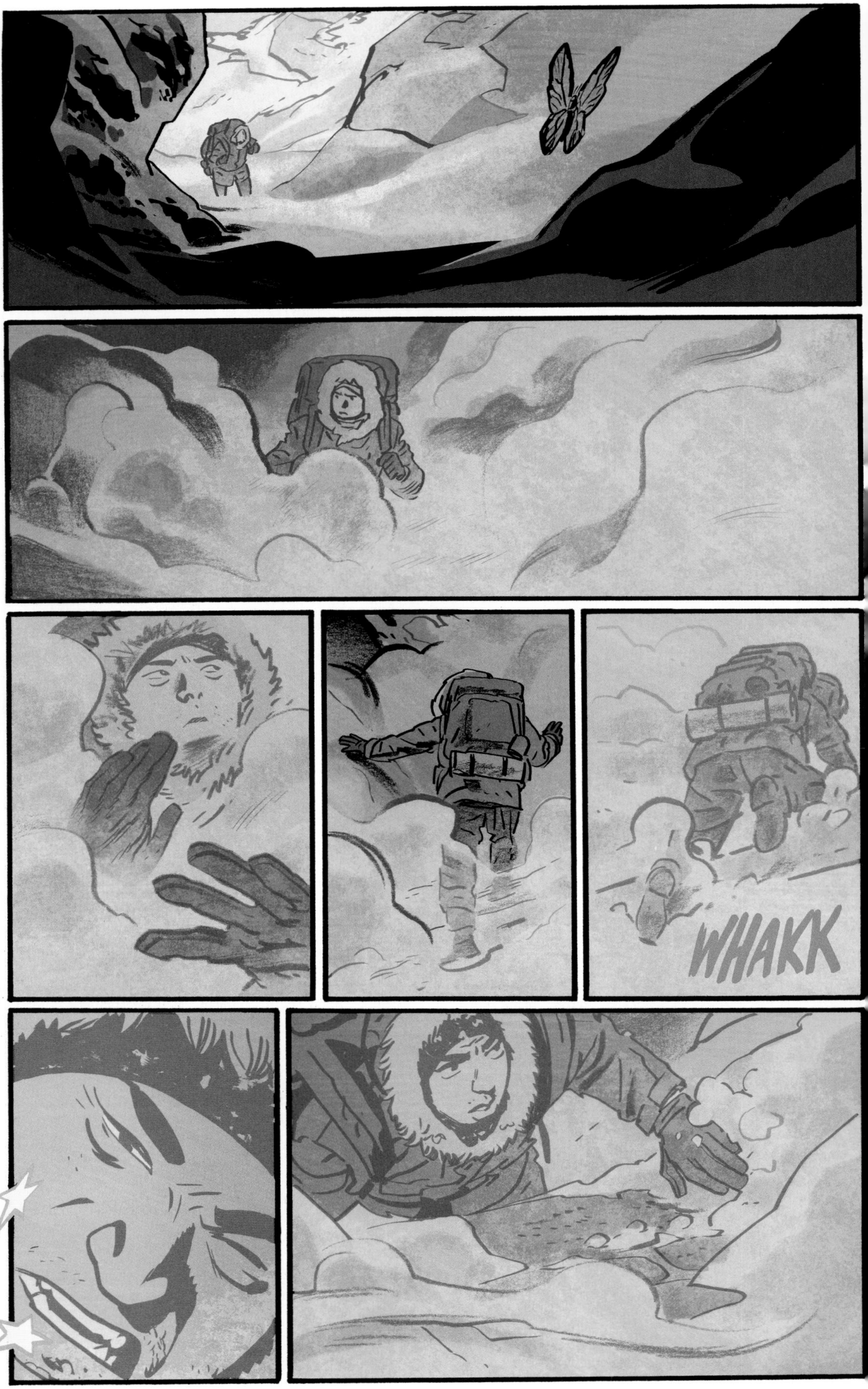
WHAKK

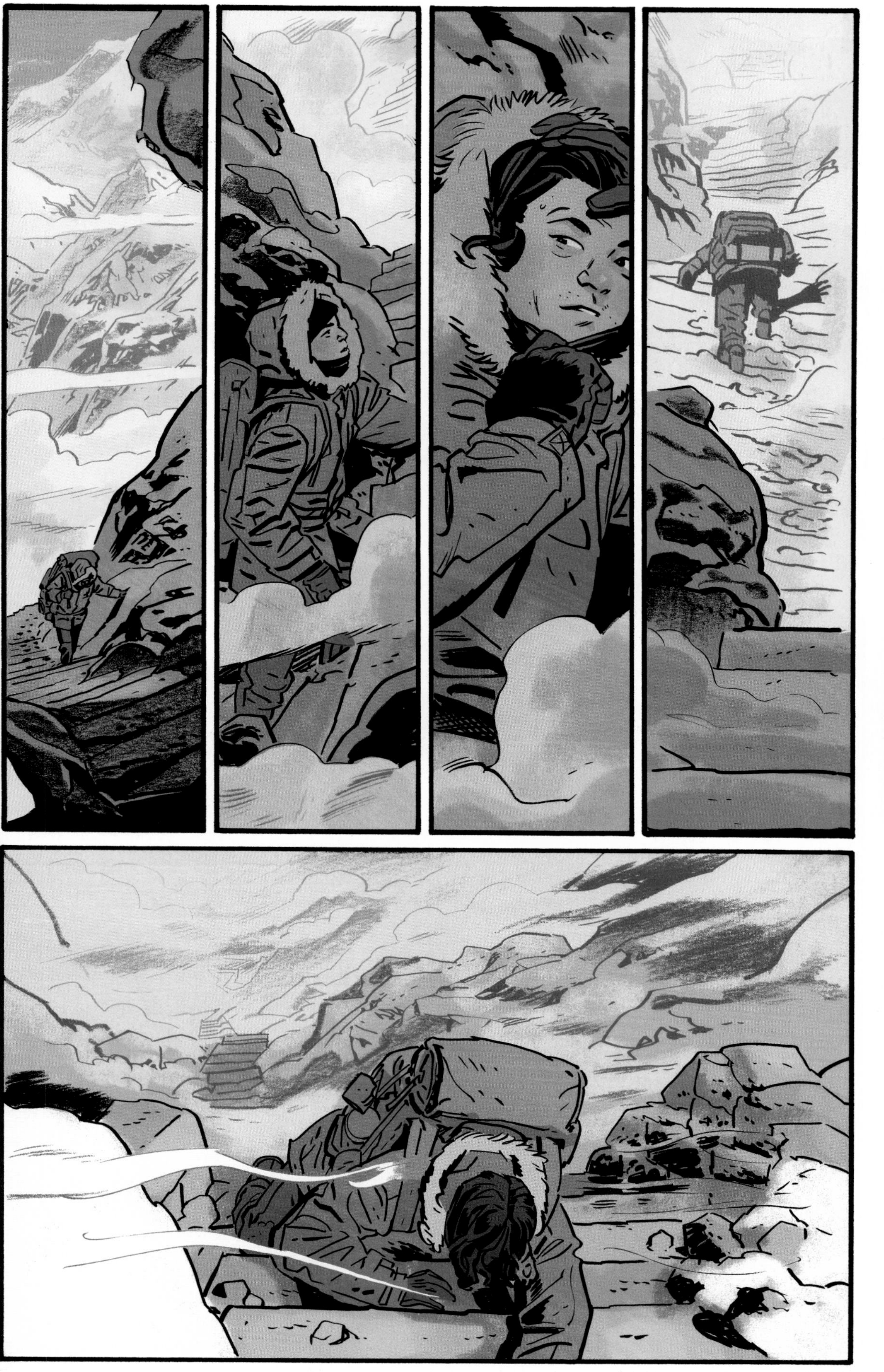

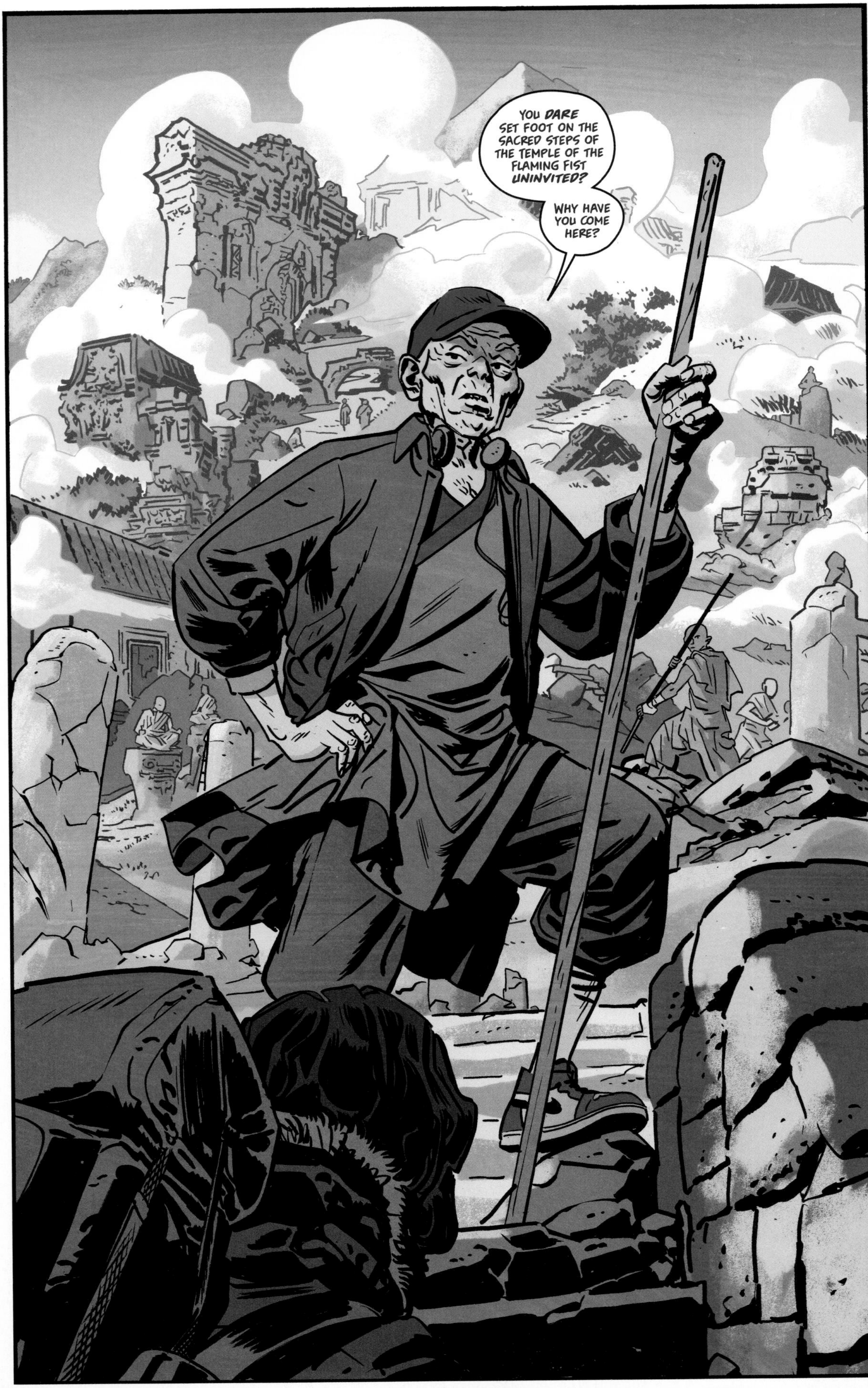
YOU DARE SET FOOT ON THE SACRED STEPS OF THE TEMPLE OF THE FLAMING FIST UNINVITED?
WHY HAVE YOU COME HERE?

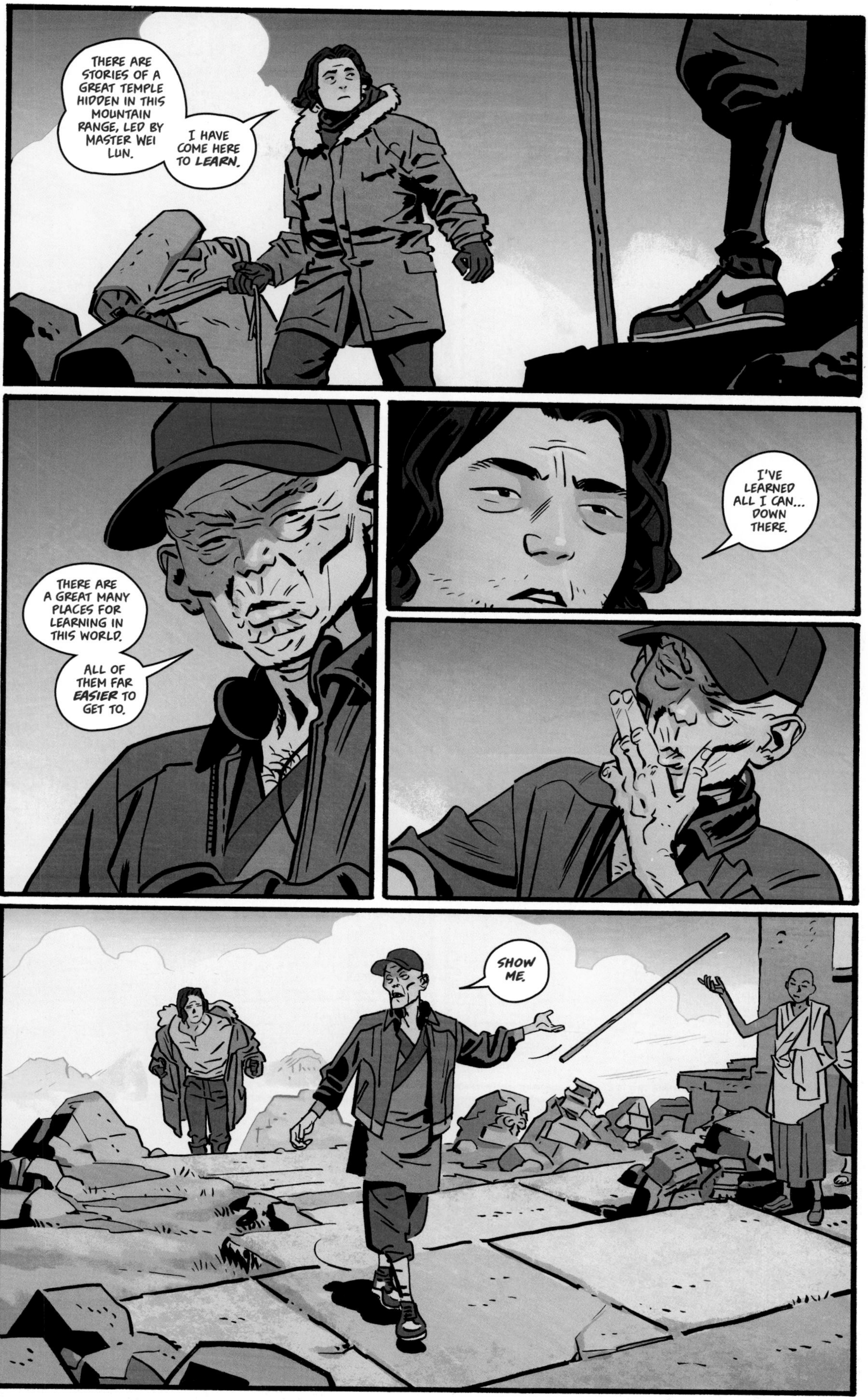
THERE ARE STORIES OF A GREAT TEMPLE HIDDEN IN THIS MOUNTAIN RANGE, LED BY MASTER WEI LUN.
I HAVE COME HERE TO *LEARN.*
THERE ARE A GREAT MANY PLACES FOR LEARNING IN THIS WORLD.
ALL OF THEM FAR *EASIER* TO GET TO.
I'VE LEARNED ALL I CAN... DOWN THERE.
SHOW ME.

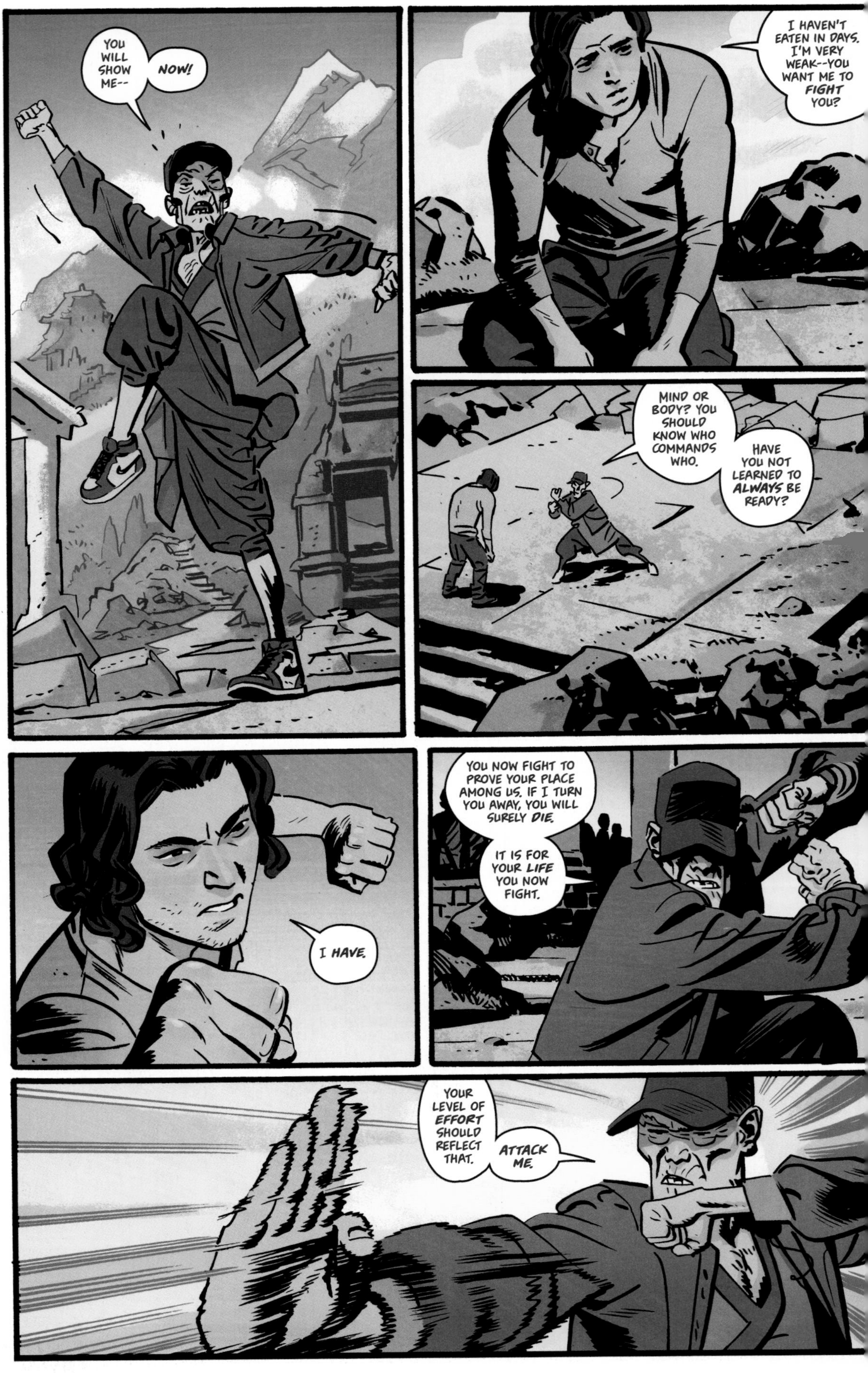
YOU WILL SHOW ME--
NOW!
I HAVEN'T EATEN IN DAYS. I'M VERY WEAK--YOU WANT ME TO FIGHT YOU?
MIND OR BODY? YOU SHOULD KNOW WHO COMMANDS WHO.
HAVE YOU NOT LEARNED TO ALWAYS BE READY?
I HAVE.
YOU NOW FIGHT TO PROVE YOUR PLACE AMONG US. IF I TURN YOU AWAY, YOU WILL SURELY DIE.
IT IS FOR YOUR LIFE YOU NOW FIGHT.
YOUR LEVEL OF EFFORT SHOULD REFLECT THAT.
ATTACK ME.

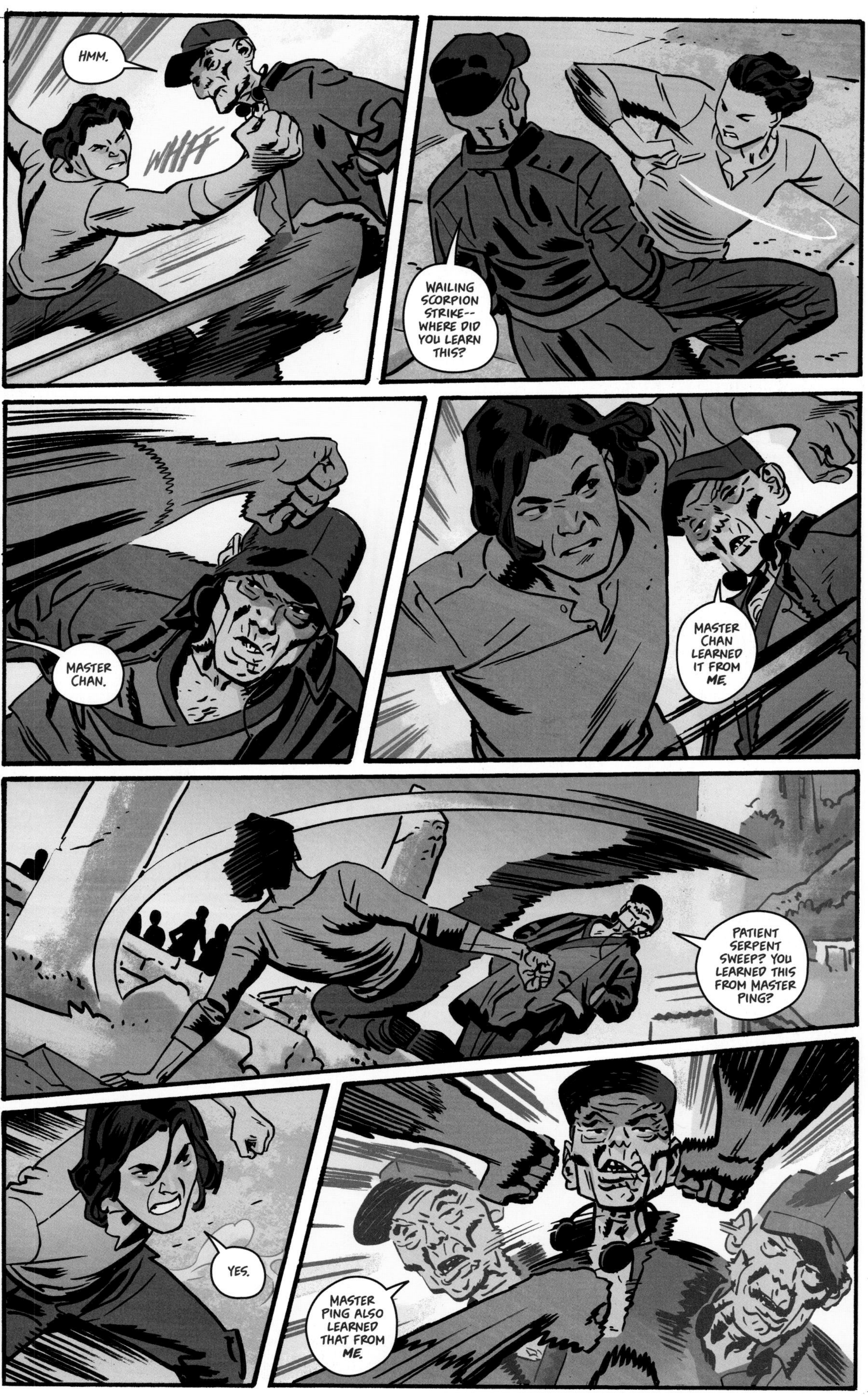
HMM.
WHFF
WAILING SCORPION STRIKE-- WHERE DID YOU LEARN THIS?
MASTER CHAN.
MASTER CHAN LEARNED IT FROM ME.
PATIENT SERPENT SWEEP? YOU LEARNED THIS FROM MASTER PING?
YES.
MASTER PING ALSO LEARNED THAT FROM ME.

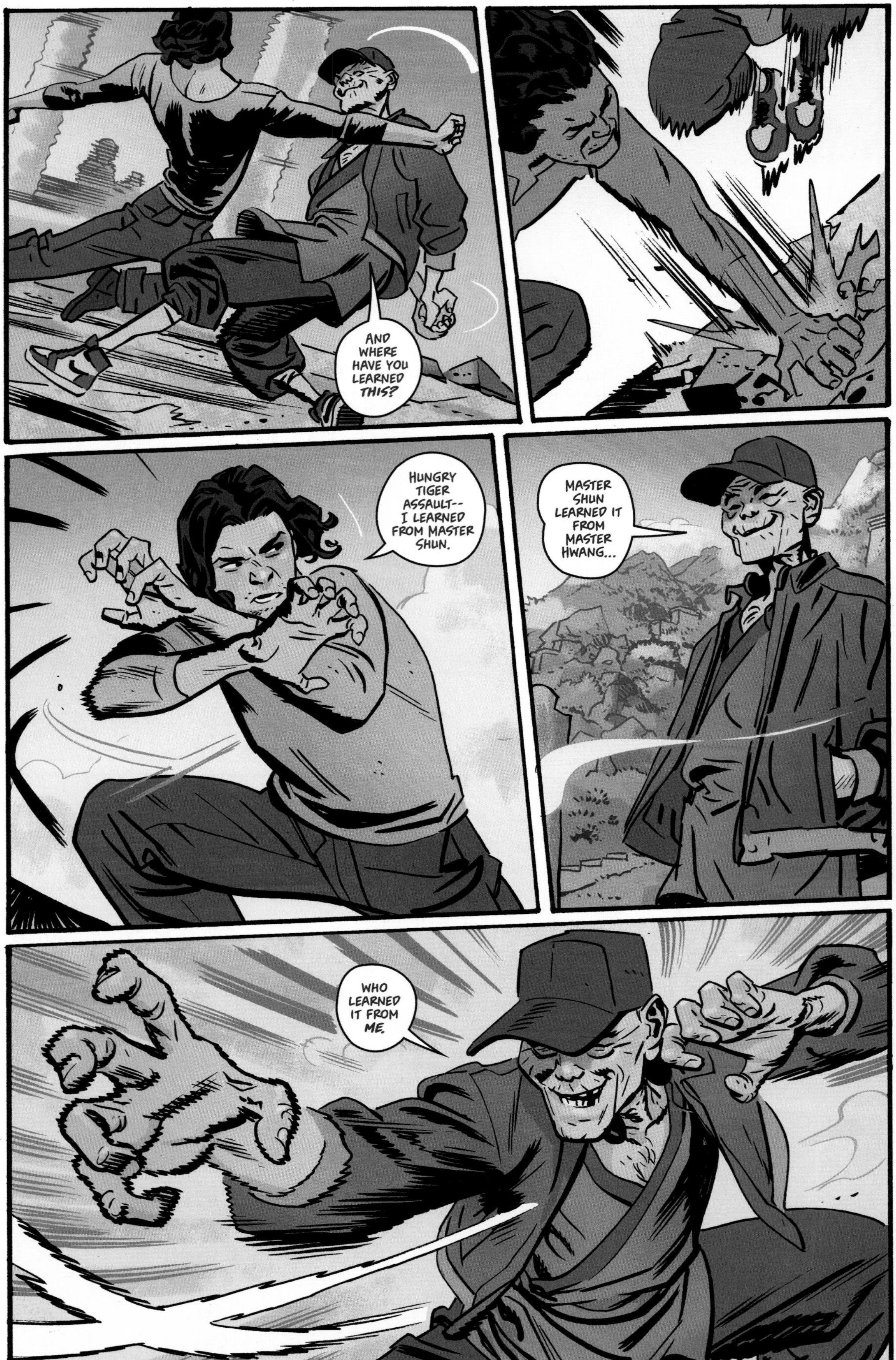
AND WHERE HAVE YOU LEARNED THIS?
HUNGRY TIGER ASSAULT-- I LEARNED FROM MASTER SHUN.
MASTER SHUN LEARNED IT FROM MASTER HWANG...
WHO LEARNED IT FROM ME.

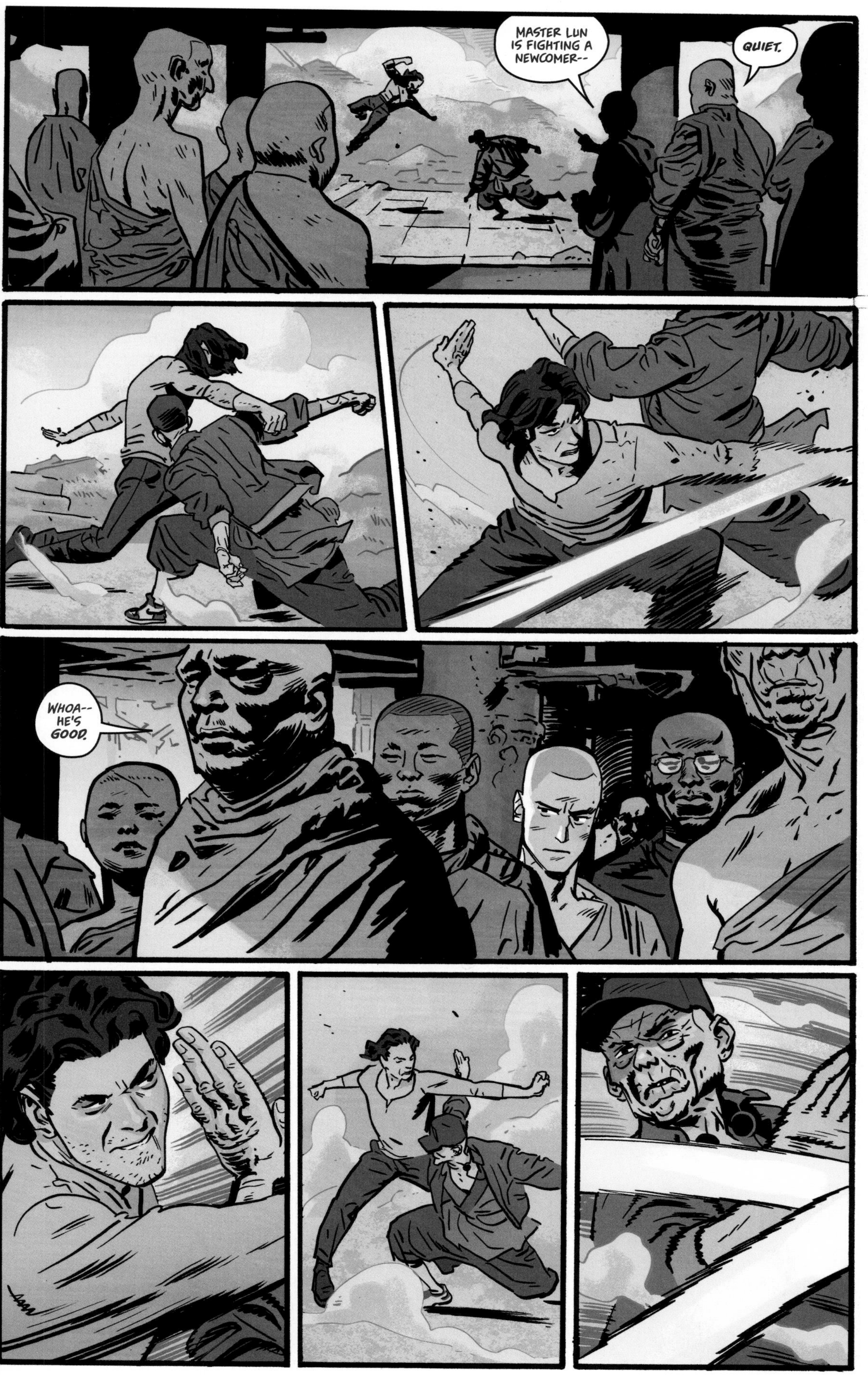
MASTER LUN IS FIGHTING A NEWCOMER--
QUIET.
WHOA-- HE'S GOOD.

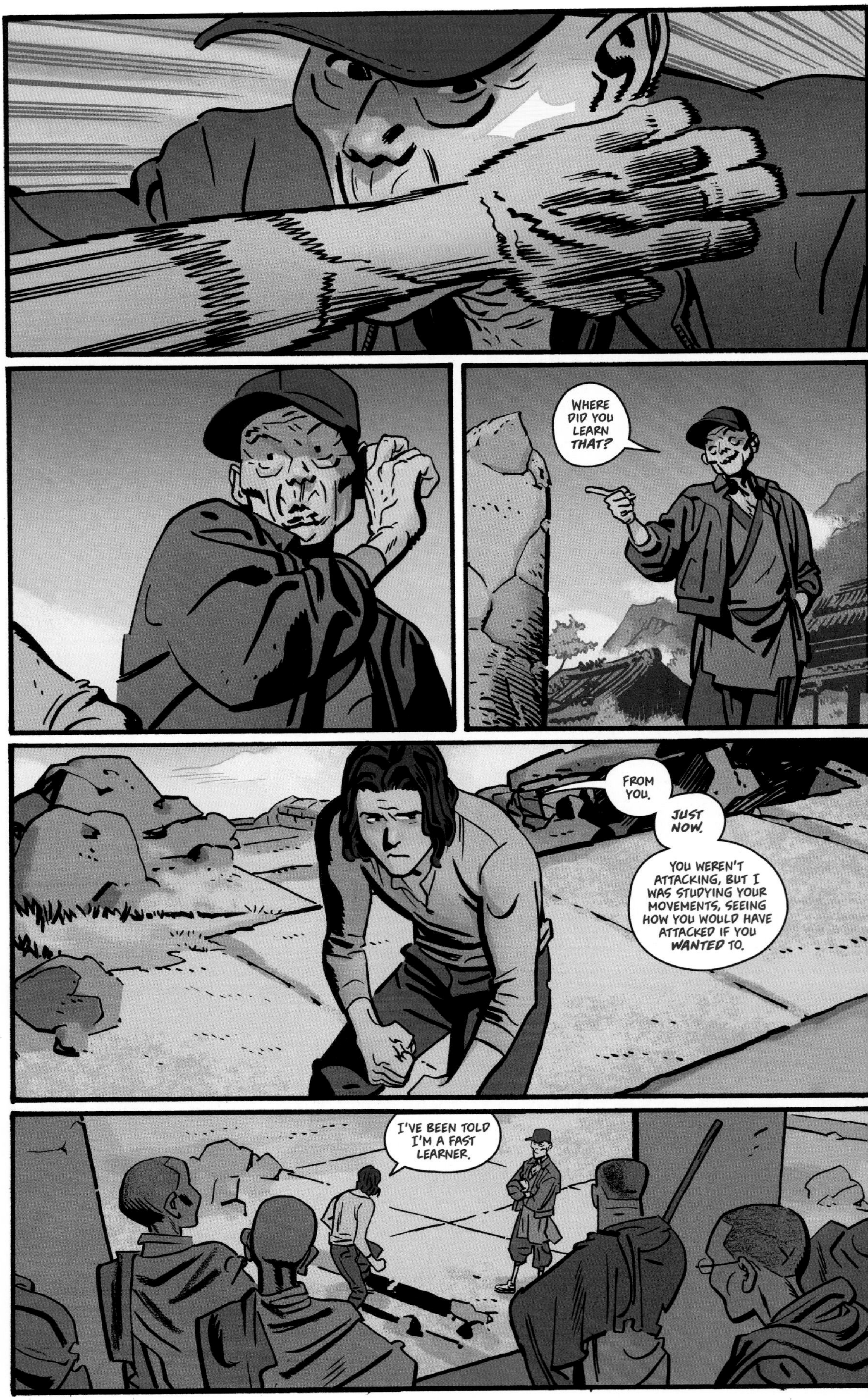
WHERE DID YOU LEARN THAT?
FROM YOU.
JUST NOW.
YOU WEREN'T ATTACKING, BUT I WAS STUDYING YOUR MOVEMENTS, SEEING HOW YOU WOULD HAVE ATTACKED IF YOU WANTED TO.
I'VE BEEN TOLD I'M A FAST LEARNER.

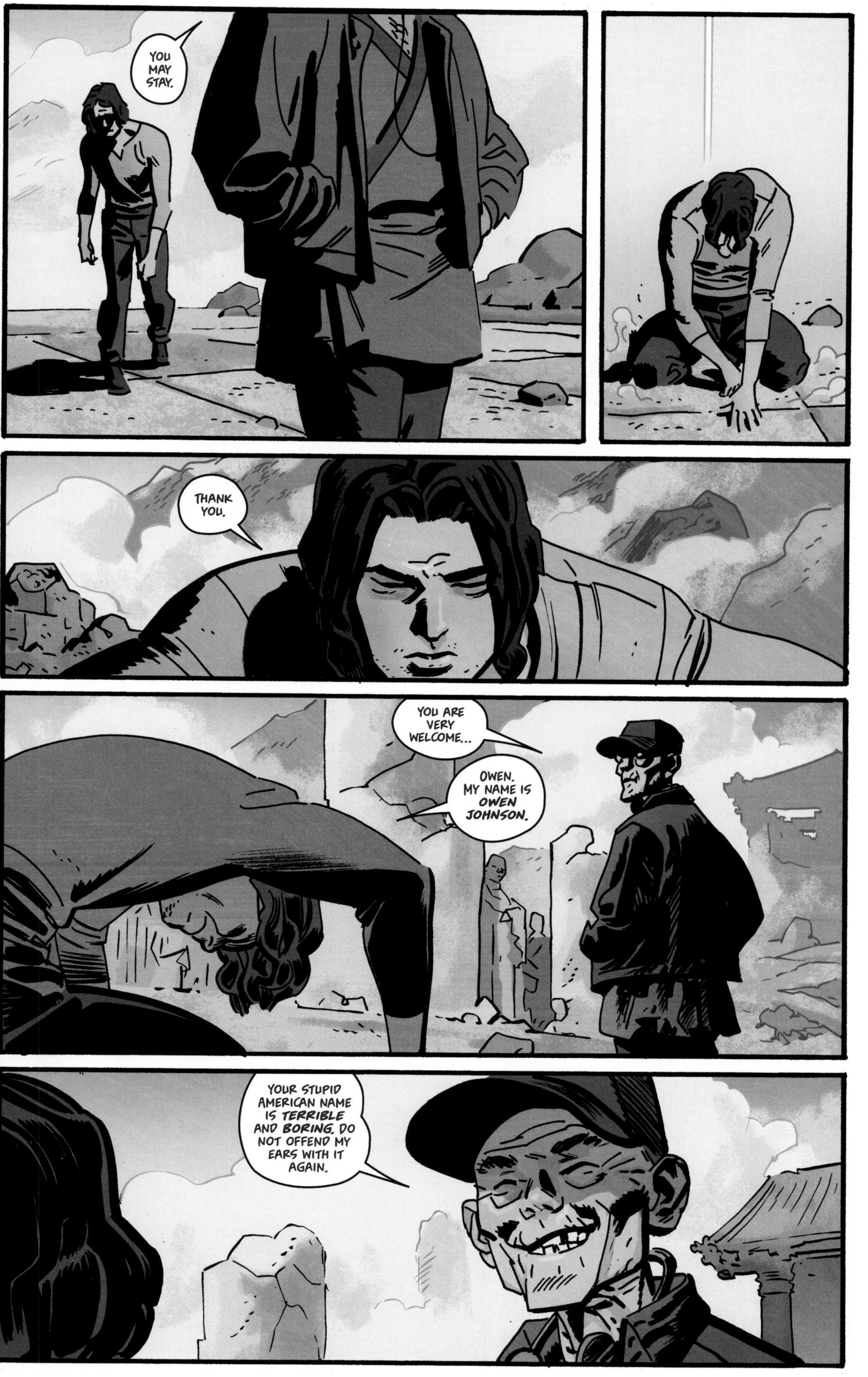
YOU MAY STAY.
THANK YOU.
YOU ARE VERY WELCOME...
OWEN. MY NAME IS OWEN JOHNSON.
YOUR STUPID AMERICAN NAME IS TERRIBLE AND BORING. DO NOT OFFEND MY EARS WITH IT AGAIN.

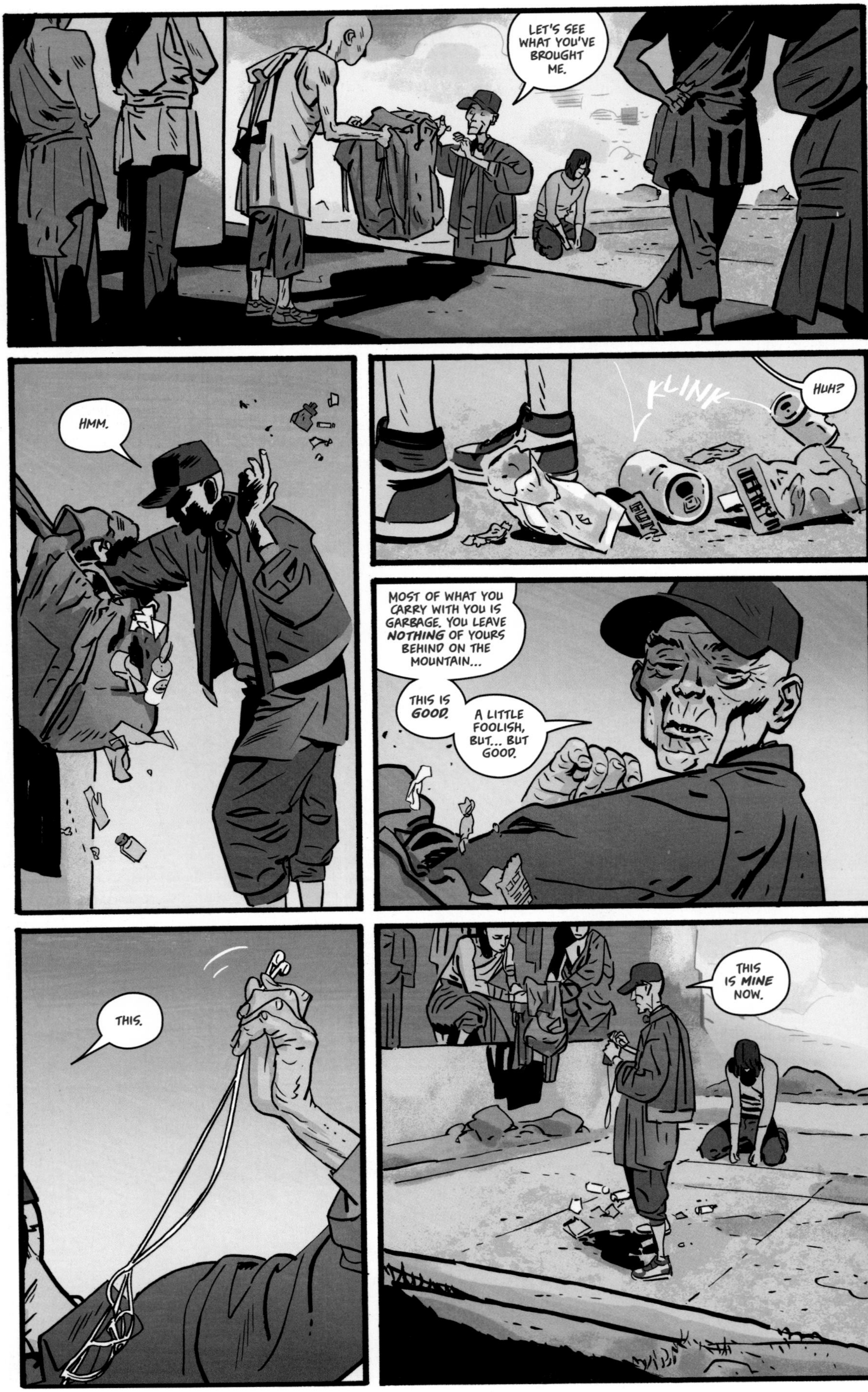
LET'S SEE WHAT YOU'VE BROUGHT ME.
HMM.
KLINK
HUH?
MOST OF WHAT YOU CARRY WITH YOU IS GARBAGE. YOU LEAVE NOTHING OF YOURS BEHIND ON THE MOUNTAIN...
THIS IS GOOD.
A LITTLE FOOLISH, BUT... BUT GOOD.
THIS.
THIS IS MINE NOW.

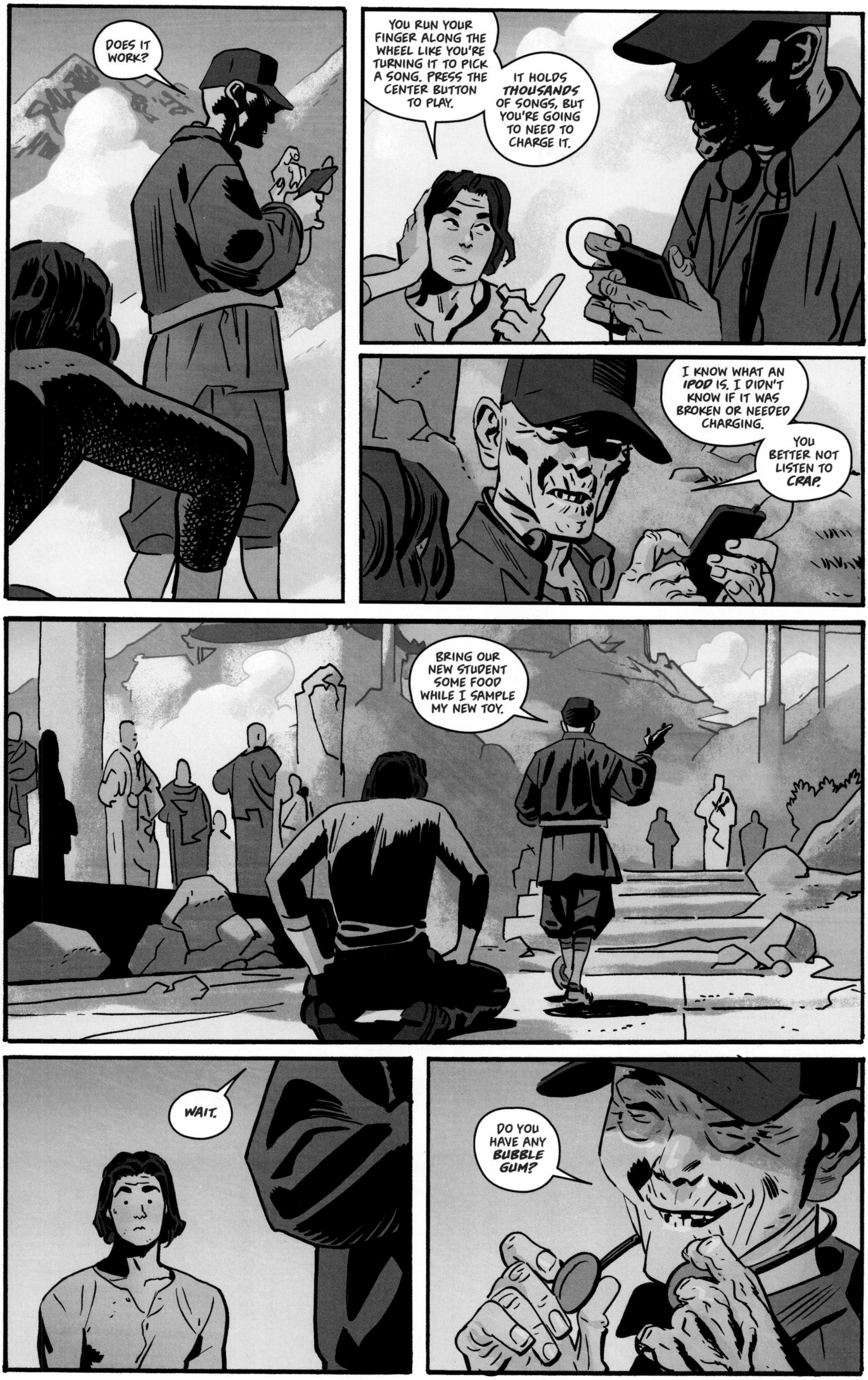
DOES IT WORK?
YOU RUN YOUR FINGER ALONG THE WHEEL LIKE YOU'RE TURNING IT TO PICK A SONG. PRESS THE CENTER BUTTON TO PLAY.
IT HOLDS THOUSANDS OF SONGS, BUT YOU'RE GOING TO NEED TO CHARGE IT.
I KNOW WHAT AN IPOD IS. I DIDN'T KNOW IF IT WAS BROKEN OR NEEDED CHARGING.
YOU BETTER NOT LISTEN TO CRAP.
BRING OUR NEW STUDENT SOME FOOD WHILE I SAMPLE MY NEW TOY.
WAIT.
DO YOU HAVE ANY BUBBLE GUM?

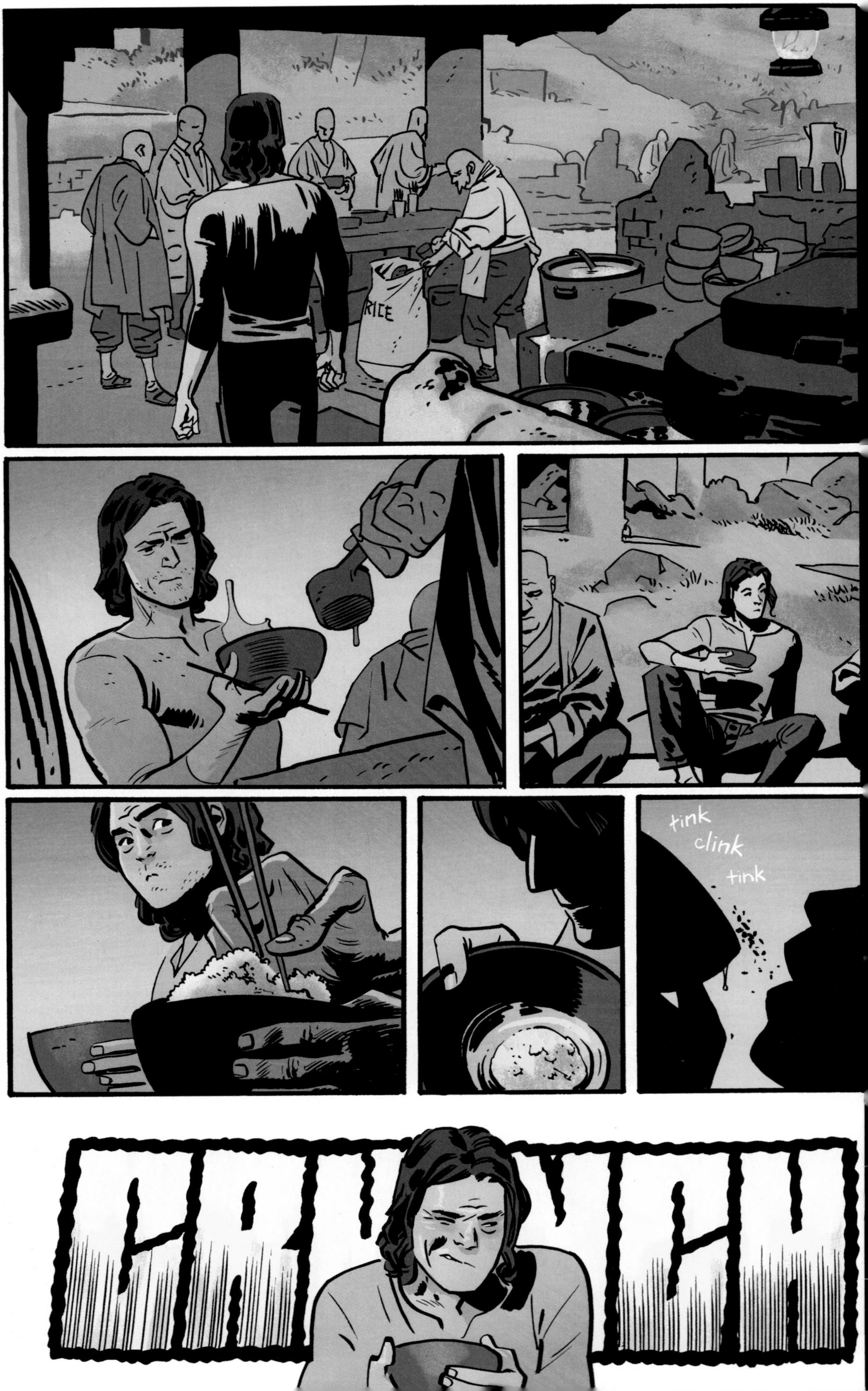

RICE
tink
clink
tink

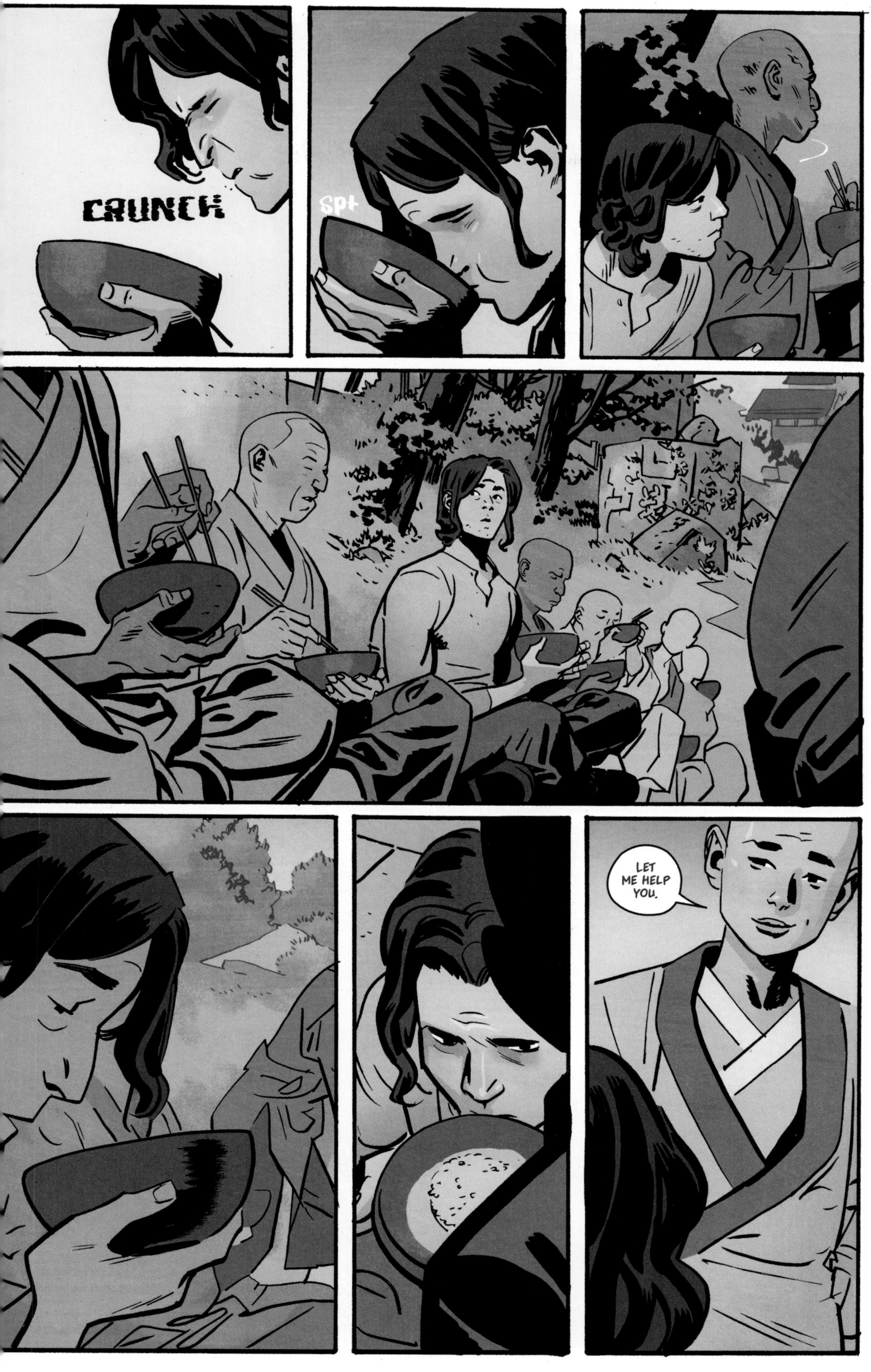
CRUNCH
SPT
LET ME HELP YOU.

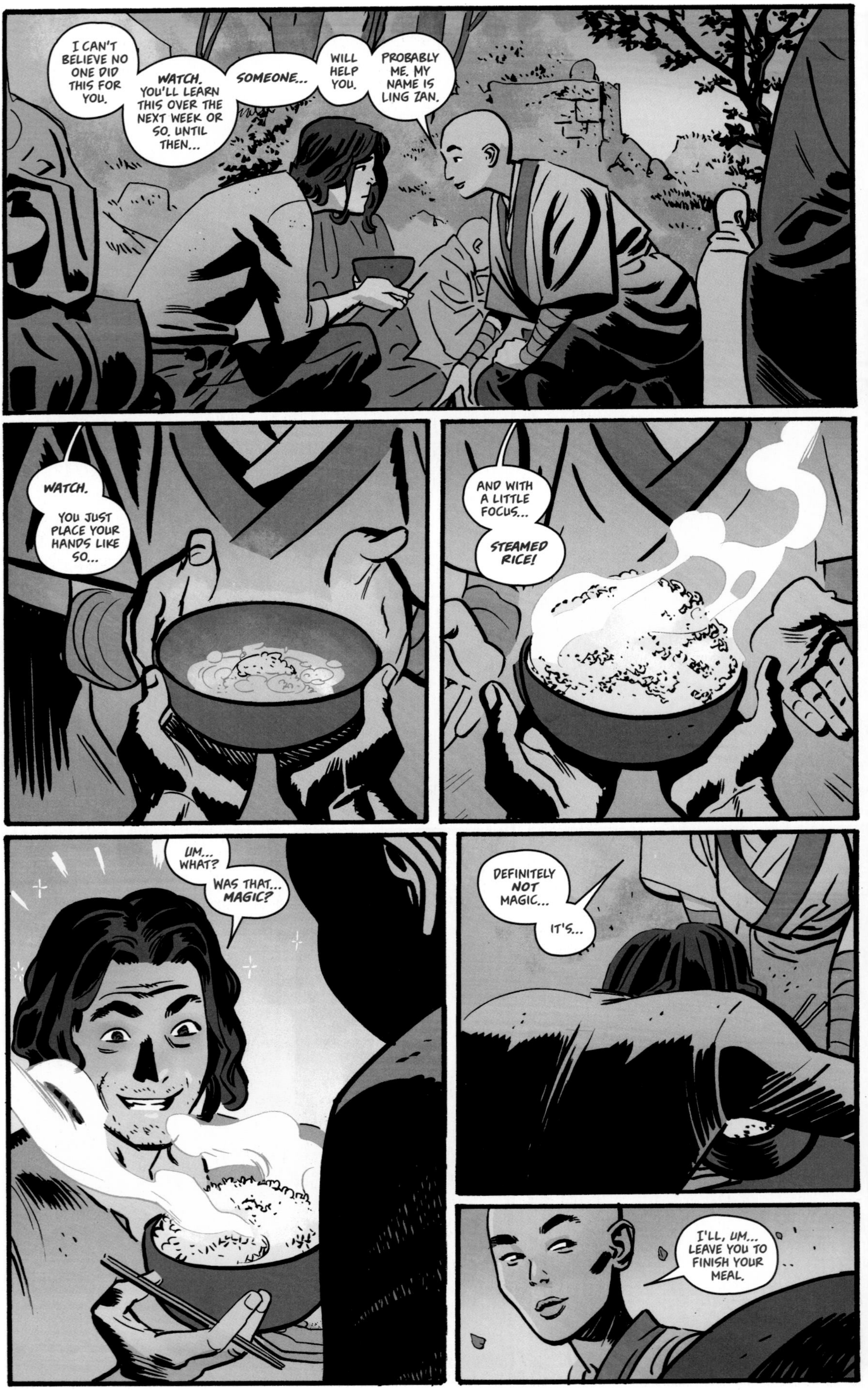
I CAN'T BELIEVE NO ONE DID THIS FOR YOU.
WATCH. YOU'LL LEARN THIS OVER THE NEXT WEEK OR SO. UNTIL THEN...
SOMEONE...
WILL HELP YOU.
PROBABLY ME. MY NAME IS LING ZAN.
WATCH.
YOU JUST PLACE YOUR HANDS LIKE SO...
AND WITH A LITTLE FOCUS...
STEAMED RICE!
UM... WHAT?
WAS THAT... MAGIC?
DEFINITELY NOT MAGIC...
IT'S...
I'LL, UM... LEAVE YOU TO FINISH YOUR MEAL.

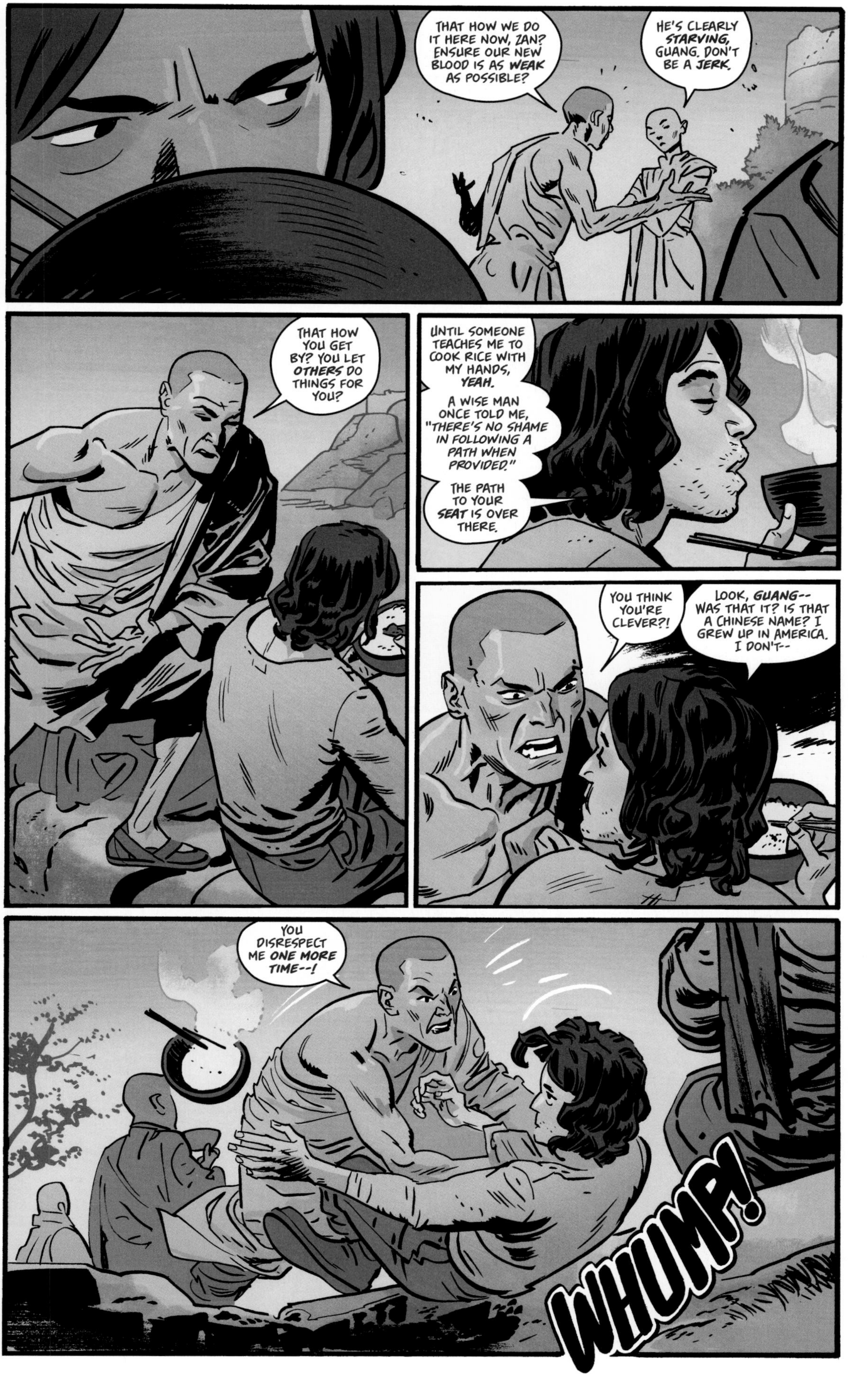
THAT HOW WE DO IT HERE NOW, ZAN? ENSURE OUR NEW BLOOD IS AS WEAK AS POSSIBLE?
HE'S CLEARLY STARVING, GUANG. DON'T BE A JERK.
THAT HOW YOU GET BY? YOU LET OTHERS DO THINGS FOR YOU?
UNTIL SOMEONE TEACHES ME TO COOK RICE WITH MY HANDS, YEAH.
A WISE MAN ONCE TOLD ME, "THERE'S NO SHAME IN FOLLOWING A PATH WHEN PROVIDED."
THE PATH TO YOUR SEAT IS OVER THERE.
YOU THINK YOU'RE CLEVER?!
LOOK, GUANG-- WAS THAT IT? IS THAT A CHINESE NAME? I GREW UP IN AMERICA. I DON'T--
YOU DISRESPECT ME ONE MORE TIME--!
WHUMP!

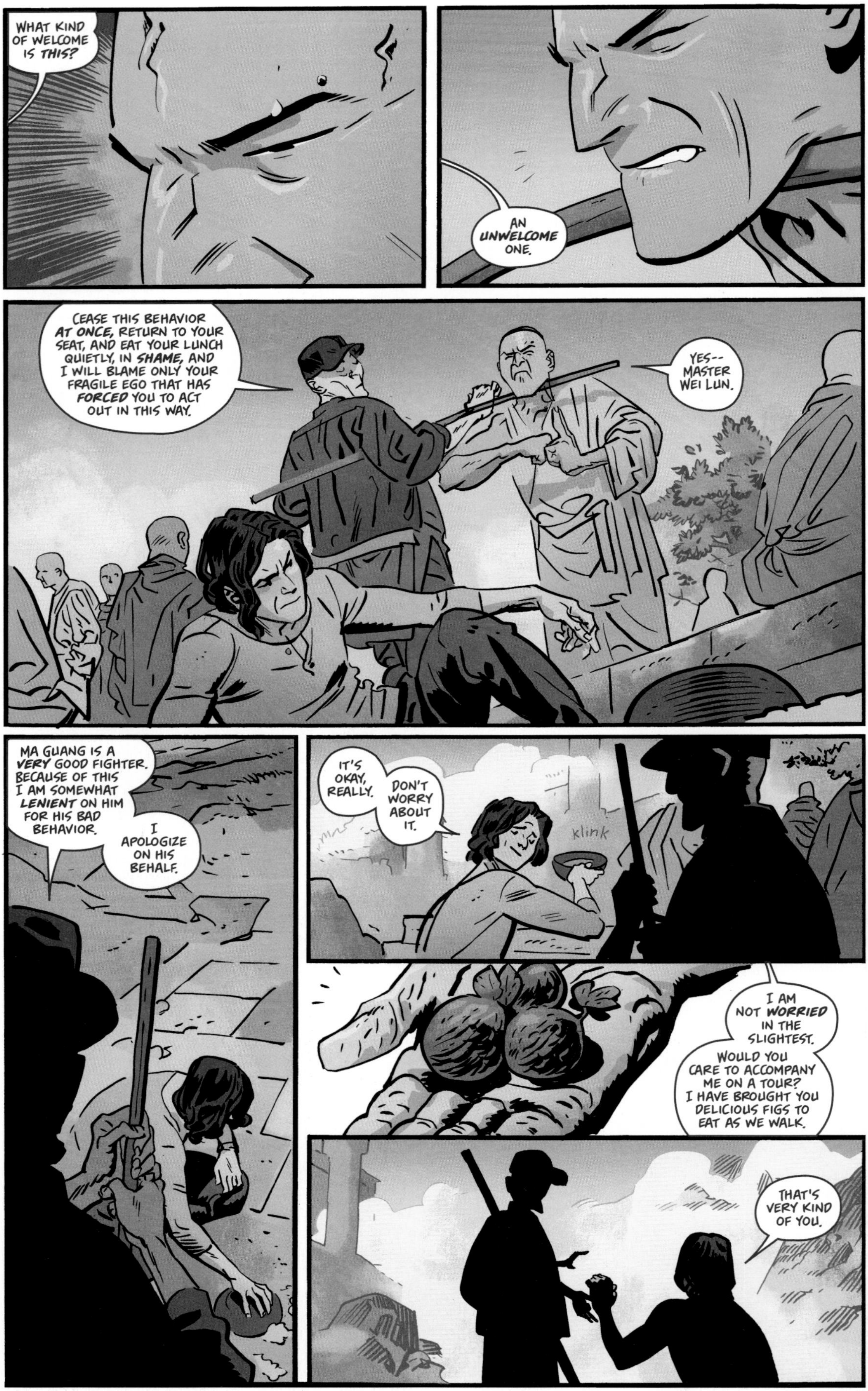
WHAT KIND OF WELCOME IS THIS?
AN UNWELCOME ONE.
CEASE THIS BEHAVIOR AT ONCE, RETURN TO YOUR SEAT, AND EAT YOUR LUNCH QUIETLY, IN SHAME, AND I WILL BLAME ONLY YOUR FRAGILE EGO THAT HAS FORCED YOU TO ACT OUT IN THIS WAY.
YES-- MASTER WEI LUN.
MA GUANG IS A VERY GOOD FIGHTER. BECAUSE OF THIS I AM SOMEWHAT LENIENT ON HIM FOR HIS BAD BEHAVIOR.
I APOLOGIZE ON HIS BEHALF.
IT'S OKAY, REALLY.
DON'T WORRY ABOUT IT.
klink
I AM NOT WORRIED IN THE SLIGHTEST.
WOULD YOU CARE TO ACCOMPANY ME ON A TOUR? I HAVE BROUGHT YOU DELICIOUS FIGS TO EAT AS WE WALK.
THAT'S VERY KIND OF YOU.

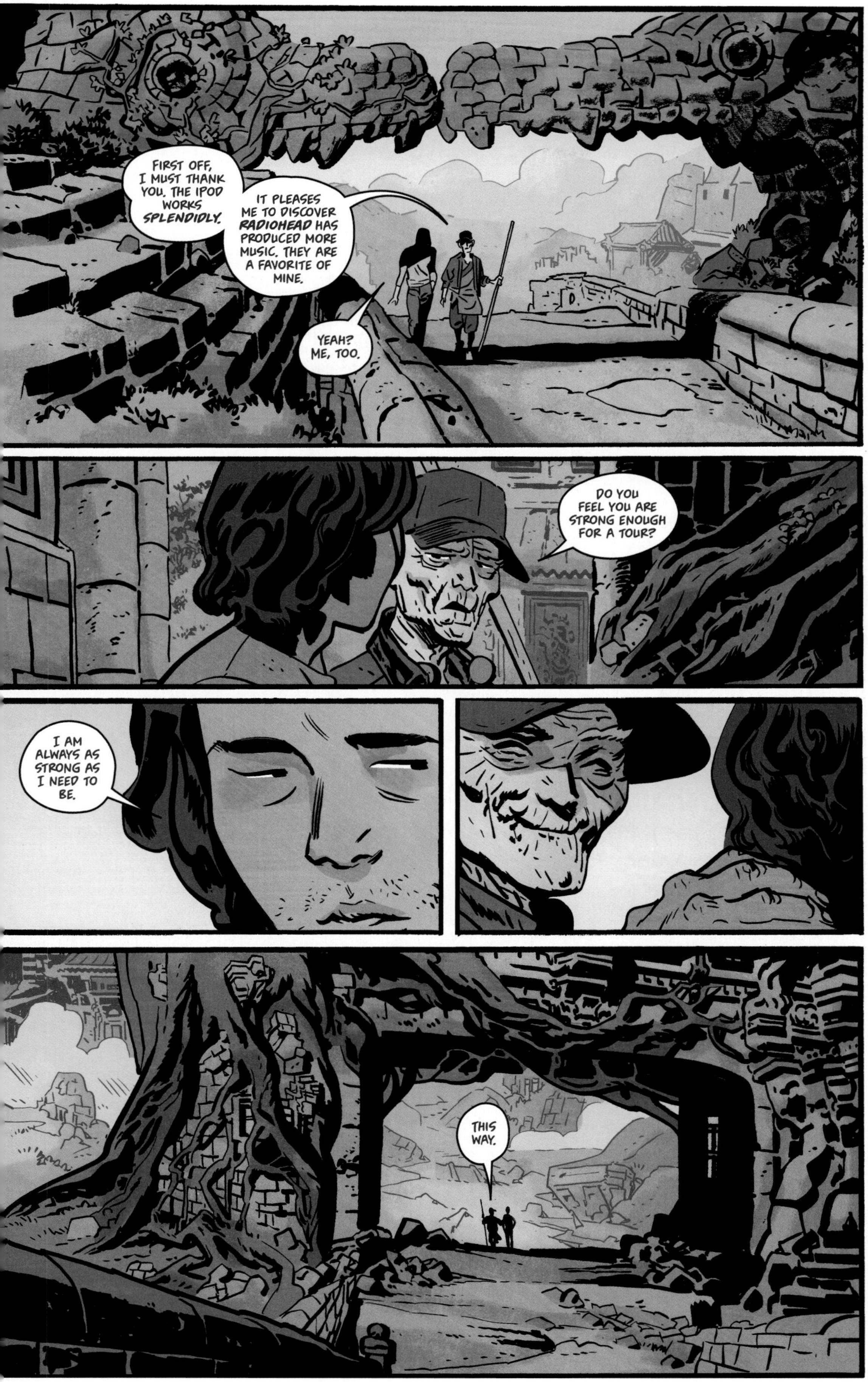
FIRST OFF, I MUST THANK YOU. THE IPOD WORKS SPLENDIDLY.
IT PLEASES ME TO DISCOVER RADIOHEAD HAS PRODUCED MORE MUSIC. THEY ARE A FAVORITE OF MINE.
YEAH? ME, TOO.
DO YOU FEEL YOU ARE STRONG ENOUGH FOR A TOUR?
I AM ALWAYS AS STRONG AS I NEED TO BE.
THIS WAY.

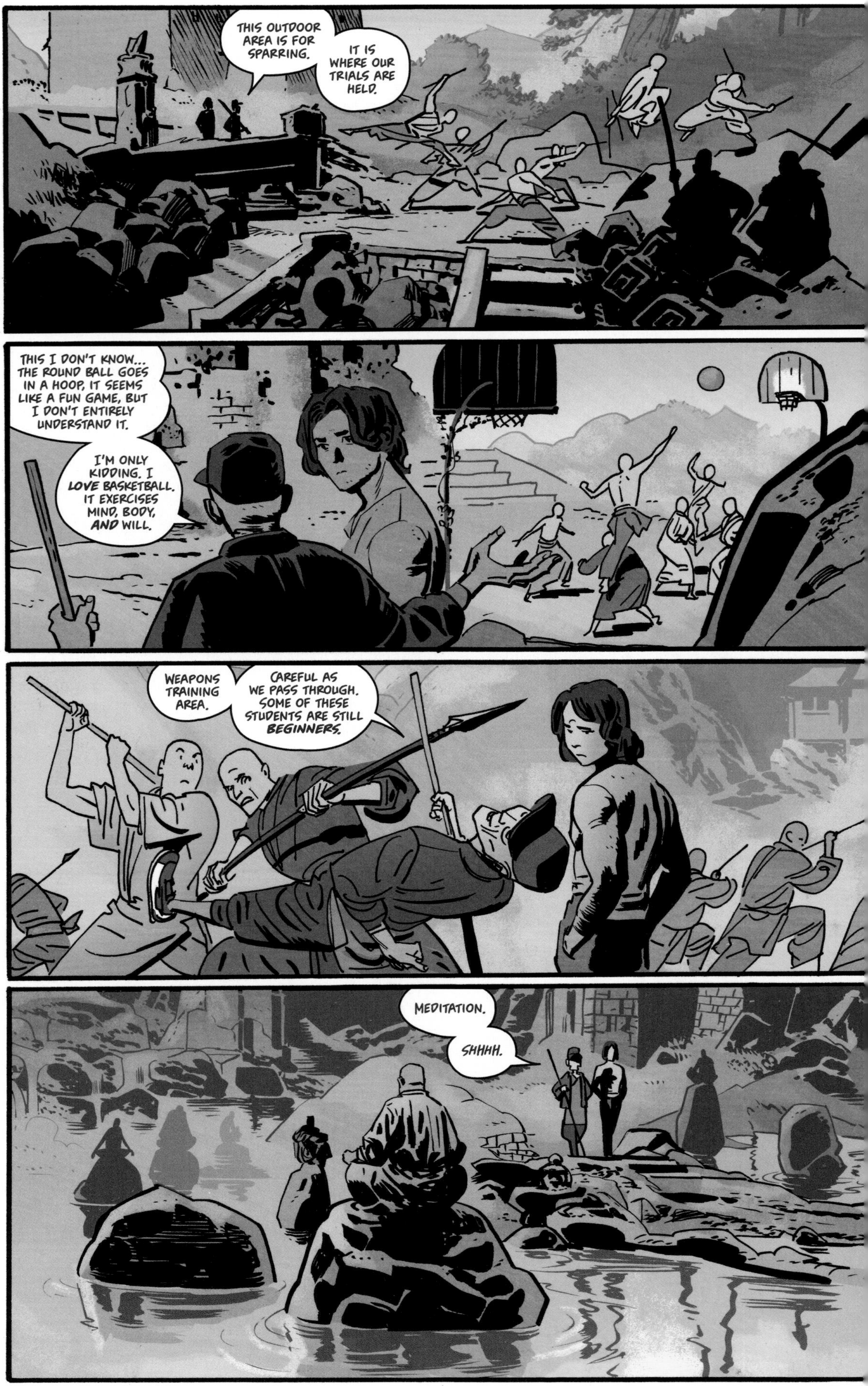
THIS OUTDOOR AREA IS FOR SPARRING.
IT IS WHERE OUR TRIALS ARE HELD.
THIS I DON'T KNOW... THE ROUND BALL GOES IN A HOOP, IT SEEMS LIKE A FUN GAME, BUT I DON'T ENTIRELY UNDERSTAND IT.
I'M ONLY KIDDING. I LOVE BASKETBALL. IT EXERCISES MIND, BODY, AND WILL.
WEAPONS TRAINING AREA.
CAREFUL AS WE PASS THROUGH. SOME OF THESE STUDENTS ARE STILL BEGINNERS.
MEDITATION.
SHHHH.

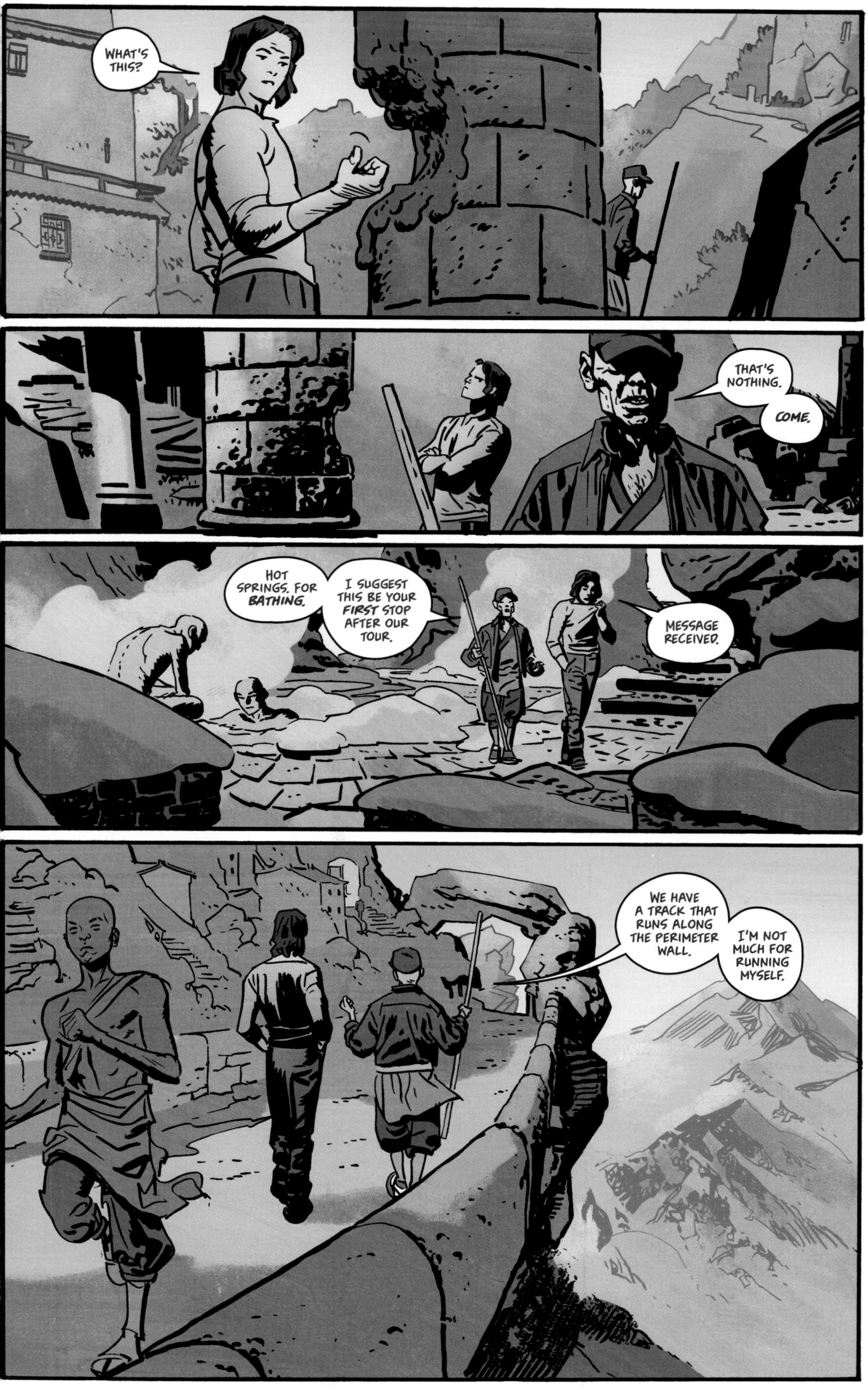
WHAT'S THIS?
THAT'S NOTHING.
COME.
HOT SPRINGS. FOR BATHING.
I SUGGEST THIS BE YOUR FIRST STOP AFTER OUR TOUR.
MESSAGE RECEIVED.
WE HAVE A TRACK THAT RUNS ALONG THE PERIMETER WALL.
I'M NOT MUCH FOR RUNNING MYSELF.

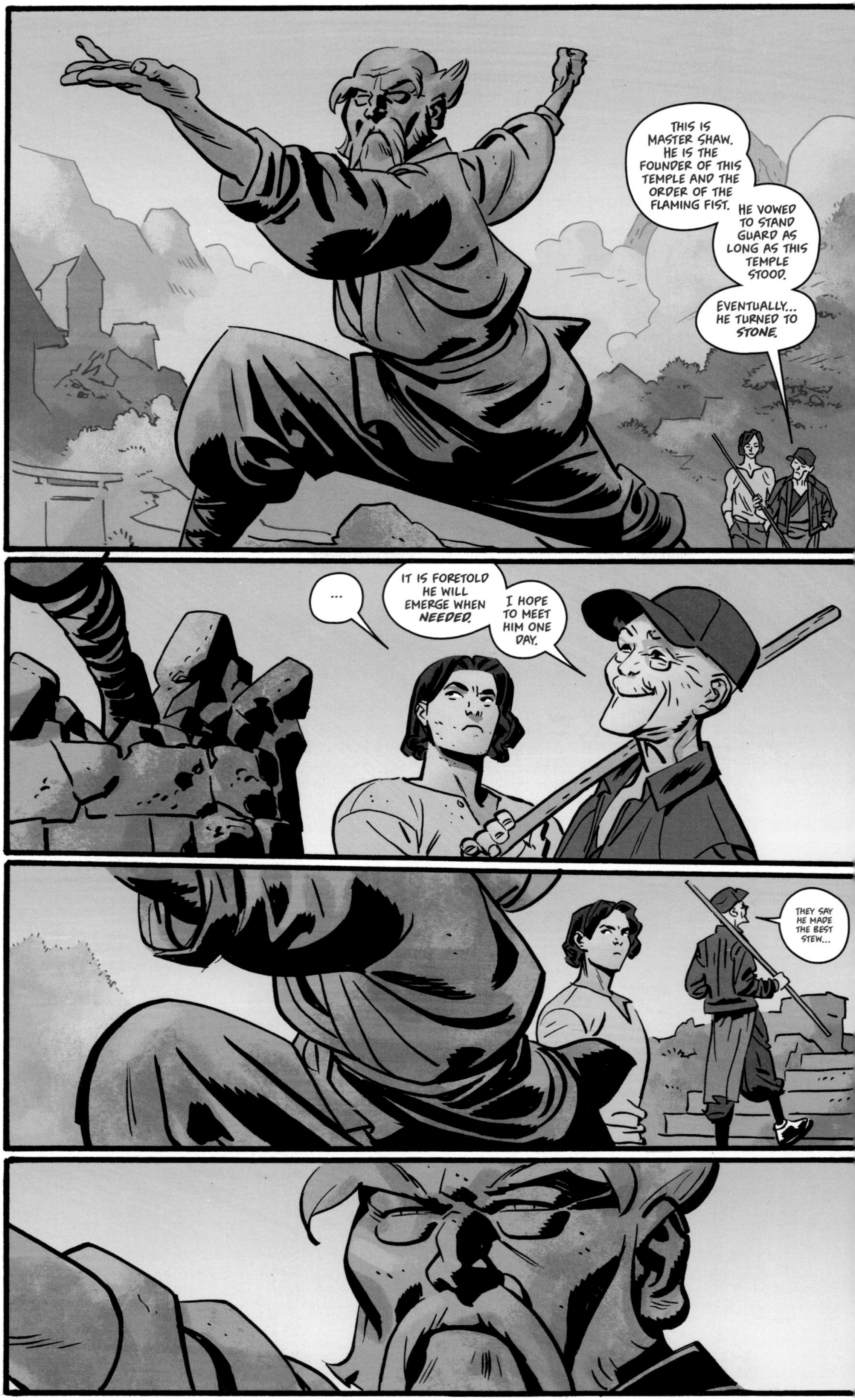
THIS IS MASTER SHAW. HE IS THE FOUNDER OF THIS TEMPLE AND THE ORDER OF THE FLAMING FIST.
HE VOWED TO STAND GUARD AS LONG AS THIS TEMPLE STOOD.
EVENTUALLY... HE TURNED TO STONE.
...
IT IS FORETOLD HE WILL EMERGE WHEN NEEDED.
I HOPE TO MEET HIM ONE DAY.
THEY SAY HE MADE THE BEST STEW...

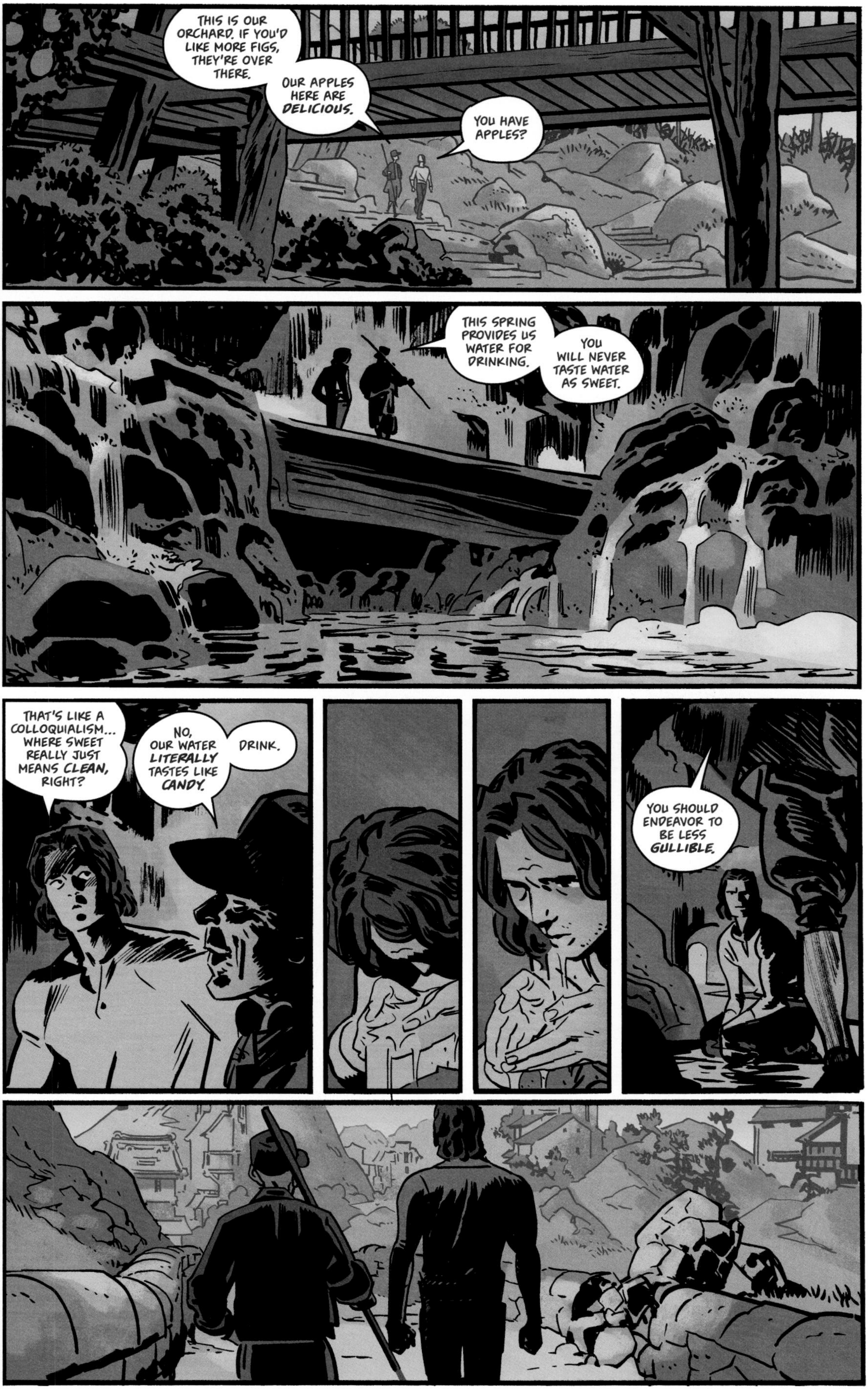
THIS IS OUR ORCHARD, IF YOU'D LIKE MORE FIGS, THEY'RE OVER THERE.
OUR APPLES HERE ARE DELICIOUS.
YOU HAVE APPLES?
THIS SPRING PROVIDES US WATER FOR DRINKING.
YOU WILL NEVER TASTE WATER AS SWEET.
THAT'S LIKE A COLLOQUIALISM... WHERE SWEET REALLY JUST MEANS CLEAN, RIGHT?
NO, OUR WATER LITERALLY TASTES LIKE CANDY.
DRINK.
YOU SHOULD ENDEAVOR TO BE LESS GULLIBLE.

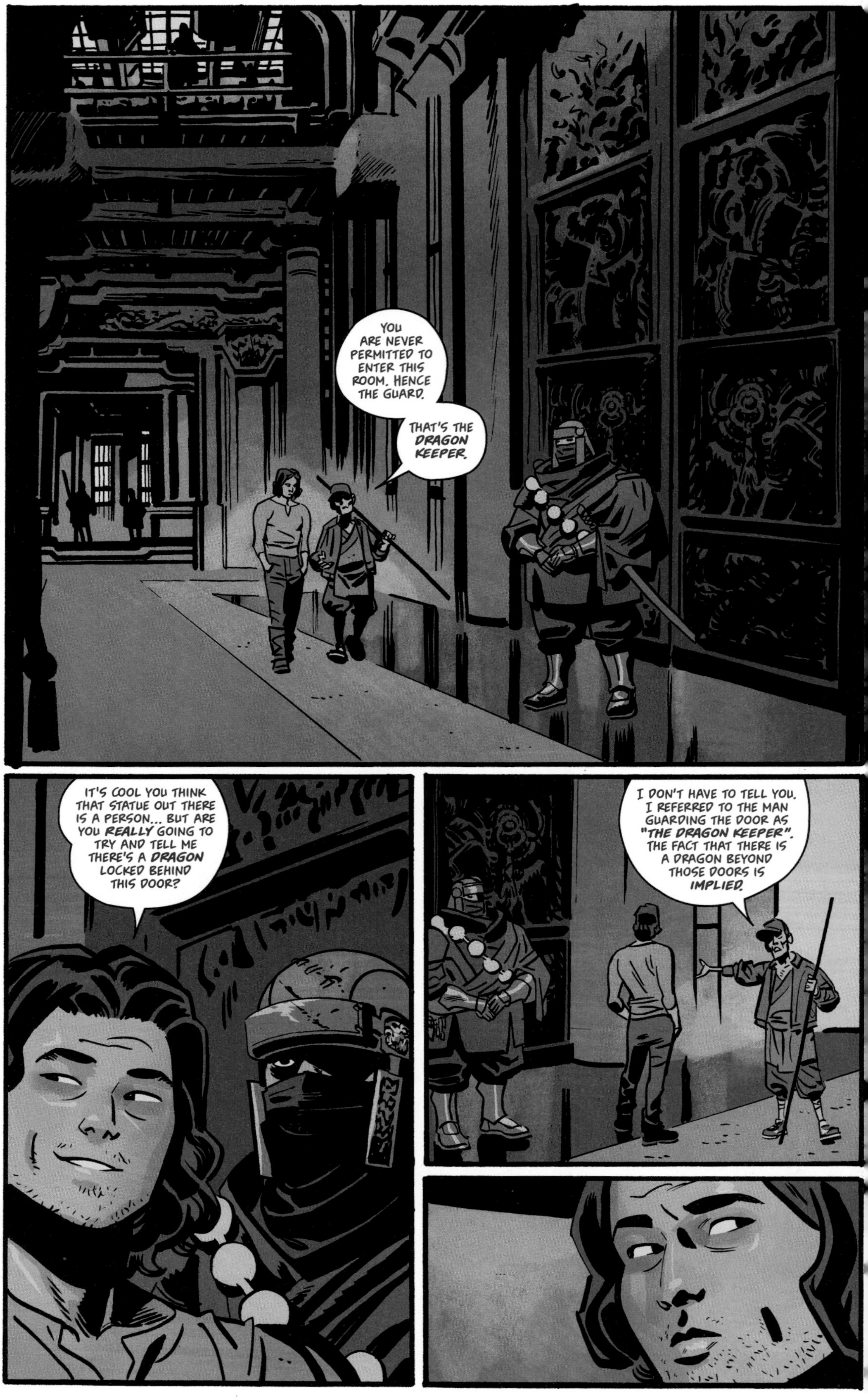
YOU ARE NEVER PERMITTED TO ENTER THIS ROOM. HENCE THE GUARD.
THAT'S THE DRAGON KEEPER.
IT'S COOL YOU THINK THAT STATUE OUT THERE IS A PERSON... BUT ARE YOU REALLY GOING TO TRY AND TELL ME THERE'S A DRAGON LOCKED BEHIND THIS DOOR?
I DON'T HAVE TO TELL YOU. I REFERRED TO THE MAN GUARDING THE DOOR AS "THE DRAGON KEEPER". THE FACT THAT THERE IS A DRAGON BEYOND THOSE DOORS IS IMPLIED.
...

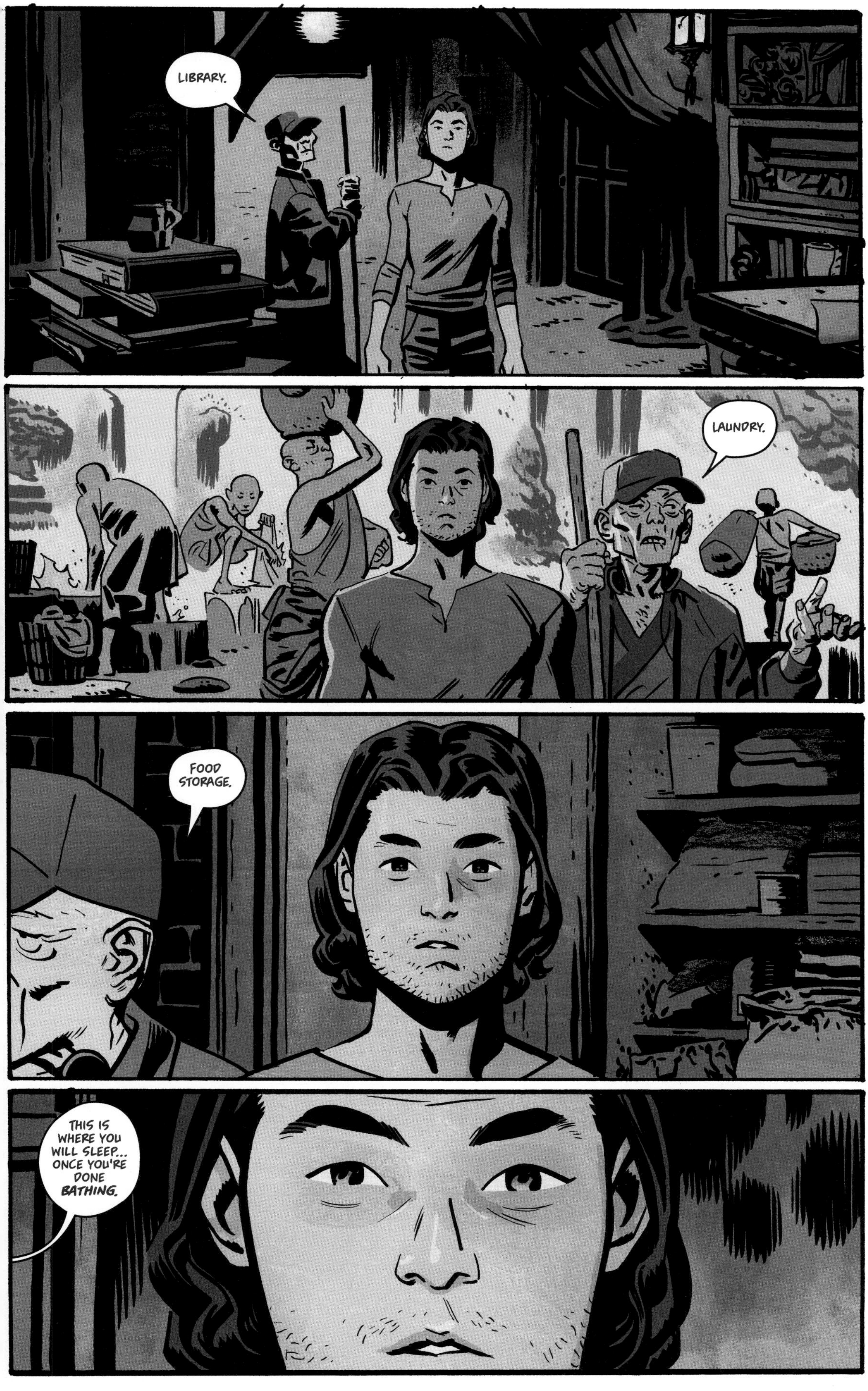
LIBRARY.
LAUNDRY.
FOOD STORAGE.
THIS IS WHERE YOU WILL SLEEP... ONCE YOU'RE DONE *BATHING*.

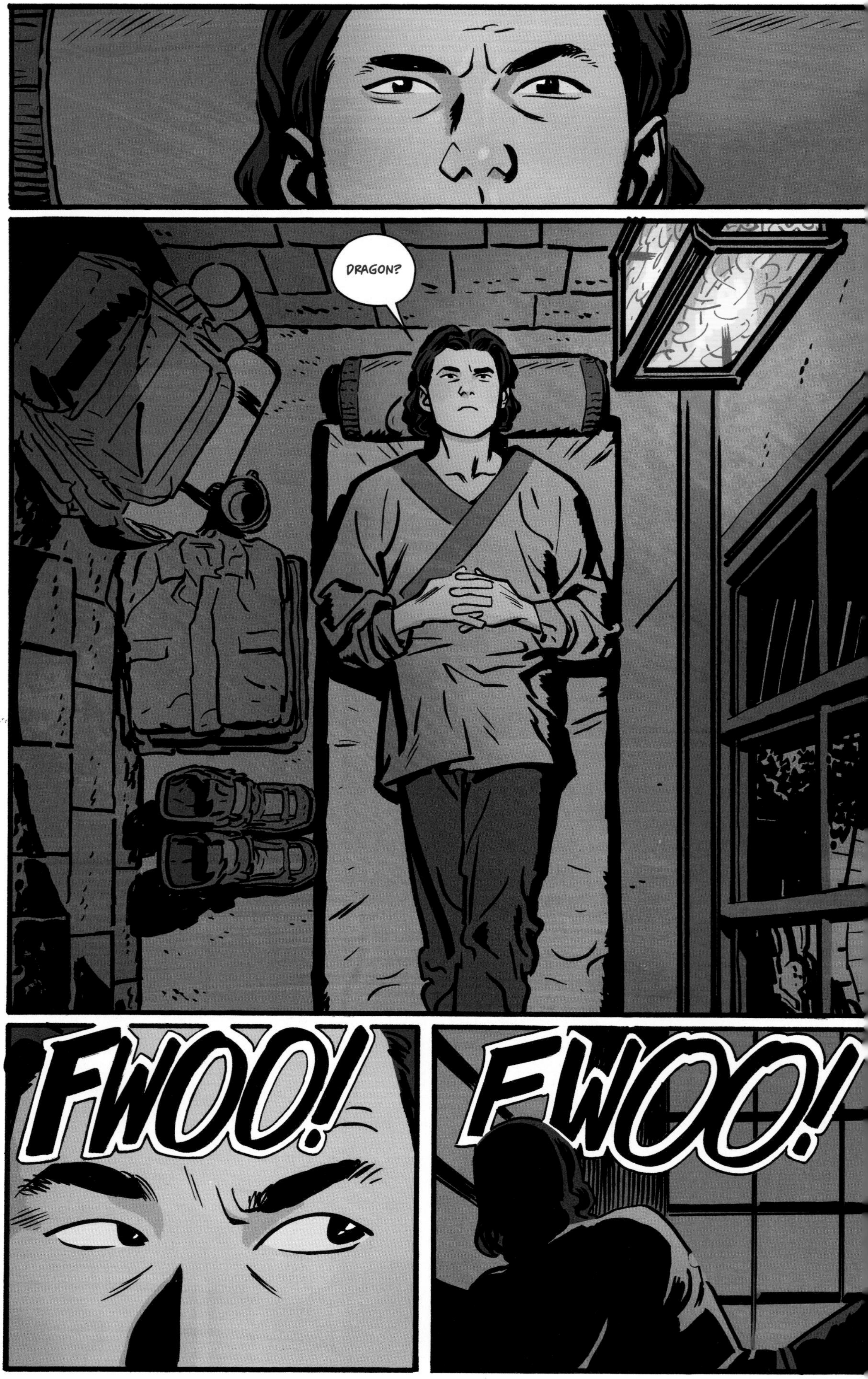
DRAGON?
FWOO!
FWOO!

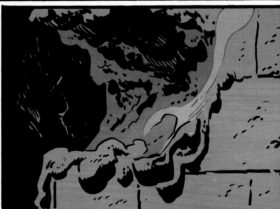

FWOO!

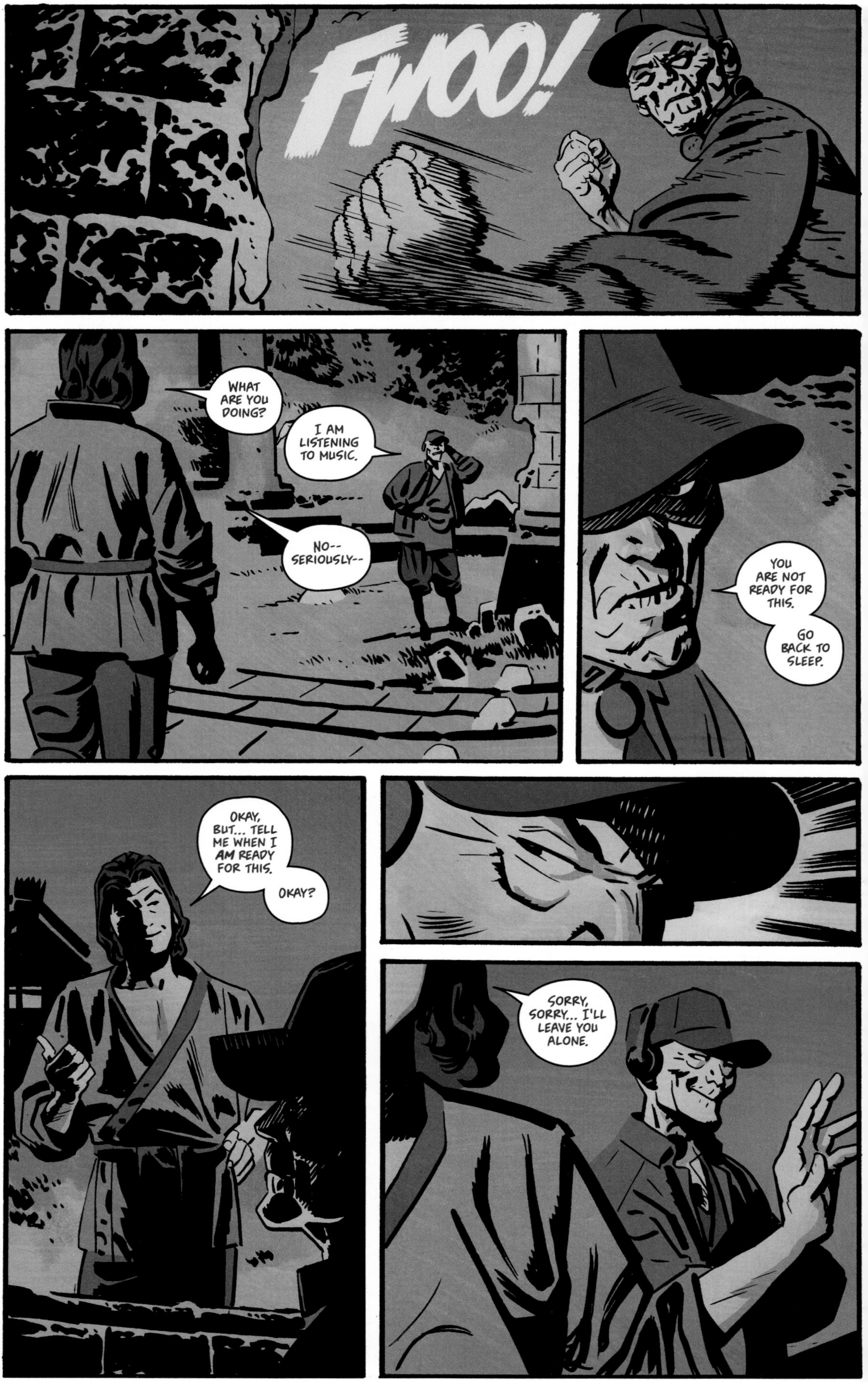
FWOO!
WHAT ARE YOU DOING?
I AM LISTENING TO MUSIC.
NO-- SERIOUSLY--
YOU ARE NOT READY FOR THIS.
GO BACK TO SLEEP.
OKAY, BUT... TELL ME WHEN I AM READY FOR THIS.
OKAY?
SORRY, SORRY... I'LL LEAVE YOU ALONE.

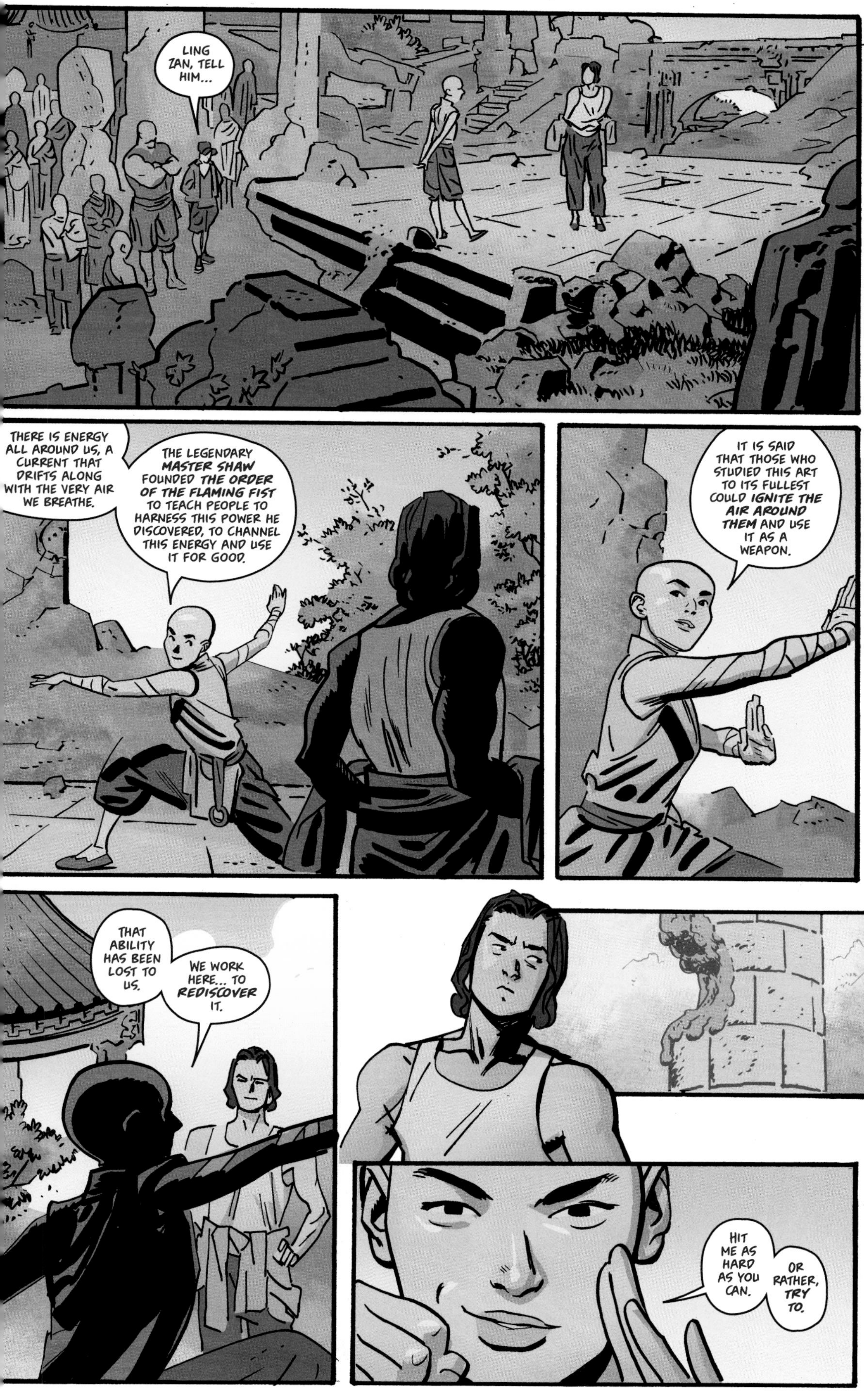
LING ZAN, TELL HIM...
THERE IS ENERGY ALL AROUND US, A CURRENT THAT DRIFTS ALONG WITH THE VERY AIR WE BREATHE.
THE LEGENDARY **MASTER SHAW** FOUNDED **THE ORDER OF THE FLAMING FIST** TO TEACH PEOPLE TO HARNESS THIS POWER HE DISCOVERED, TO CHANNEL THIS ENERGY AND USE IT FOR GOOD.
IT IS SAID THAT THOSE WHO STUDIED THIS ART TO ITS FULLEST COULD **IGNITE THE AIR AROUND THEM** AND USE IT AS A WEAPON.
THAT ABILITY HAS BEEN LOST TO US.
WE WORK HERE... TO **REDISCOVER** IT.
HIT ME AS HARD AS YOU CAN.
OR RATHER, **TRY** TO.

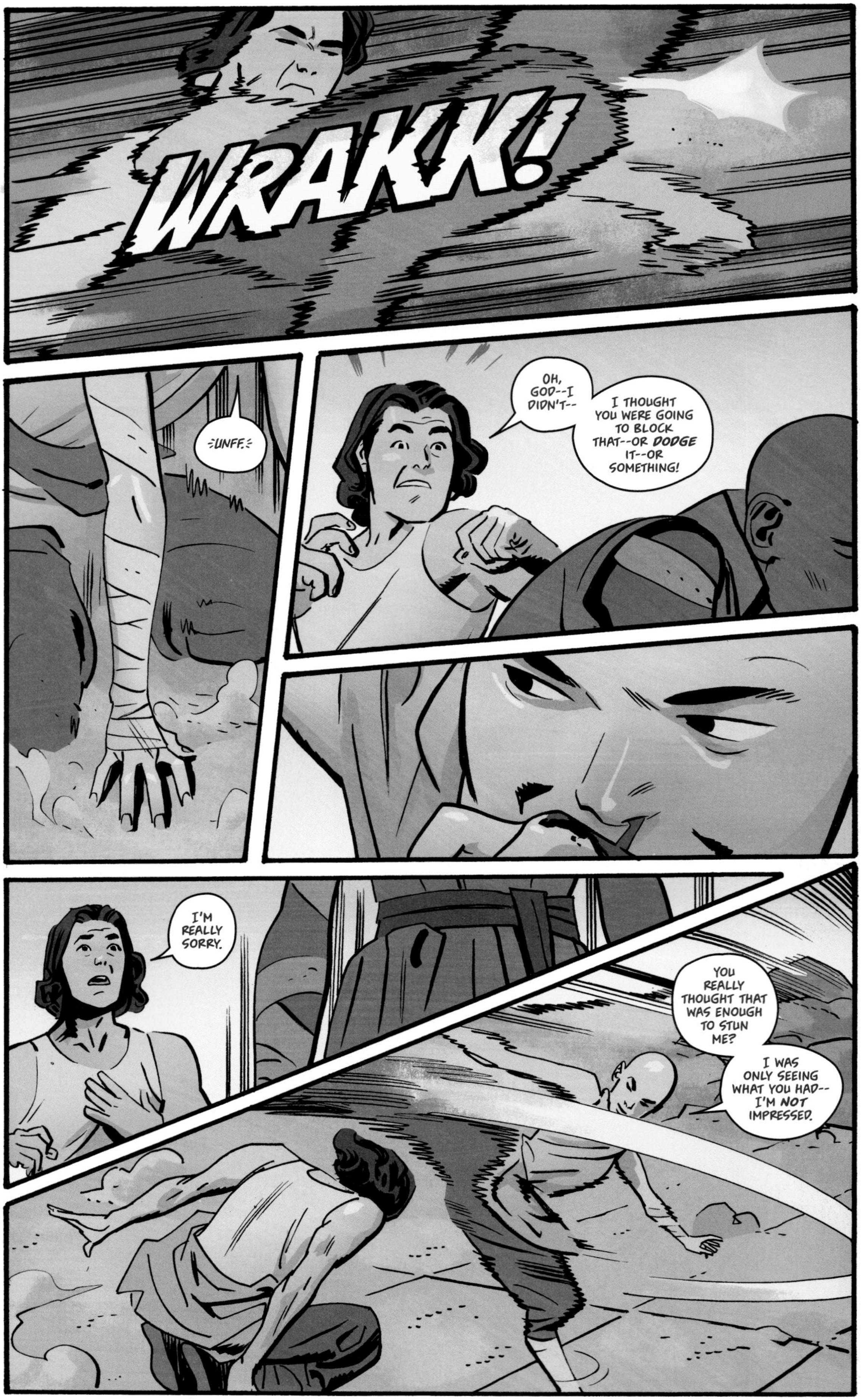
WRAKK!
UNFF.
OH, GOD--I DIDN'T--
I THOUGHT YOU WERE GOING TO BLOCK THAT--OR DODGE IT--OR SOMETHING!
I'M REALLY SORRY.
YOU REALLY THOUGHT THAT WAS ENOUGH TO STUN ME?
I WAS ONLY SEEING WHAT YOU HAD-- I'M NOT IMPRESSED.

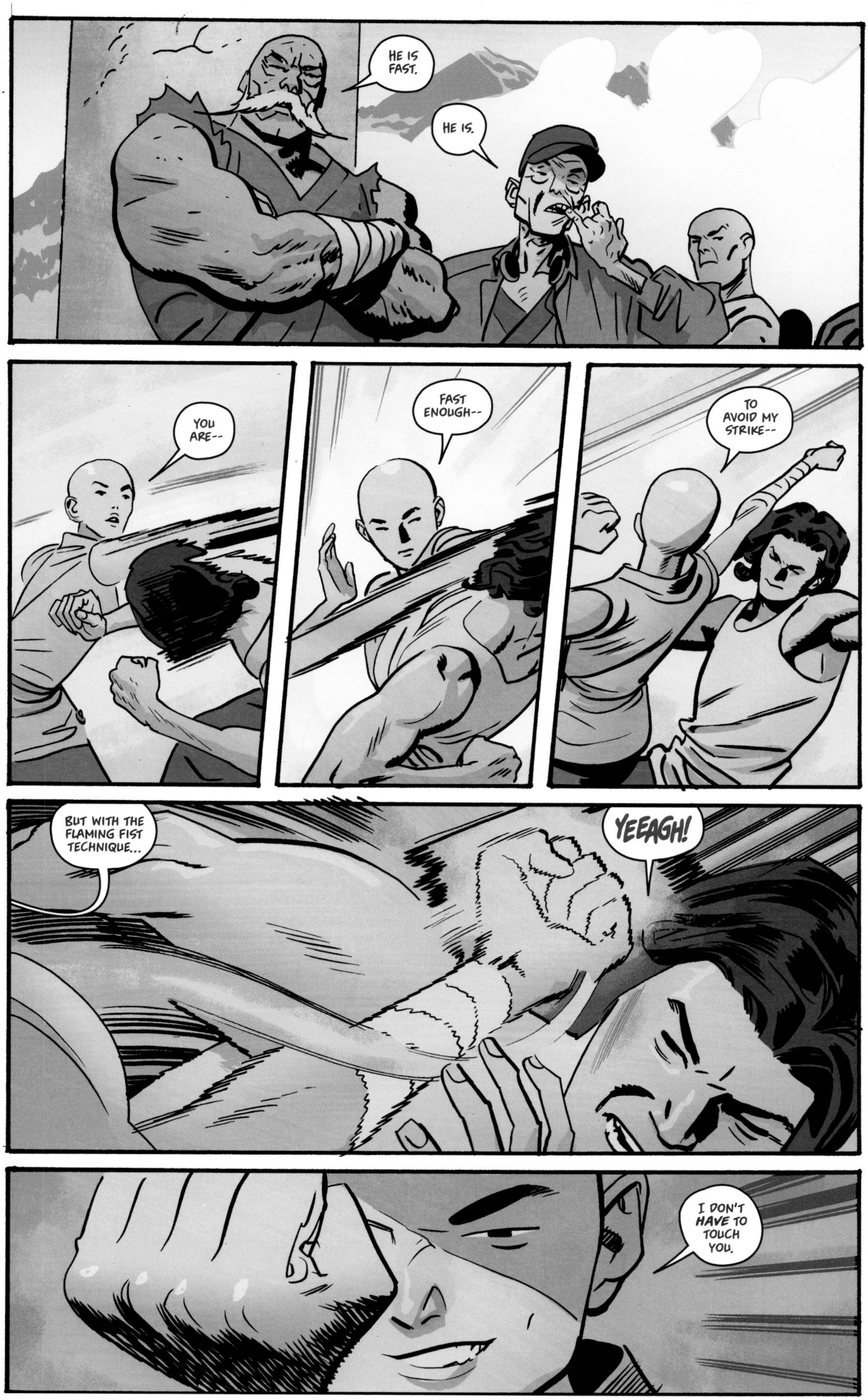
HE IS FAST.
HE IS.
YOU ARE--
FAST ENOUGH--
TO AVOID MY STRIKE--
BUT WITH THE FLAMING FIST TECHNIQUE...
YEEAGH!
I DON'T *HAVE* TO TOUCH YOU.

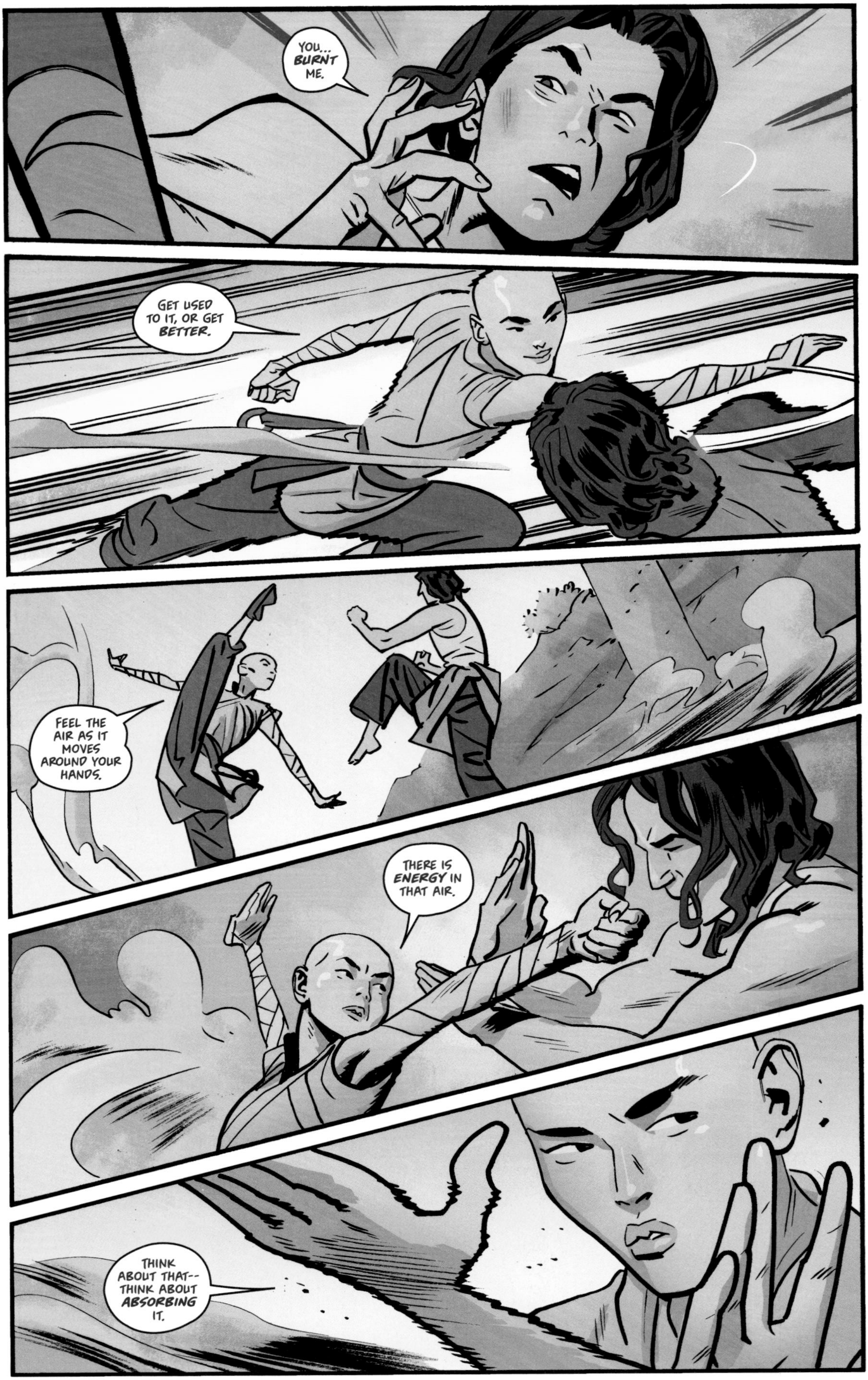
YOU... BURNT ME.
GET USED TO IT, OR GET BETTER.
FEEL THE AIR AS IT MOVES AROUND YOUR HANDS.
THERE IS ENERGY IN THAT AIR.
THINK ABOUT THAT-- THINK ABOUT ABSORBING IT.

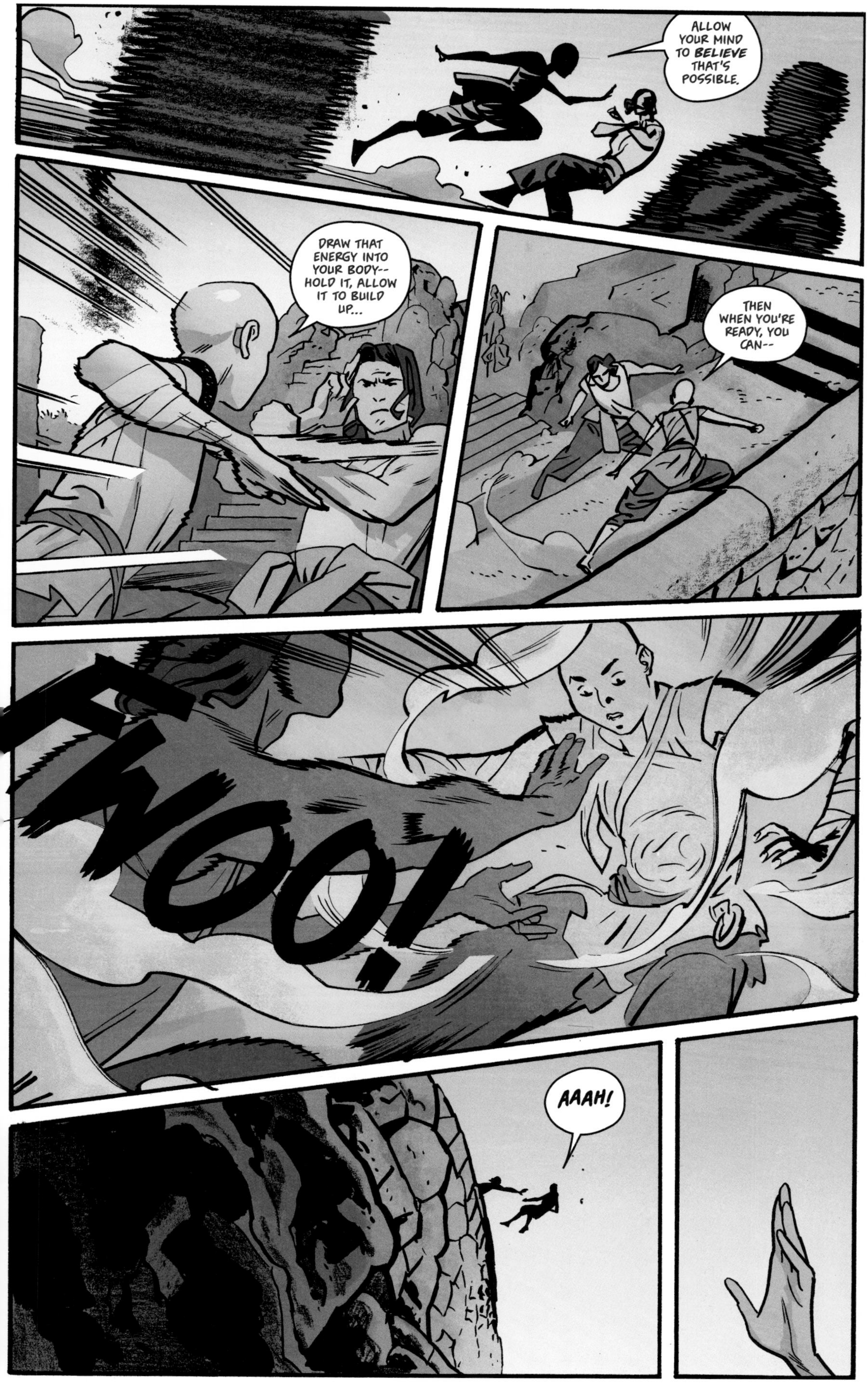
ALLOW YOUR MIND TO BELIEVE THAT'S POSSIBLE.
DRAW THAT ENERGY INTO YOUR BODY-- HOLD IT, ALLOW IT TO BUILD UP...
THEN WHEN YOU'RE READY, YOU CAN--
FWOOM!
AAAH!

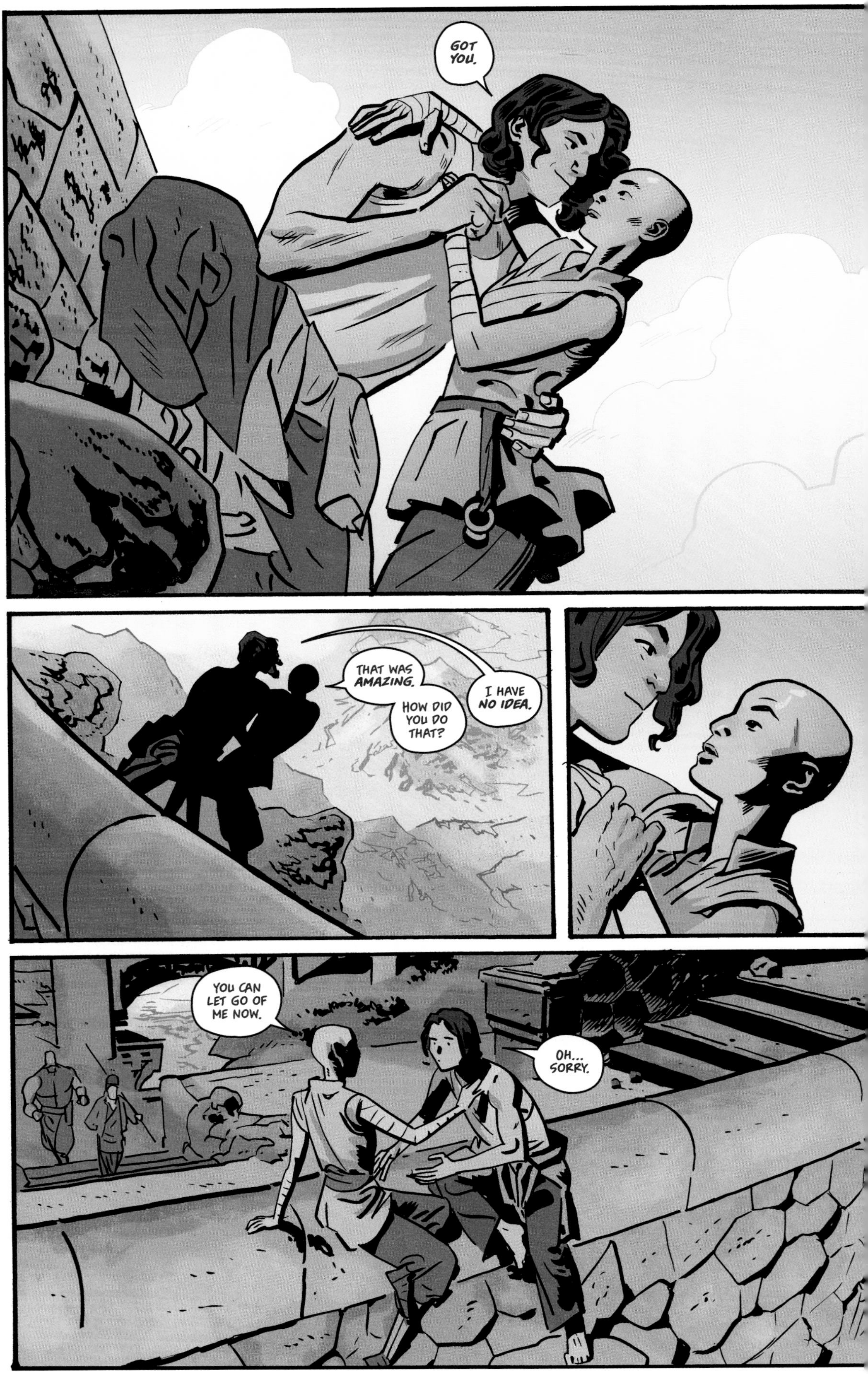
GOT YOU.
THAT WAS AMAZING.
HOW DID YOU DO THAT?
I HAVE NO IDEA.
YOU CAN LET GO OF ME NOW.
OH... SORRY.

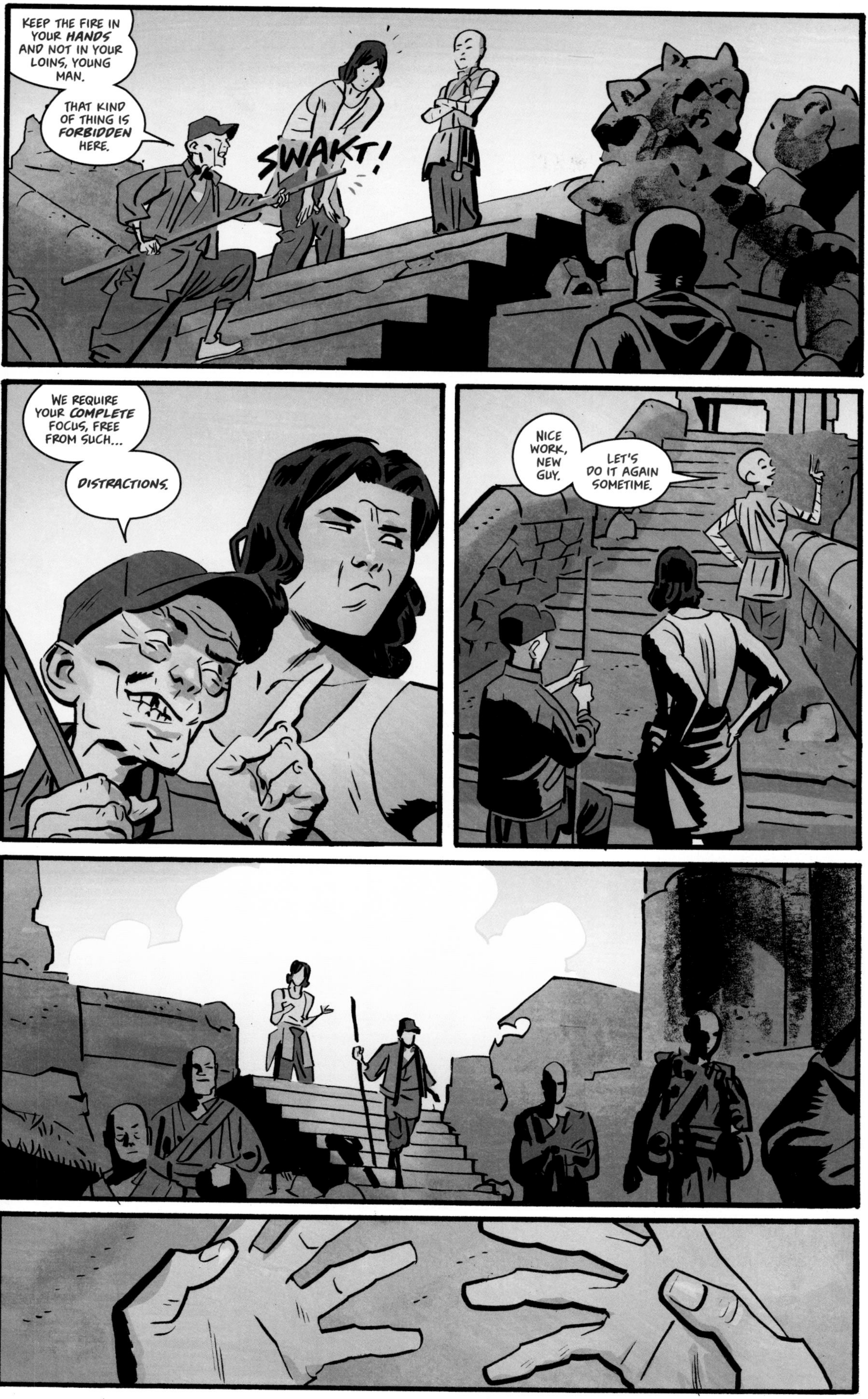
KEEP THE FIRE IN YOUR HANDS AND NOT IN YOUR LOINS, YOUNG MAN.
THAT KIND OF THING IS FORBIDDEN HERE.
SWAKT!
WE REQUIRE YOUR COMPLETE FOCUS, FREE FROM SUCH...
DISTRACTIONS.
NICE WORK, NEW GUY.
LET'S DO IT AGAIN SOMETIME.

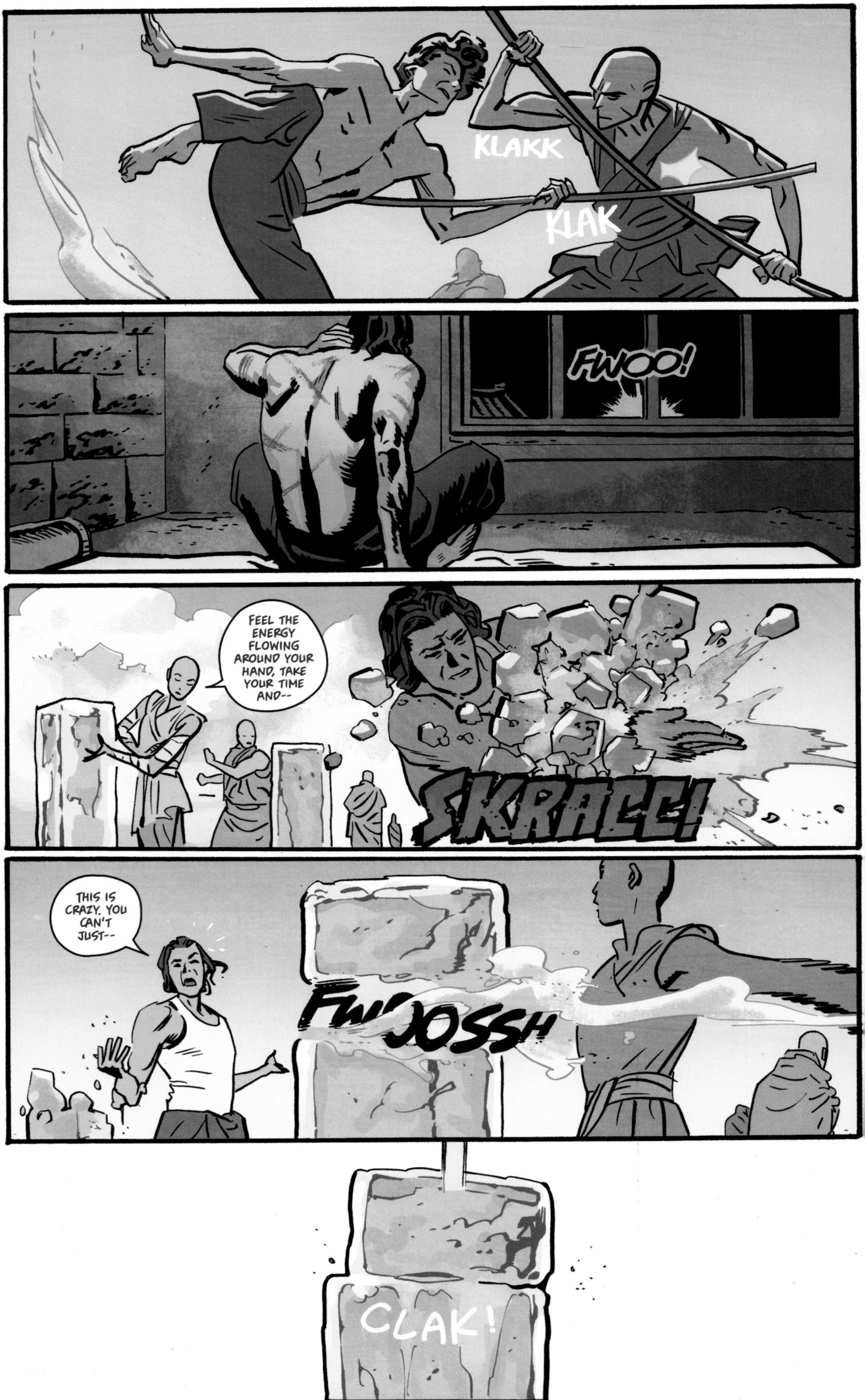
KLAKK
KLAK
FWOO!
FEEL THE ENERGY FLOWING AROUND YOUR HAND, TAKE YOUR TIME AND--
SKRACC!
THIS IS CRAZY. YOU CAN'T JUST--
FWOOSSH
CLAK!

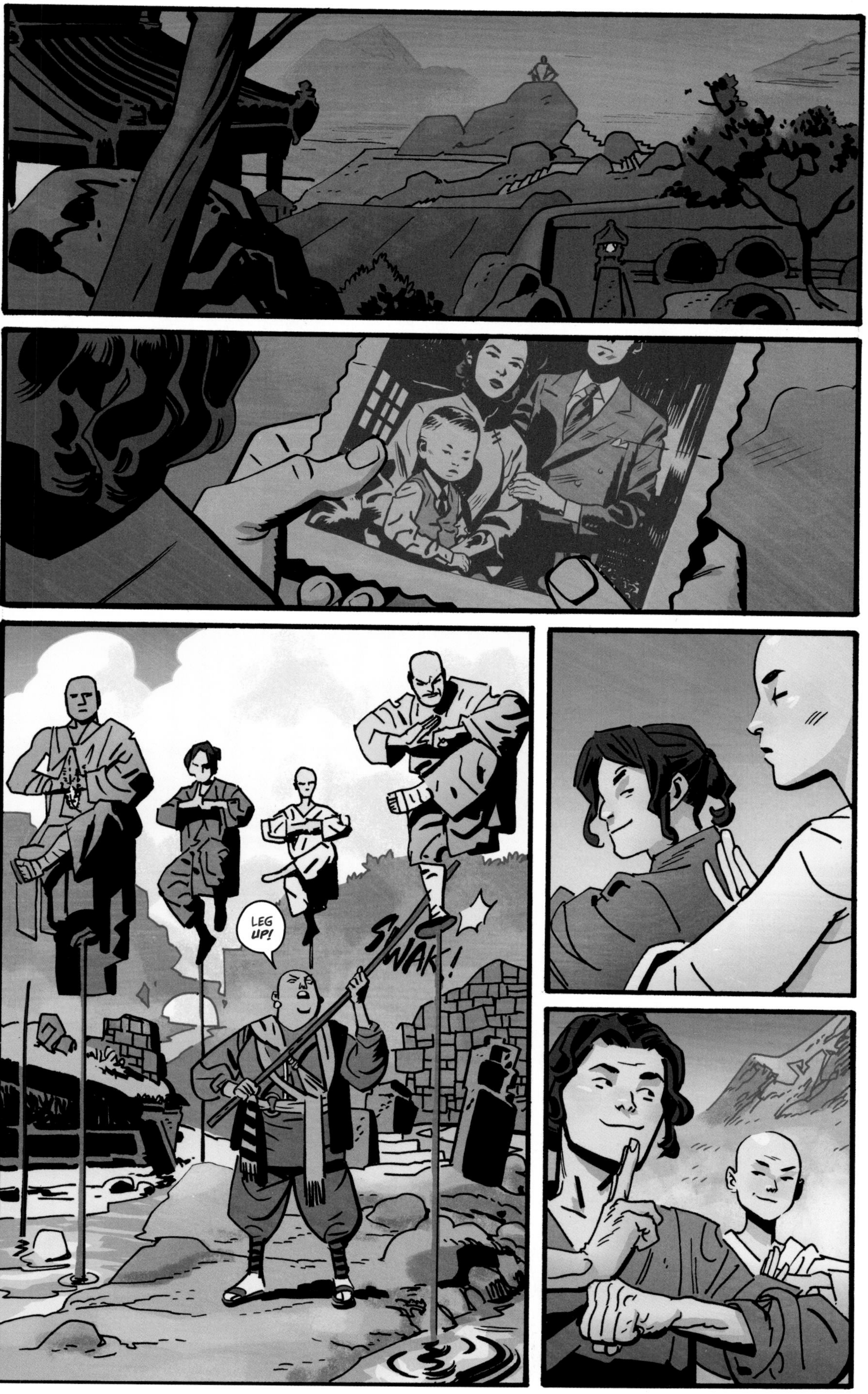
LEG UP!
SWAK!

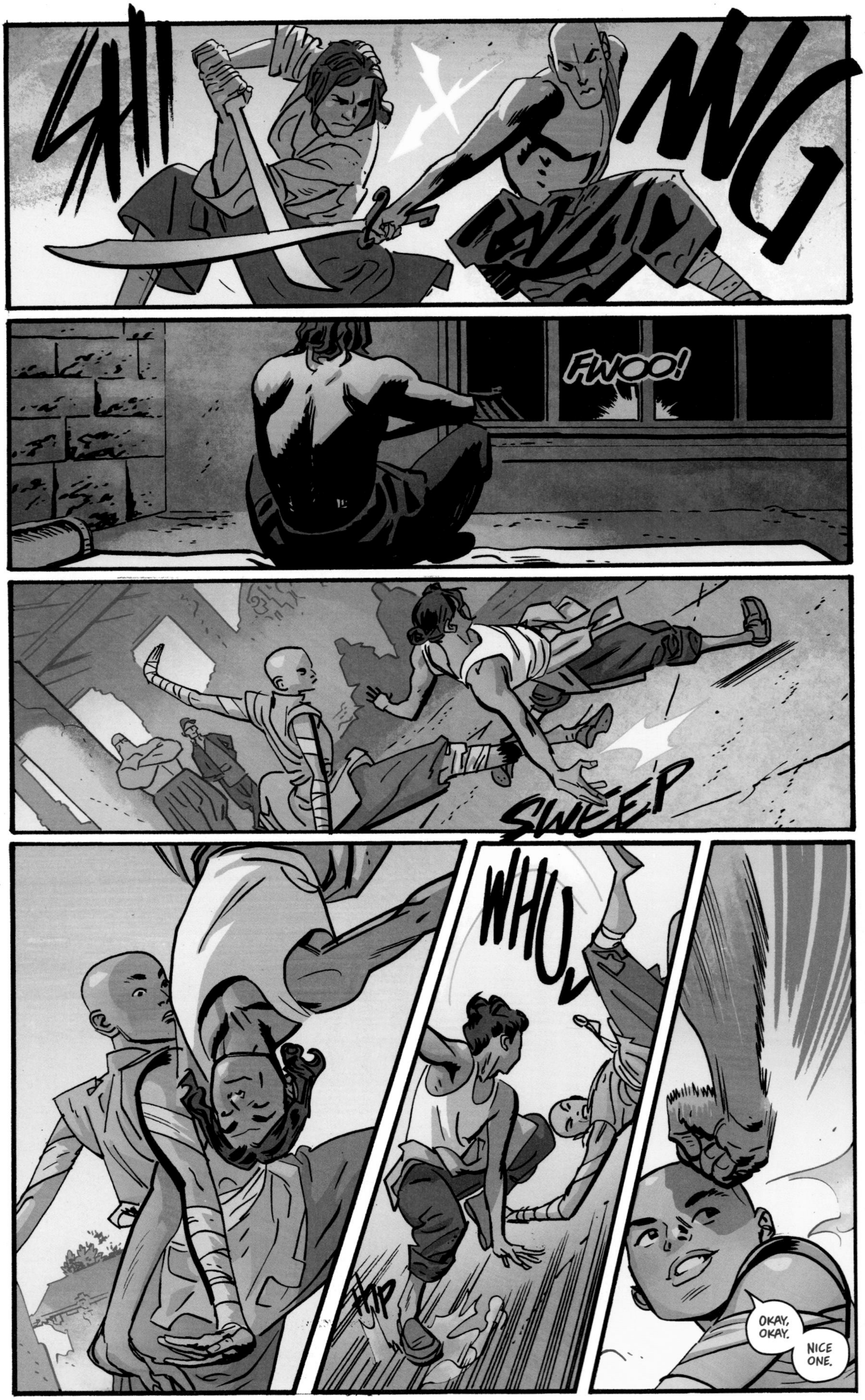
SHIING
FWOO!
SWEEP
WHUV
HUP
OKAY, OKAY.
NICE ONE.

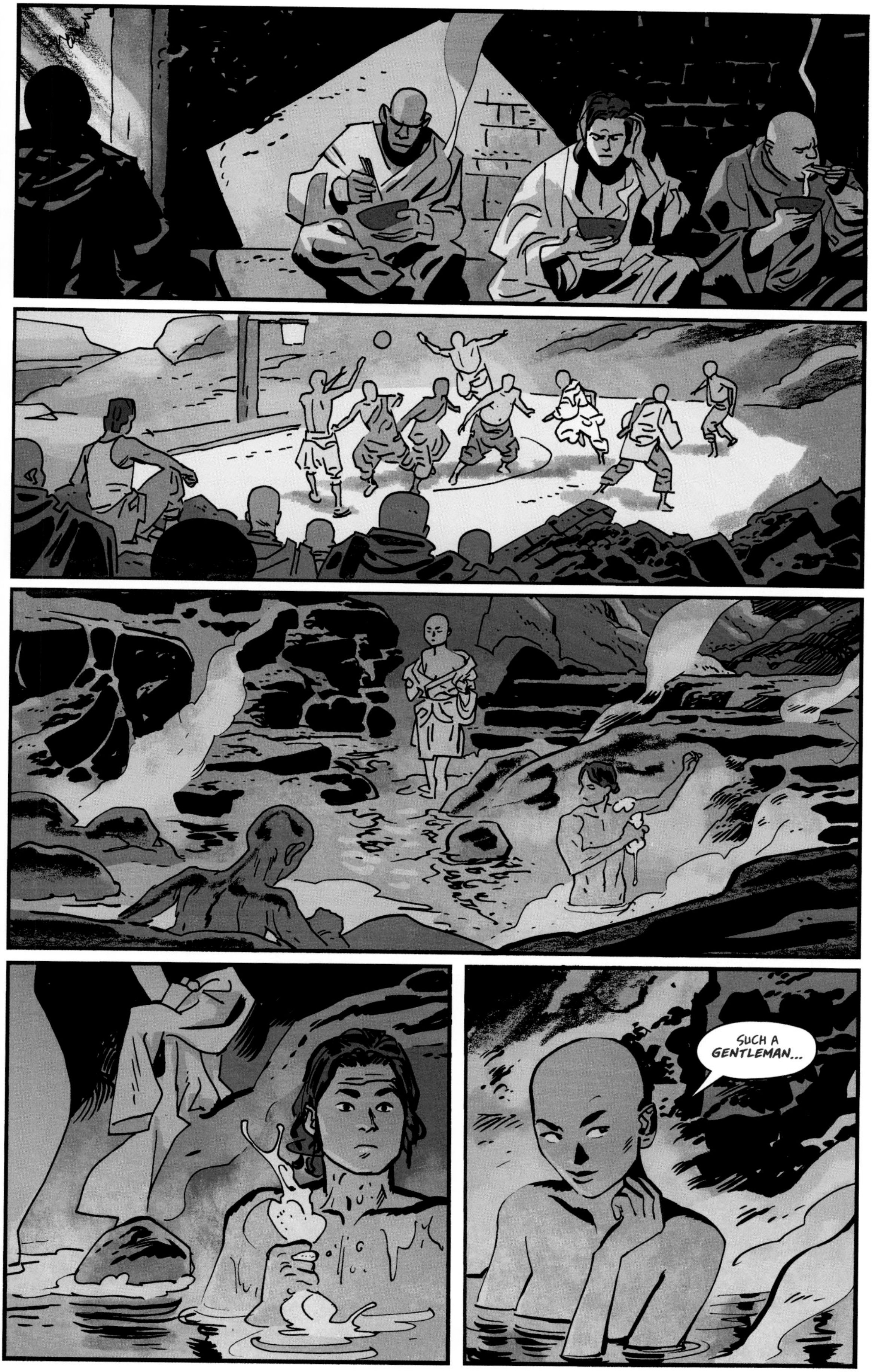
SUCH A GENTLEMAN...

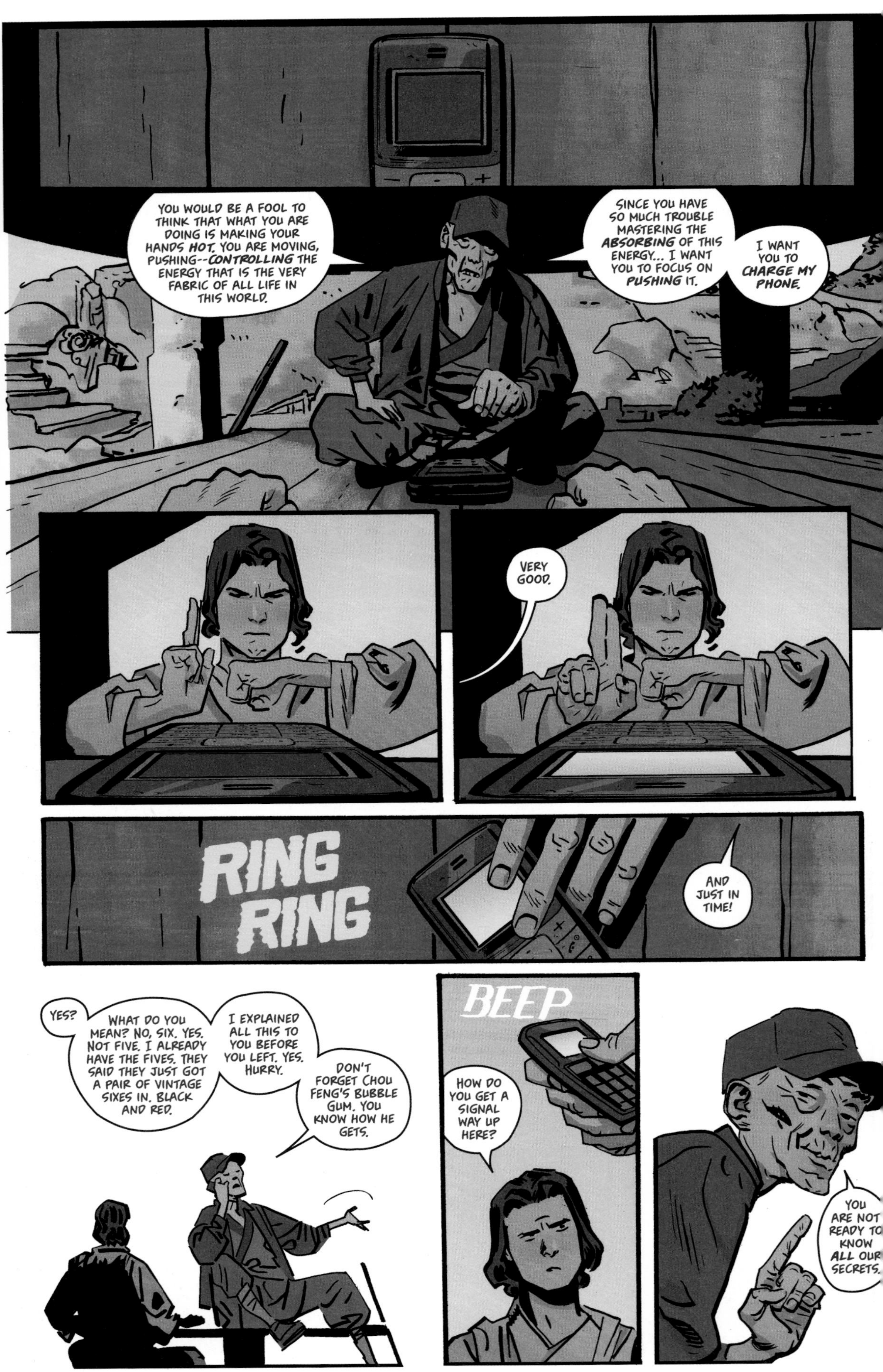
YOU WOULD BE A FOOL TO THINK THAT WHAT YOU ARE DOING IS MAKING YOUR HANDS HOT. YOU ARE MOVING, PUSHING--CONTROLLING THE ENERGY THAT IS THE VERY FABRIC OF ALL LIFE IN THIS WORLD.
SINCE YOU HAVE SO MUCH TROUBLE MASTERING THE ABSORBING OF THIS ENERGY... I WANT YOU TO FOCUS ON PUSHING IT.
I WANT YOU TO CHARGE MY PHONE.
VERY GOOD.
RING RING
AND JUST IN TIME!
YES?
WHAT DO YOU MEAN? NO, SIX. YES. NOT FIVE. I ALREADY HAVE THE FIVES. THEY SAID THEY JUST GOT A PAIR OF VINTAGE SIXES IN. BLACK AND RED.
I EXPLAINED ALL THIS TO YOU BEFORE YOU LEFT. YES. HURRY.
DON'T FORGET CHOU FENG'S BUBBLE GUM. YOU KNOW HOW HE GETS.
BEEP
HOW DO YOU GET A SIGNAL WAY UP HERE?
YOU ARE NOT READY TO KNOW ALL OUR SECRETS.

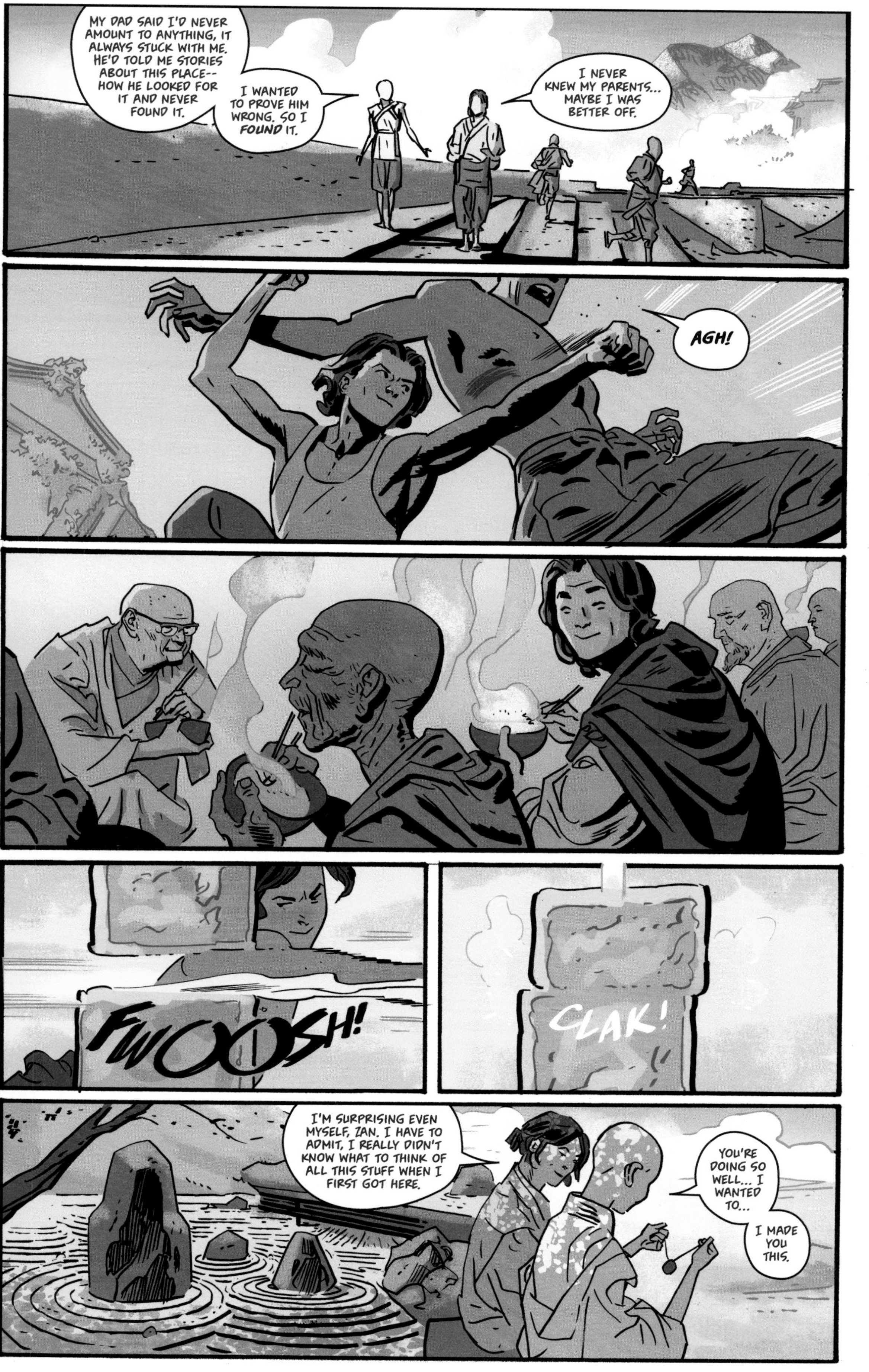
MY DAD SAID I'D NEVER AMOUNT TO ANYTHING, IT ALWAYS STUCK WITH ME. HE'D TOLD ME STORIES ABOUT THIS PLACE-- HOW HE LOOKED FOR IT AND NEVER FOUND IT.
I WANTED TO PROVE HIM WRONG. SO I FOUND IT.
I NEVER KNEW MY PARENTS... MAYBE I WAS BETTER OFF.
AGH!
FWOOOSH!
CLAK!
I'M SURPRISING EVEN MYSELF, ZAN. I HAVE TO ADMIT, I REALLY DIDN'T KNOW WHAT TO THINK OF ALL THIS STUFF WHEN I FIRST GOT HERE.
YOU'RE DOING SO WELL... I WANTED TO...
I MADE YOU THIS.

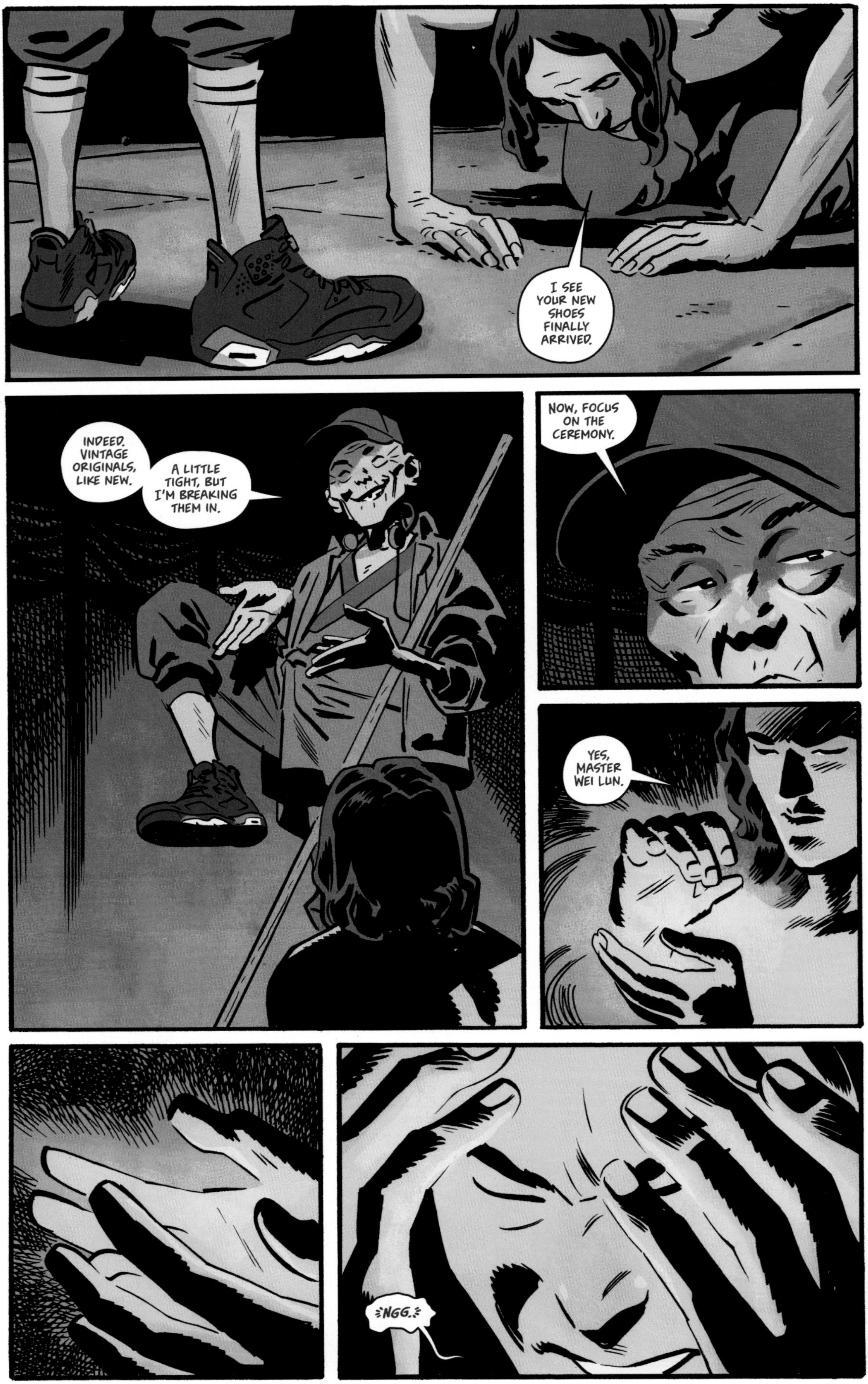
I SEE YOUR NEW SHOES FINALLY ARRIVED.
INDEED. VINTAGE ORIGINALS, LIKE NEW.
A LITTLE TIGHT, BUT I'M BREAKING THEM IN.
NOW, FOCUS ON THE CEREMONY.
YES, MASTER WEI LUN.
NGG.

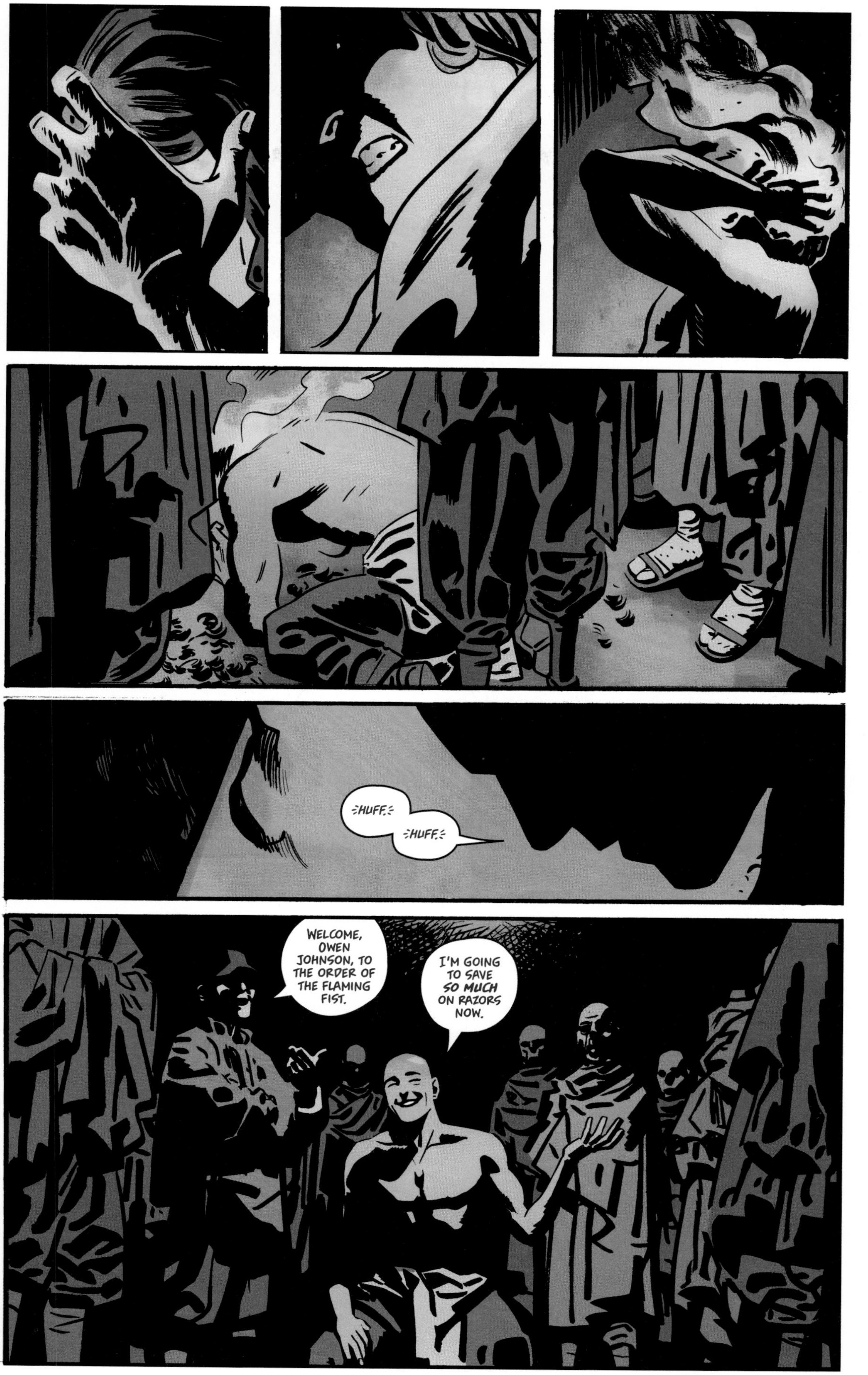
HUFF.
HUFF.
WELCOME, OWEN JOHNSON, TO THE ORDER OF THE FLAMING FIST.
I'M GOING TO SAVE SO MUCH ON RAZORS NOW.

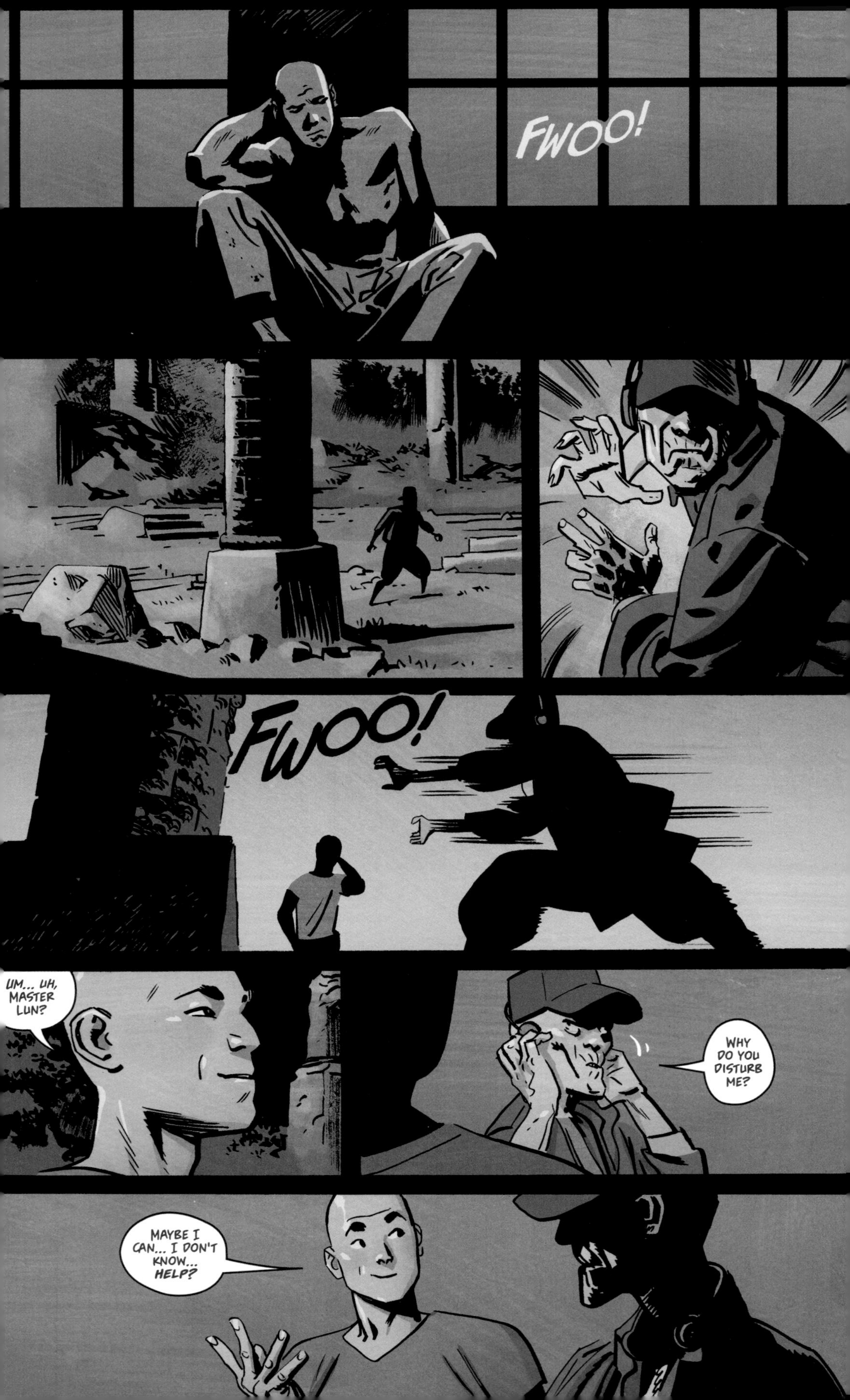
FWOO!
FWOO!
UM... UH, MASTER LUN?
WHY DO YOU DISTURB ME?
MAYBE I CAN... I DON'T KNOW... HELP?

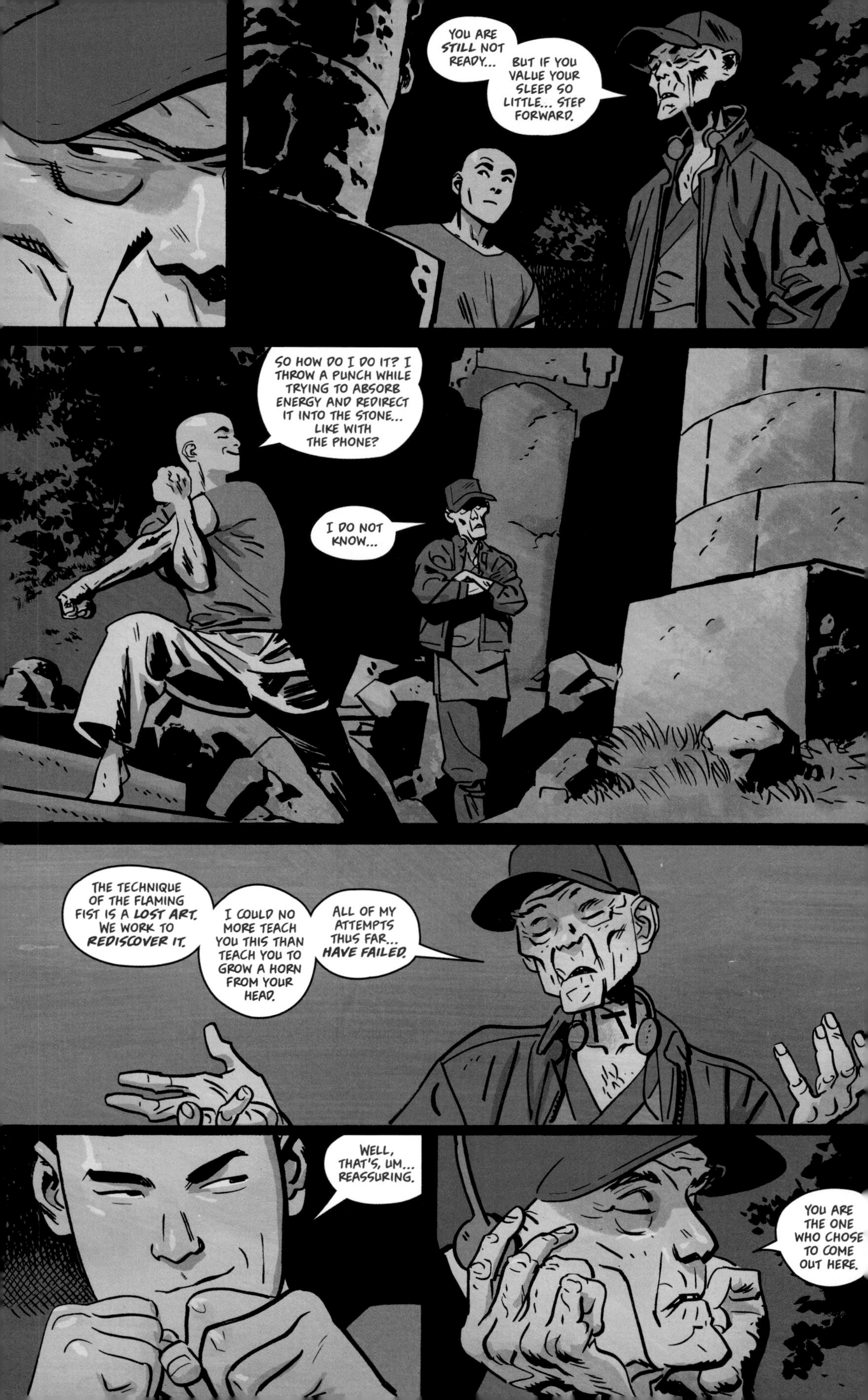

YOU ARE STILL NOT READY...
BUT IF YOU VALUE YOUR SLEEP SO LITTLE... STEP FORWARD.
SO HOW DO I DO IT? I THROW A PUNCH WHILE TRYING TO ABSORB ENERGY AND REDIRECT IT INTO THE STONE... LIKE WITH THE PHONE?
I DO NOT KNOW...
THE TECHNIQUE OF THE FLAMING FIST IS A LOST ART. WE WORK TO REDISCOVER IT.
I COULD NO MORE TEACH YOU THIS THAN TEACH YOU TO GROW A HORN FROM YOUR HEAD.
ALL OF MY ATTEMPTS THUS FAR... HAVE FAILED.
WELL, THAT'S, UM... REASSURING.
YOU ARE THE ONE WHO CHOSE TO COME OUT HERE.

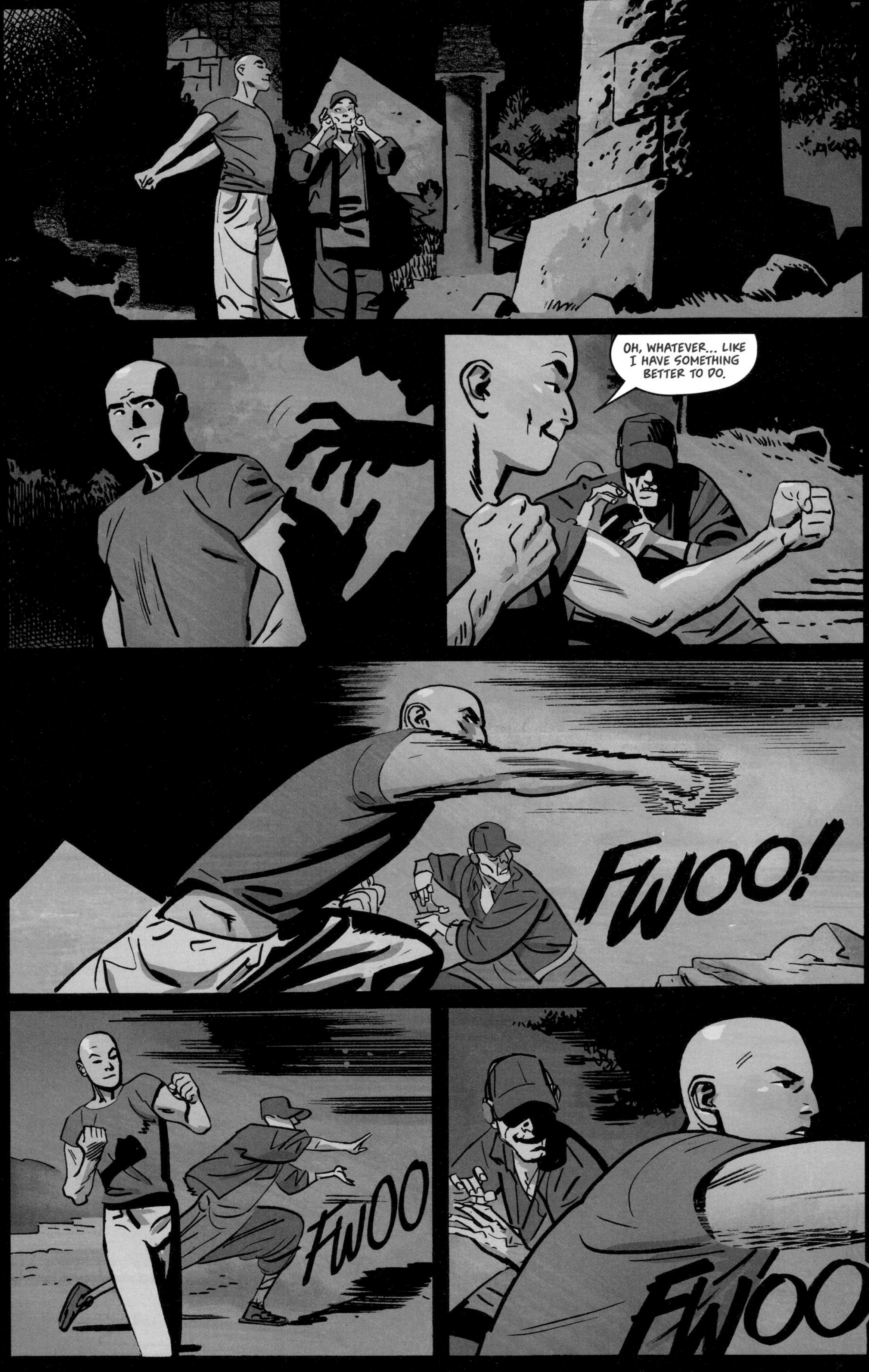
OH, WHATEVER... LIKE I HAVE SOMETHING BETTER TO DO.
FWOO!
FWOO
FWOO

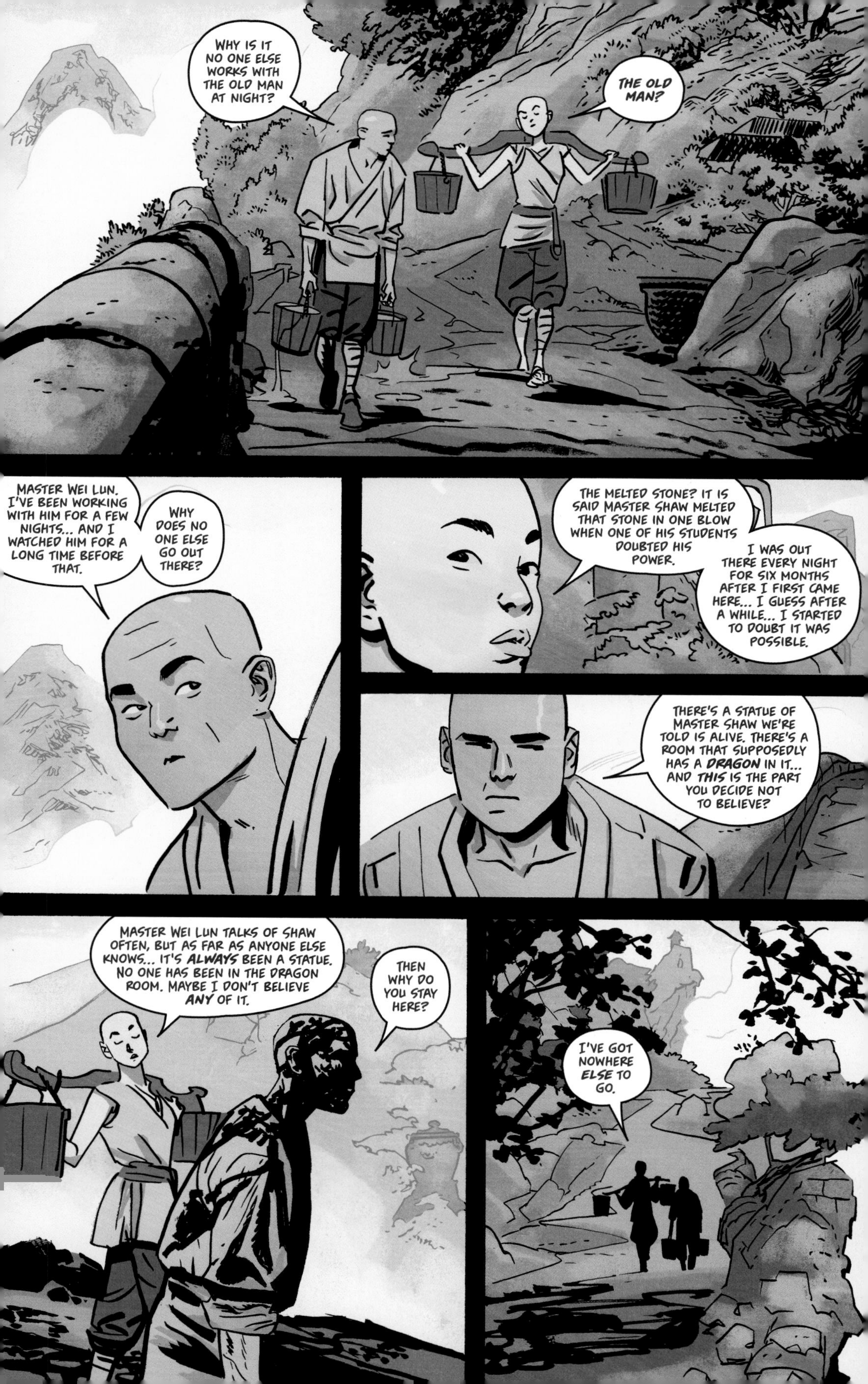
WHY IS IT NO ONE ELSE WORKS WITH THE OLD MAN AT NIGHT?
THE OLD MAN?
MASTER WEI LUN. I'VE BEEN WORKING WITH HIM FOR A FEW NIGHTS... AND I WATCHED HIM FOR A LONG TIME BEFORE THAT.
WHY DOES NO ONE ELSE GO OUT THERE?
THE MELTED STONE? IT IS SAID MASTER SHAW MELTED THAT STONE IN ONE BLOW WHEN ONE OF HIS STUDENTS DOUBTED HIS POWER.
I WAS OUT THERE EVERY NIGHT FOR SIX MONTHS AFTER I FIRST CAME HERE... I GUESS AFTER A WHILE... I STARTED TO DOUBT IT WAS POSSIBLE.
THERE'S A STATUE OF MASTER SHAW WE'RE TOLD IS ALIVE. THERE'S A ROOM THAT SUPPOSEDLY HAS A DRAGON IN IT... AND THIS IS THE PART YOU DECIDE NOT TO BELIEVE?
MASTER WEI LUN TALKS OF SHAW OFTEN, BUT AS FAR AS ANYONE ELSE KNOWS... IT'S ALWAYS BEEN A STATUE. NO ONE HAS BEEN IN THE DRAGON ROOM. MAYBE I DON'T BELIEVE ANY OF IT.
THEN WHY DO YOU STAY HERE?
I'VE GOT NOWHERE ELSE TO GO.

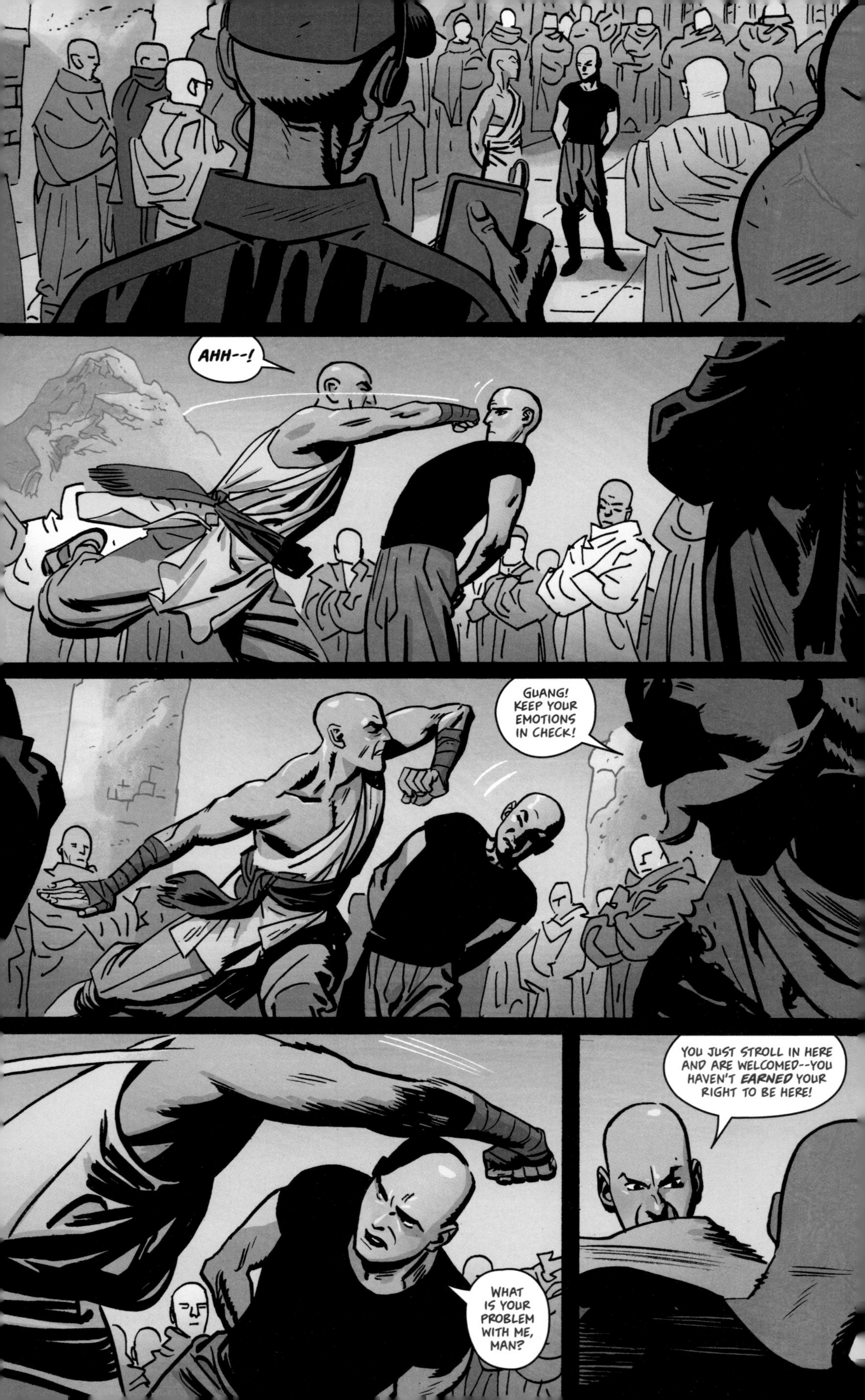
AHH--!
GUANG! KEEP YOUR EMOTIONS IN CHECK!
WHAT IS YOUR PROBLEM WITH ME, MAN?
YOU JUST STROLL IN HERE AND ARE WELCOMED--YOU HAVEN'T EARNED YOUR RIGHT TO BE HERE!

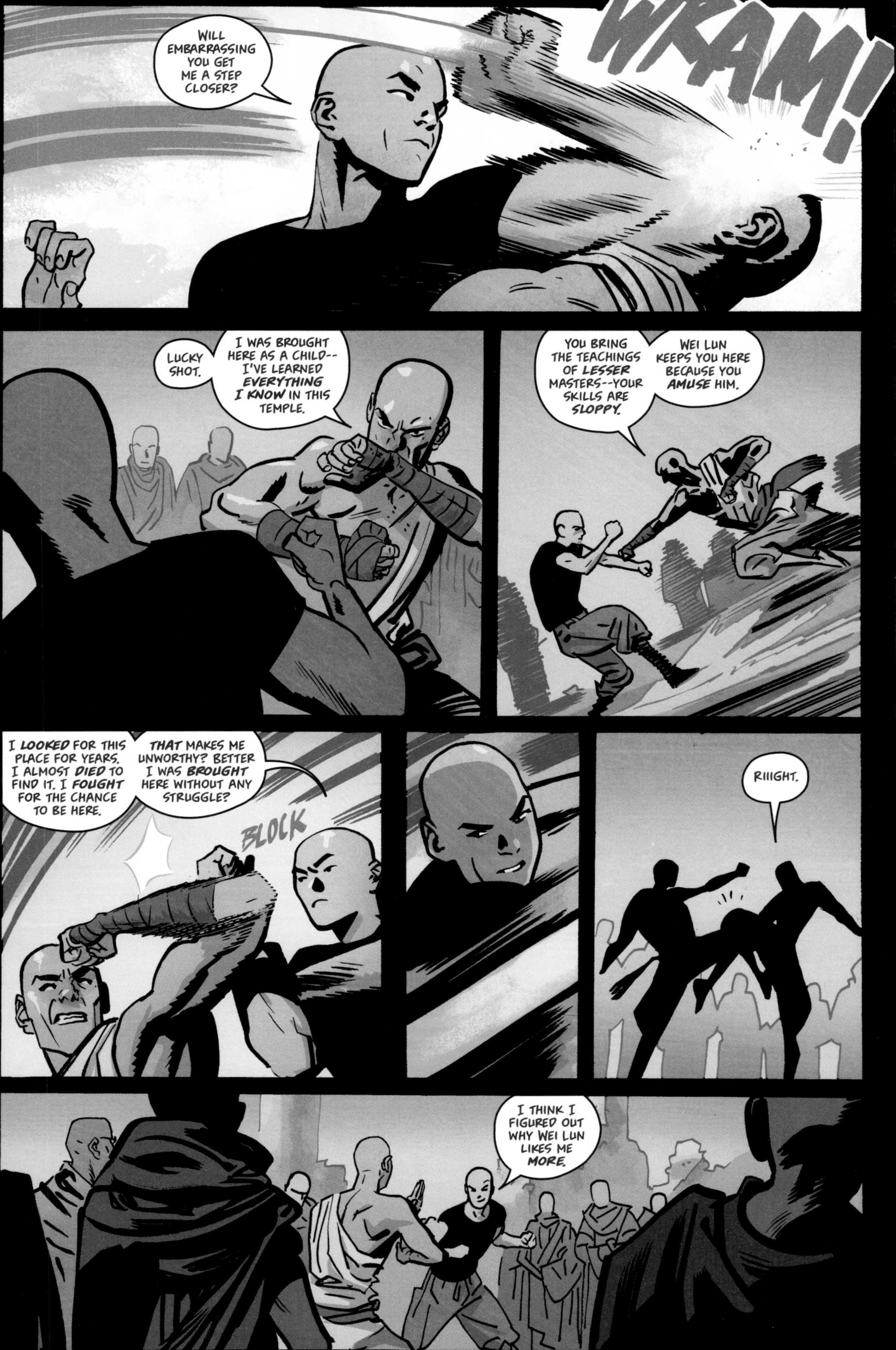

WILL EMBARRASSING YOU GET ME A STEP CLOSER?
WRAM!
LUCKY SHOT.
I WAS BROUGHT HERE AS A CHILD-- I'VE LEARNED EVERYTHING I KNOW IN THIS TEMPLE.
YOU BRING THE TEACHINGS OF LESSER MASTERS--YOUR SKILLS ARE SLOPPY.
WEI LUN KEEPS YOU HERE BECAUSE YOU AMUSE HIM.
I LOOKED FOR THIS PLACE FOR YEARS. I ALMOST DIED TO FIND IT. I FOUGHT FOR THE CHANCE TO BE HERE.
THAT MAKES ME UNWORTHY? BETTER I WAS BROUGHT HERE WITHOUT ANY STRUGGLE?
BLOCK
RIIIGHT.
I THINK I FIGURED OUT WHY WEI LUN LIKES ME MORE.

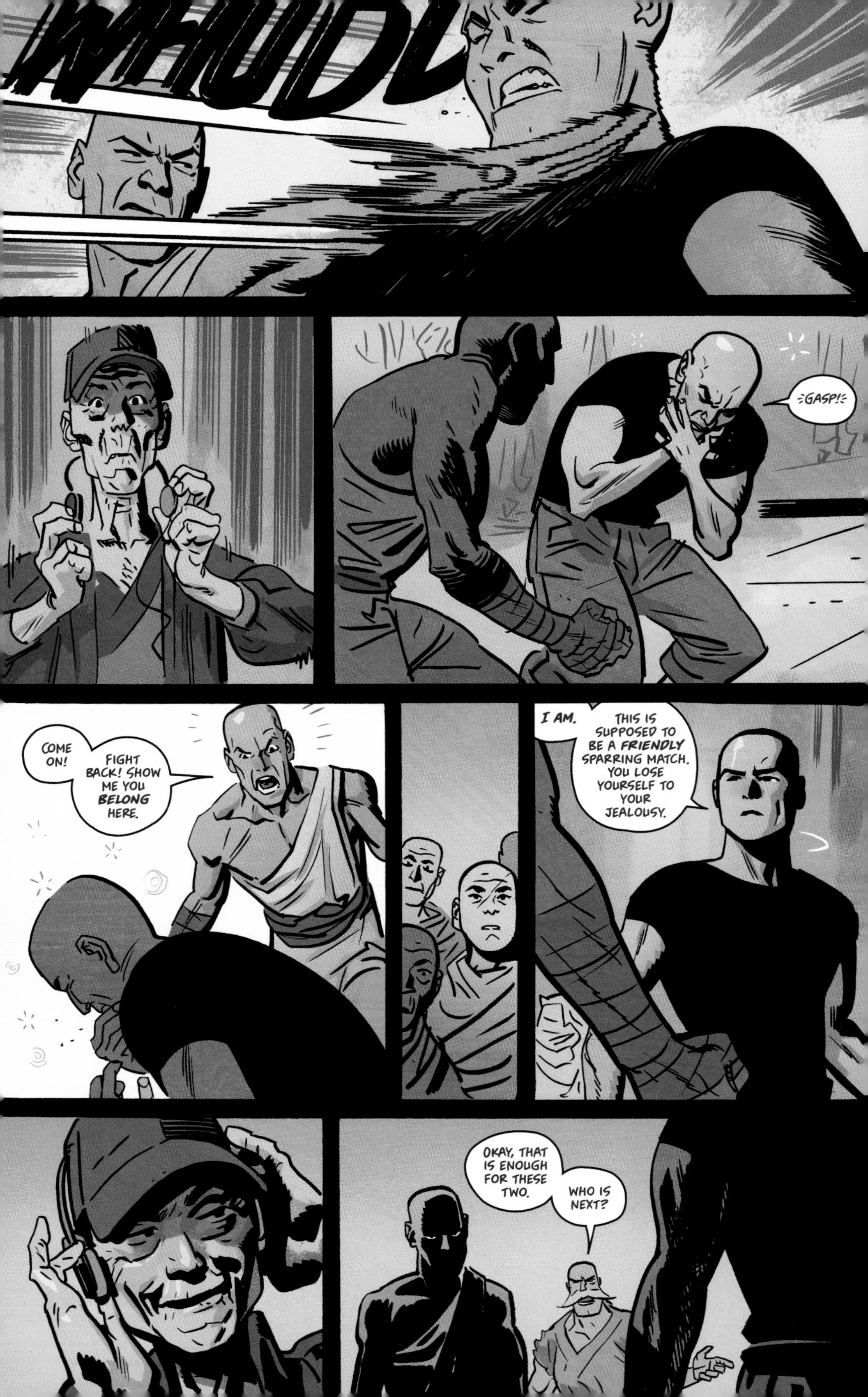
WHUDD
GASP!
COME ON!
FIGHT BACK! SHOW ME YOU BELONG HERE.
I AM.
THIS IS SUPPOSED TO BE A FRIENDLY SPARRING MATCH. YOU LOSE YOURSELF TO YOUR JEALOUSY.
OKAY, THAT IS ENOUGH FOR THESE TWO.
WHO IS NEXT?

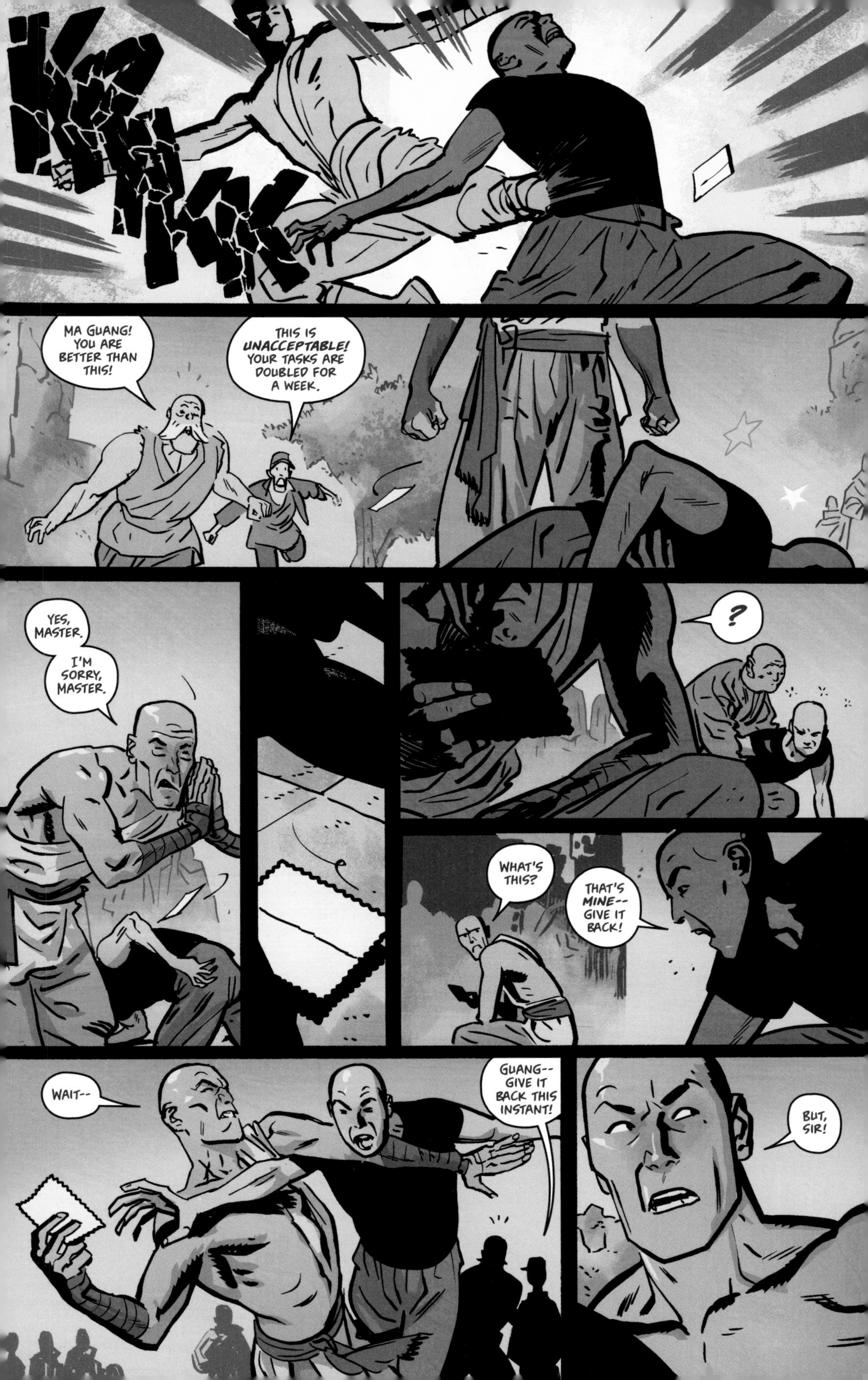
KRAKK
MA GUANG! YOU ARE BETTER THAN THIS!
THIS IS UNACCEPTABLE! YOUR TASKS ARE DOUBLED FOR A WEEK.
YES, MASTER.
I'M SORRY, MASTER.
?
WHAT'S THIS?
THAT'S MINE--GIVE IT BACK!
WAIT--
GUANG--GIVE IT BACK THIS INSTANT!
BUT, SIR!

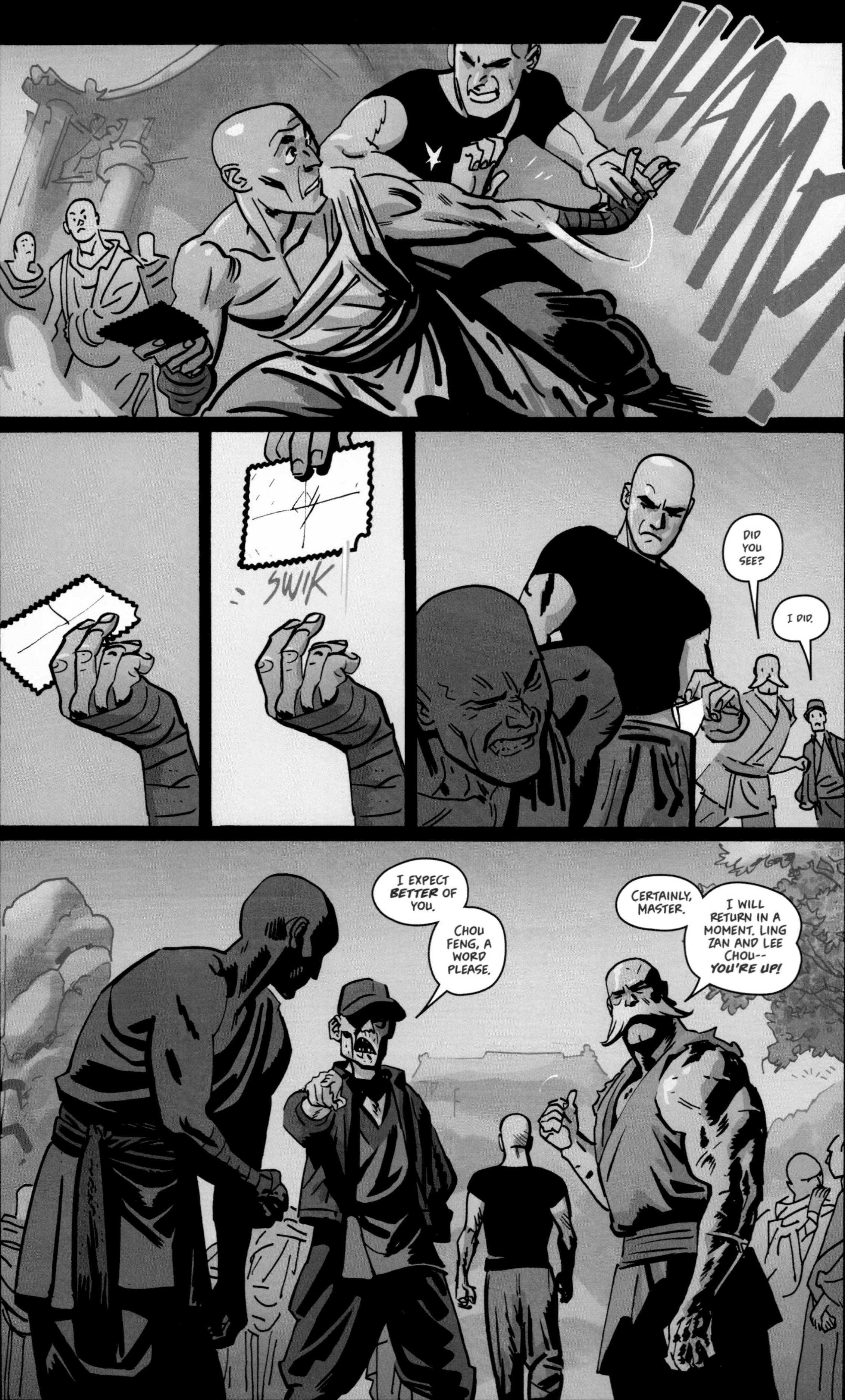
WHAMP!
SWIK
DID YOU SEE?
I DID.
I EXPECT BETTER OF YOU.
CHOU FENG, A WORD PLEASE.
CERTAINLY, MASTER.
I WILL RETURN IN A MOMENT. LING ZAN AND LEE CHOU-- YOU'RE UP!

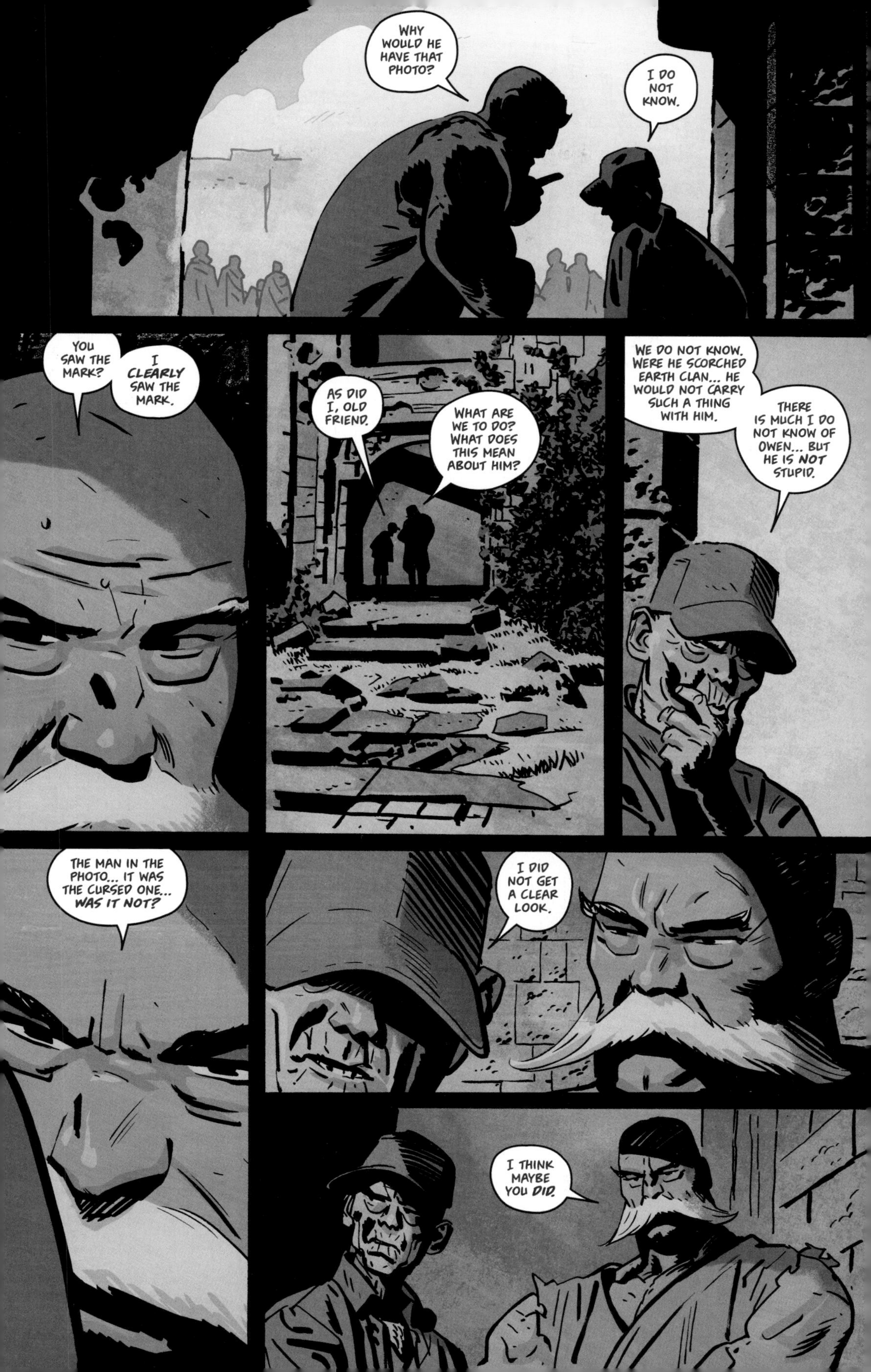
WHY WOULD HE HAVE THAT PHOTO?
I DO NOT KNOW.
YOU SAW THE MARK?
I CLEARLY SAW THE MARK.
AS DID I, OLD FRIEND.
WHAT ARE WE TO DO? WHAT DOES THIS MEAN ABOUT HIM?
WE DO NOT KNOW. WERE HE SCORCHED EARTH CLAN... HE WOULD NOT CARRY SUCH A THING WITH HIM.
THERE IS MUCH I DO NOT KNOW OF OWEN... BUT HE IS NOT STUPID.
THE MAN IN THE PHOTO... IT WAS THE CURSED ONE... WAS IT NOT?
I DID NOT GET A CLEAR LOOK.
I THINK MAYBE YOU DID.

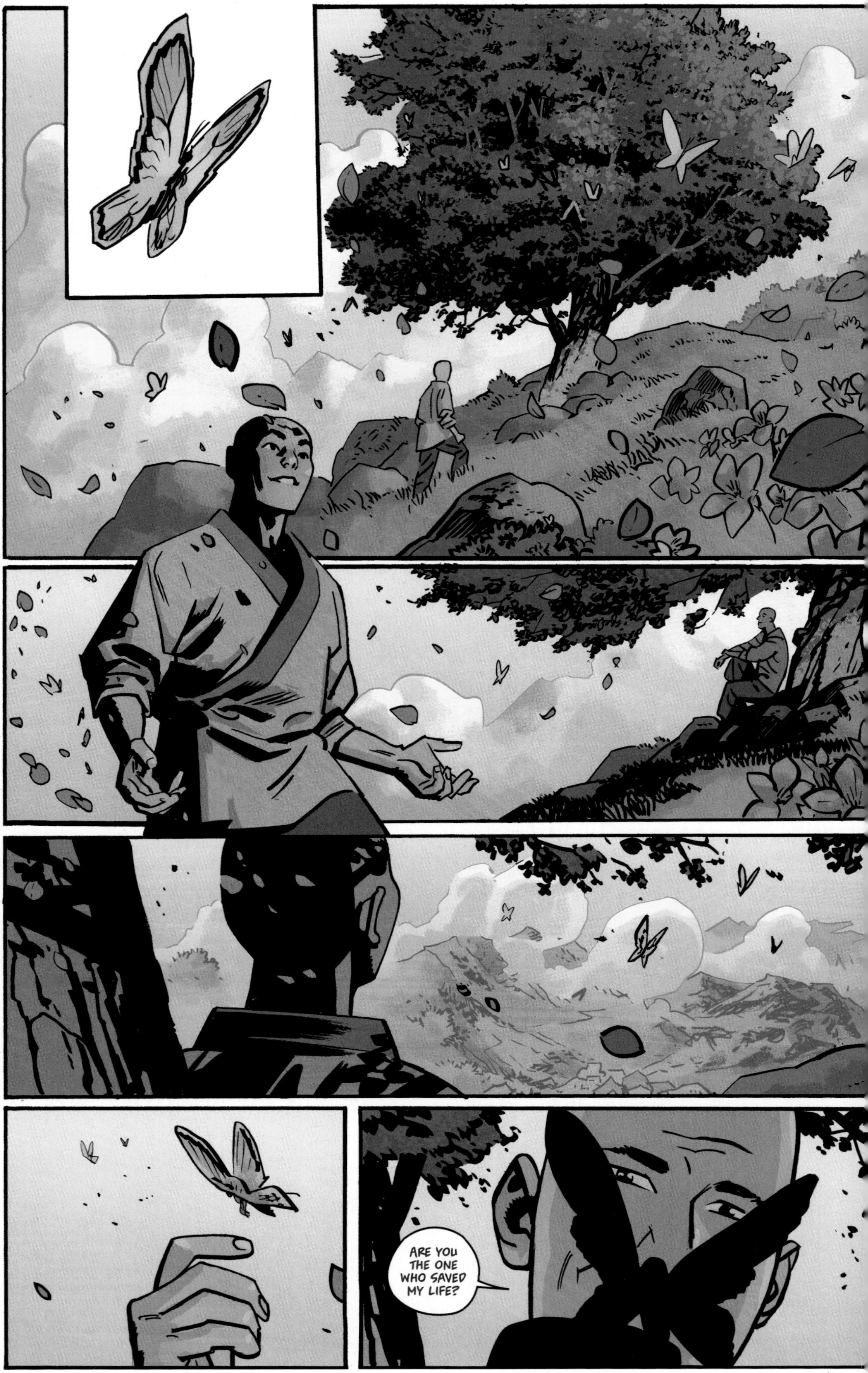
ARE YOU THE ONE WHO SAVED MY LIFE?

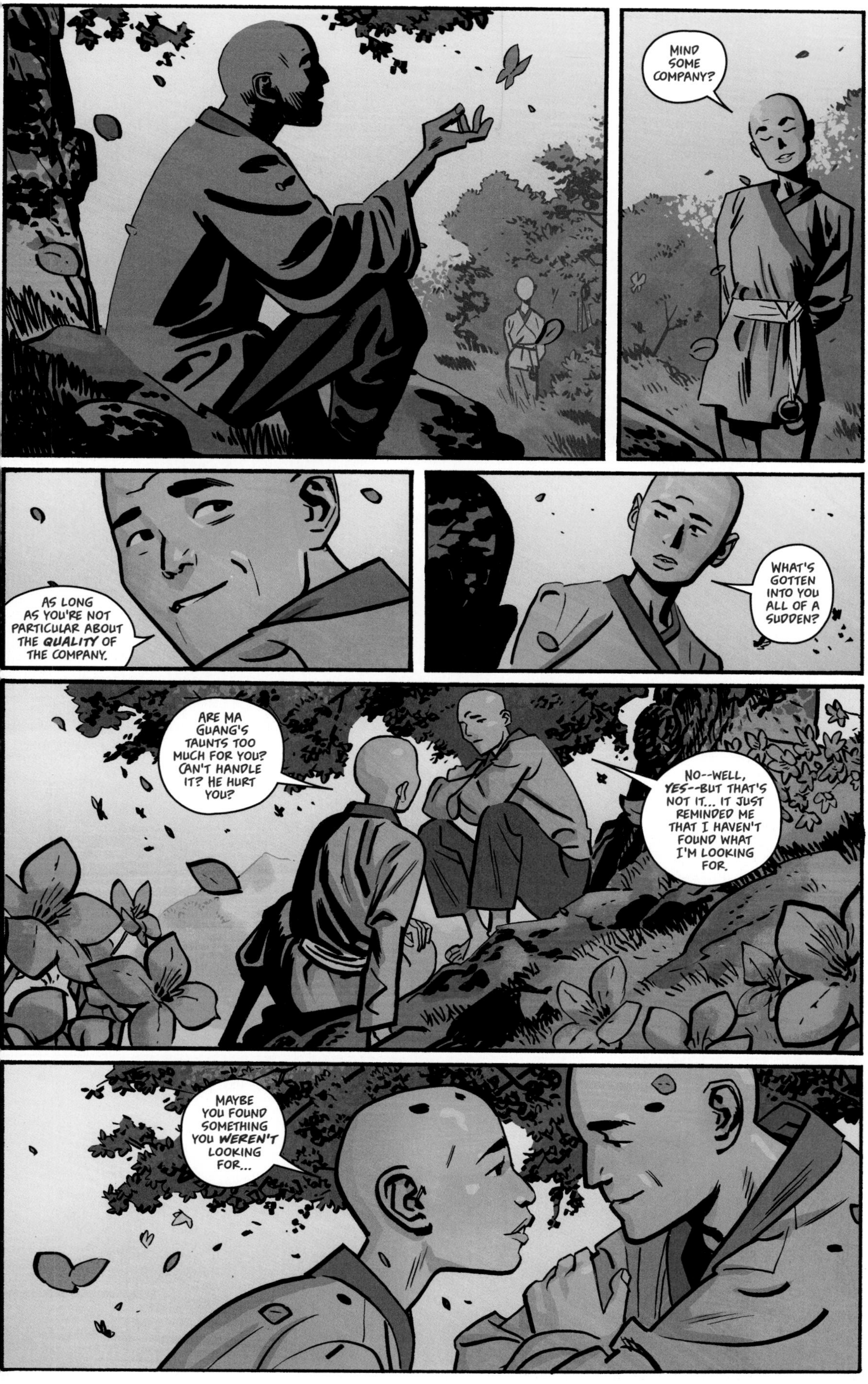
MIND SOME COMPANY?
AS LONG AS YOU'RE NOT PARTICULAR ABOUT THE QUALITY OF THE COMPANY.
WHAT'S GOTTEN INTO YOU ALL OF A SUDDEN?
ARE MA GUANG'S TAUNTS TOO MUCH FOR YOU? CAN'T HANDLE IT? HE HURT YOU?
NO--WELL, YES--BUT THAT'S NOT IT... IT JUST REMINDED ME THAT I HAVEN'T FOUND WHAT I'M LOOKING FOR.
MAYBE YOU FOUND SOMETHING YOU WEREN'T LOOKING FOR...

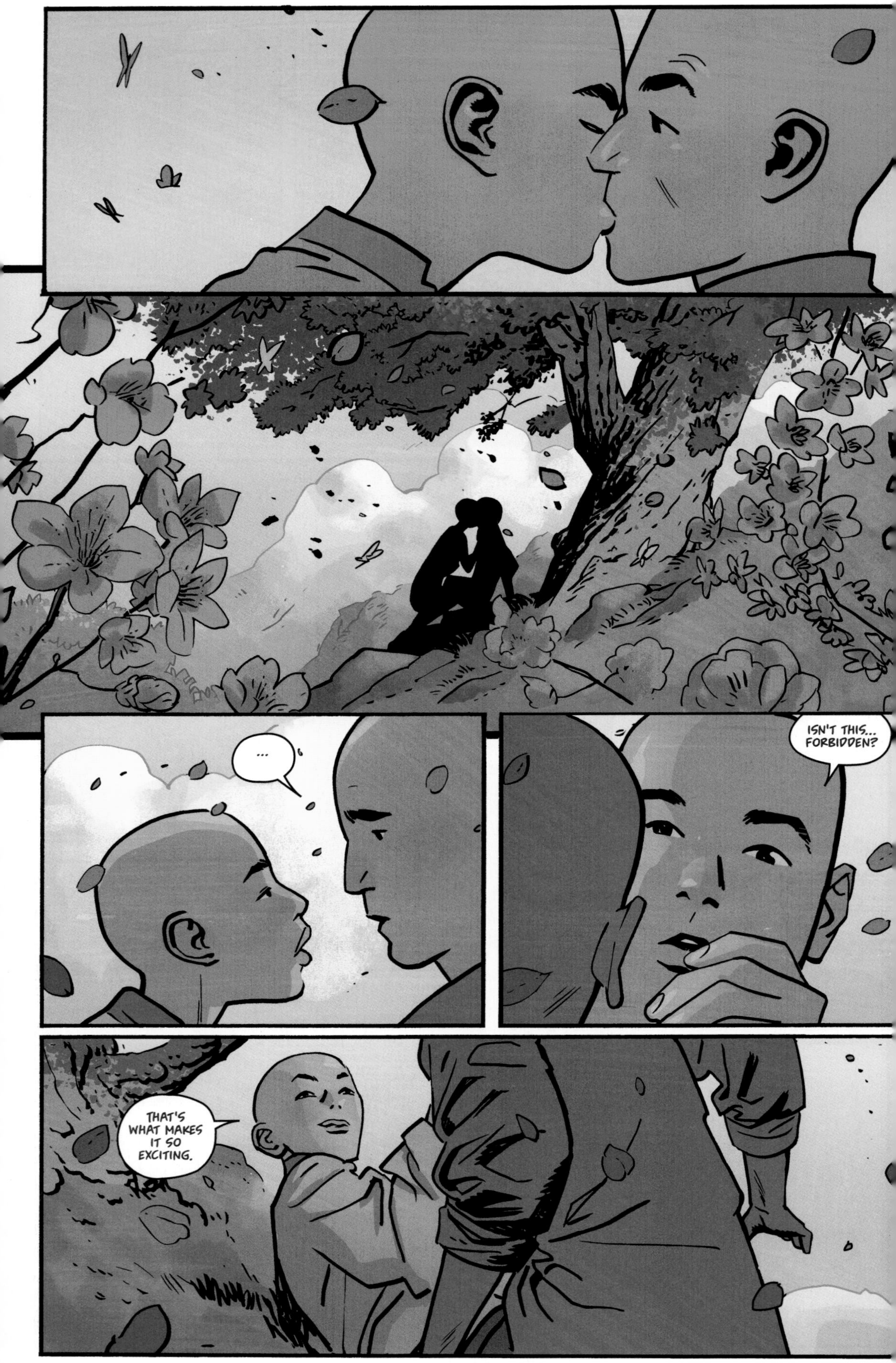
...
ISN'T THIS... FORBIDDEN?
THAT'S WHAT MAKES IT SO EXCITING.

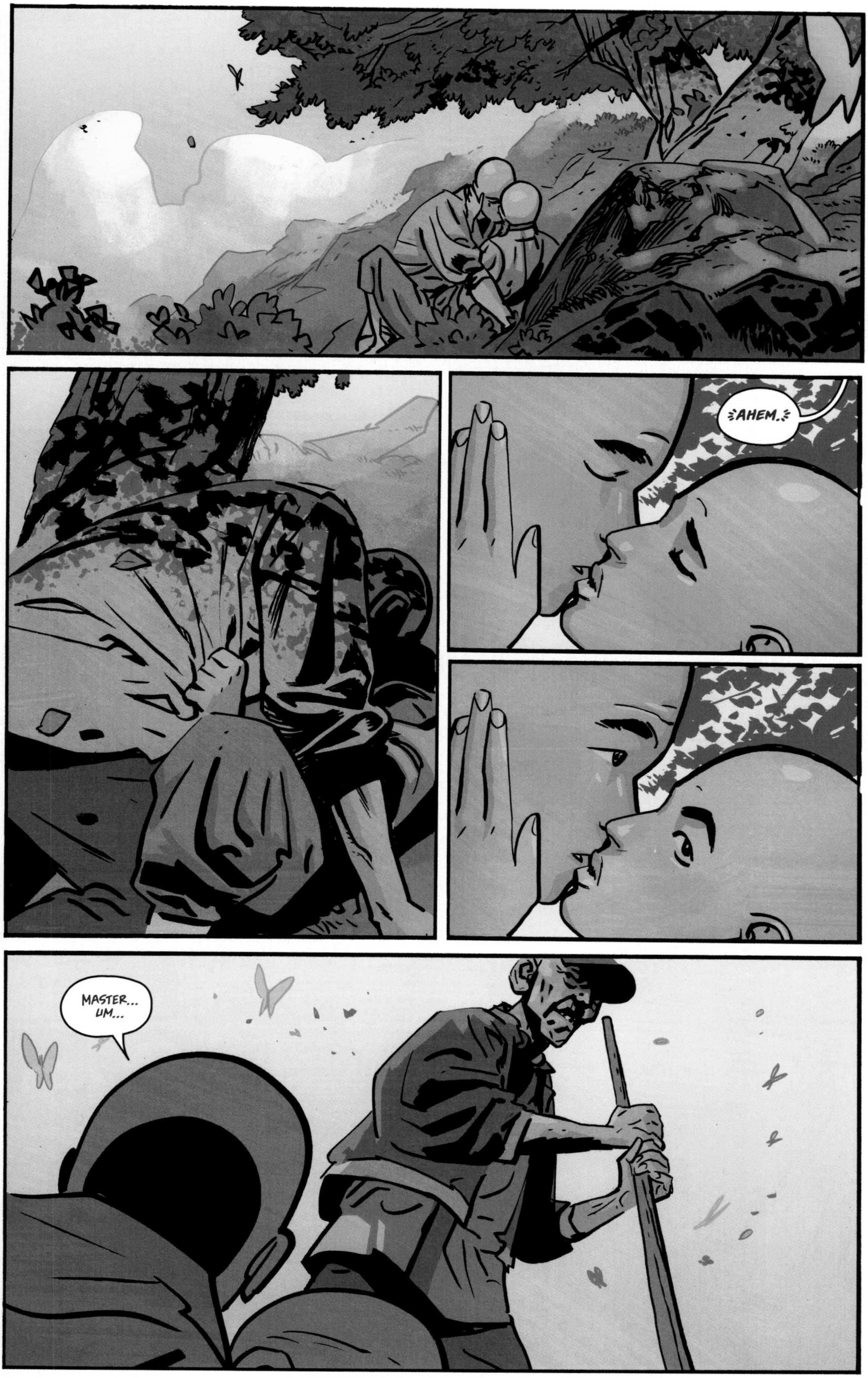
AHEM.
MASTER... UM...

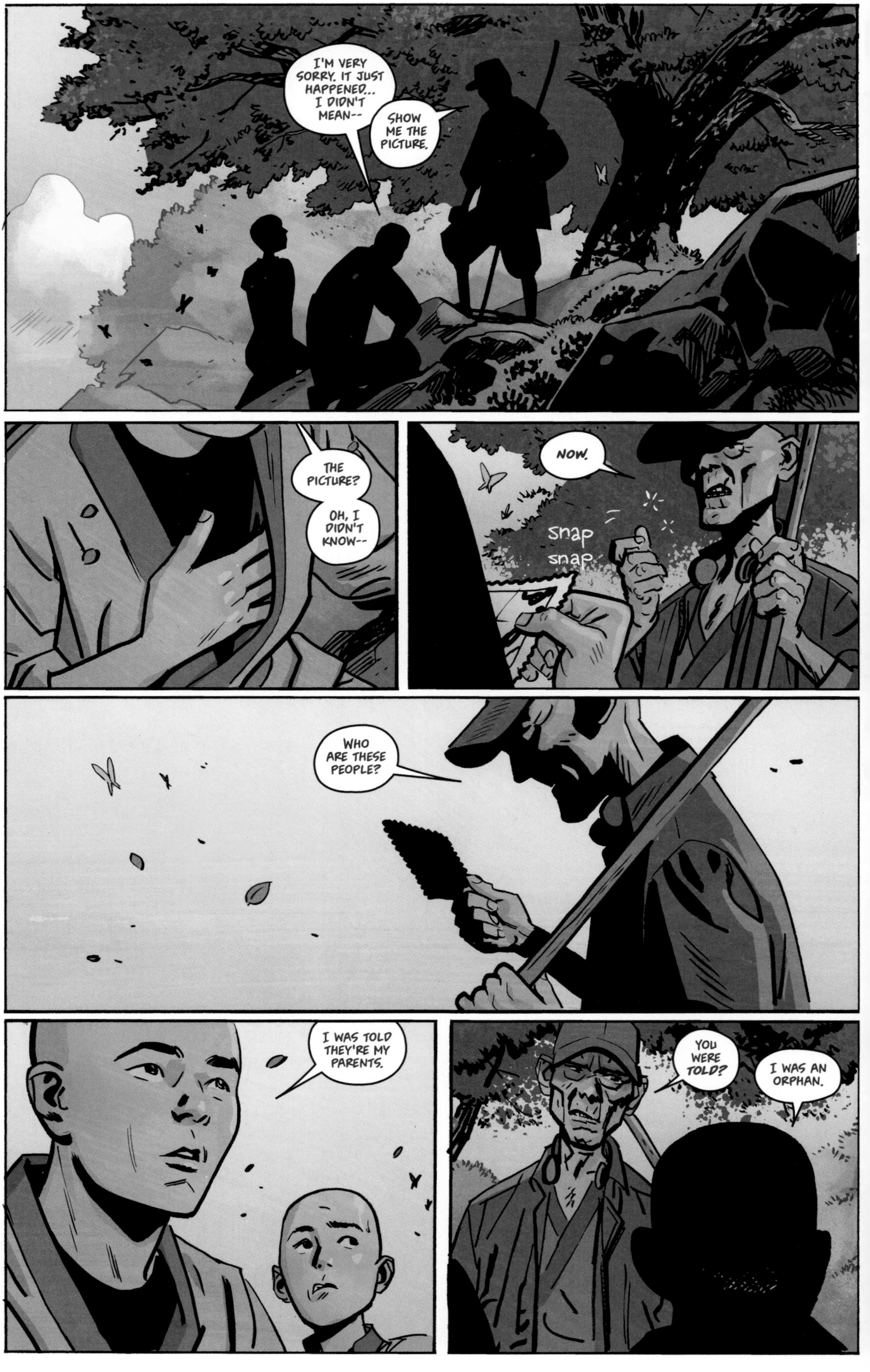
I'M VERY SORRY. IT JUST HAPPENED... I DIDN'T MEAN--
SHOW ME THE PICTURE.
THE PICTURE?
OH, I DIDN'T KNOW--
NOW.
snap
snap
WHO ARE THESE PEOPLE?
I WAS TOLD THEY'RE MY PARENTS.
YOU WERE *TOLD*?
I WAS AN ORPHAN.

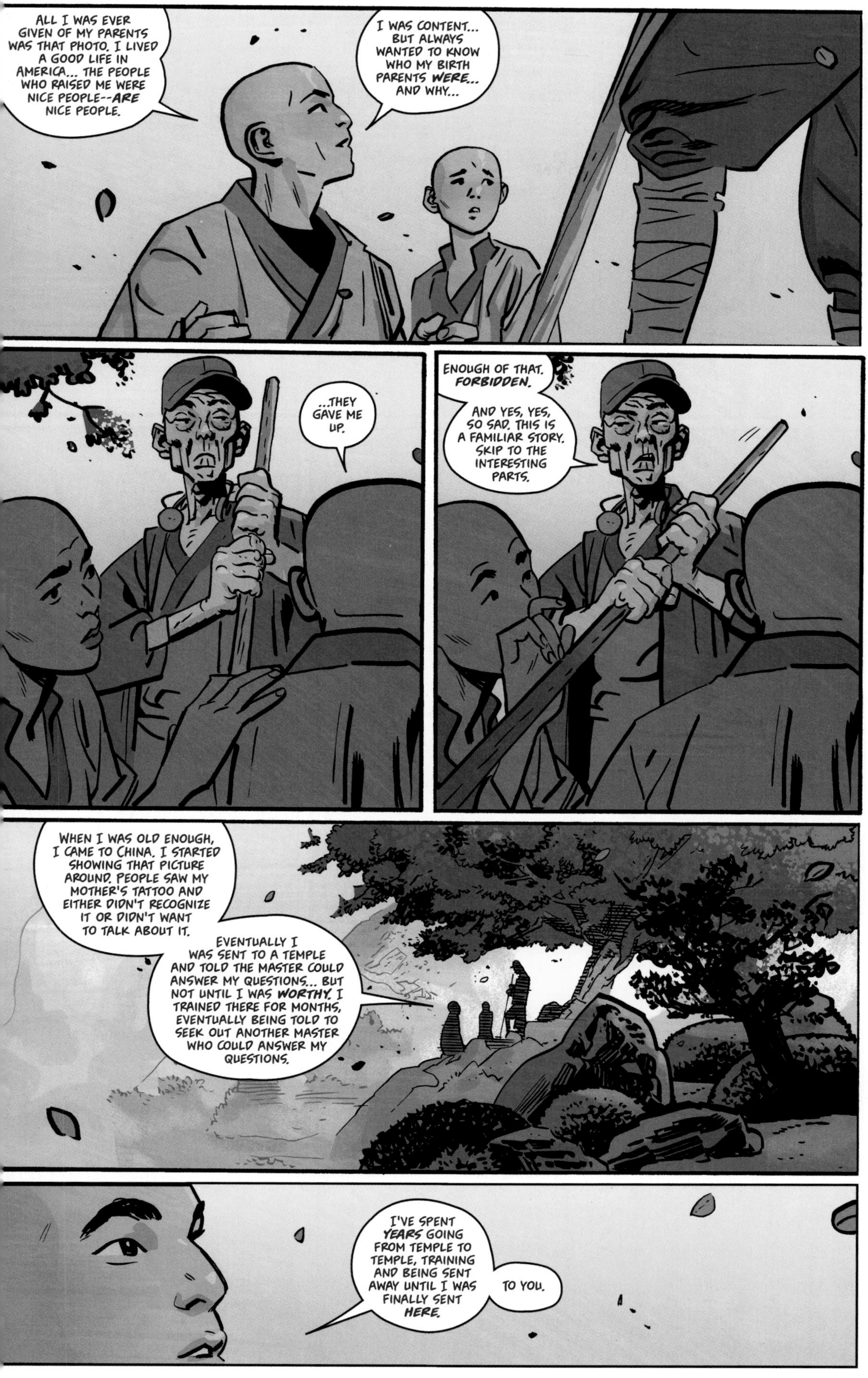

ALL I WAS EVER GIVEN OF MY PARENTS WAS THAT PHOTO. I LIVED A GOOD LIFE IN AMERICA... THE PEOPLE WHO RAISED ME WERE NICE PEOPLE--ARE NICE PEOPLE.
I WAS CONTENT... BUT ALWAYS WANTED TO KNOW WHO MY BIRTH PARENTS WERE... AND WHY...
...THEY GAVE ME UP.
ENOUGH OF THAT. FORBIDDEN.
AND YES, YES, SO SAD. THIS IS A FAMILIAR STORY. SKIP TO THE INTERESTING PARTS.
WHEN I WAS OLD ENOUGH, I CAME TO CHINA. I STARTED SHOWING THAT PICTURE AROUND. PEOPLE SAW MY MOTHER'S TATTOO AND EITHER DIDN'T RECOGNIZE IT OR DIDN'T WANT TO TALK ABOUT IT.
EVENTUALLY I WAS SENT TO A TEMPLE AND TOLD THE MASTER COULD ANSWER MY QUESTIONS... BUT NOT UNTIL I WAS WORTHY. I TRAINED THERE FOR MONTHS, EVENTUALLY BEING TOLD TO SEEK OUT ANOTHER MASTER WHO COULD ANSWER MY QUESTIONS.
I'VE SPENT YEARS GOING FROM TEMPLE TO TEMPLE, TRAINING AND BEING SENT AWAY UNTIL I WAS FINALLY SENT HERE.
TO YOU.

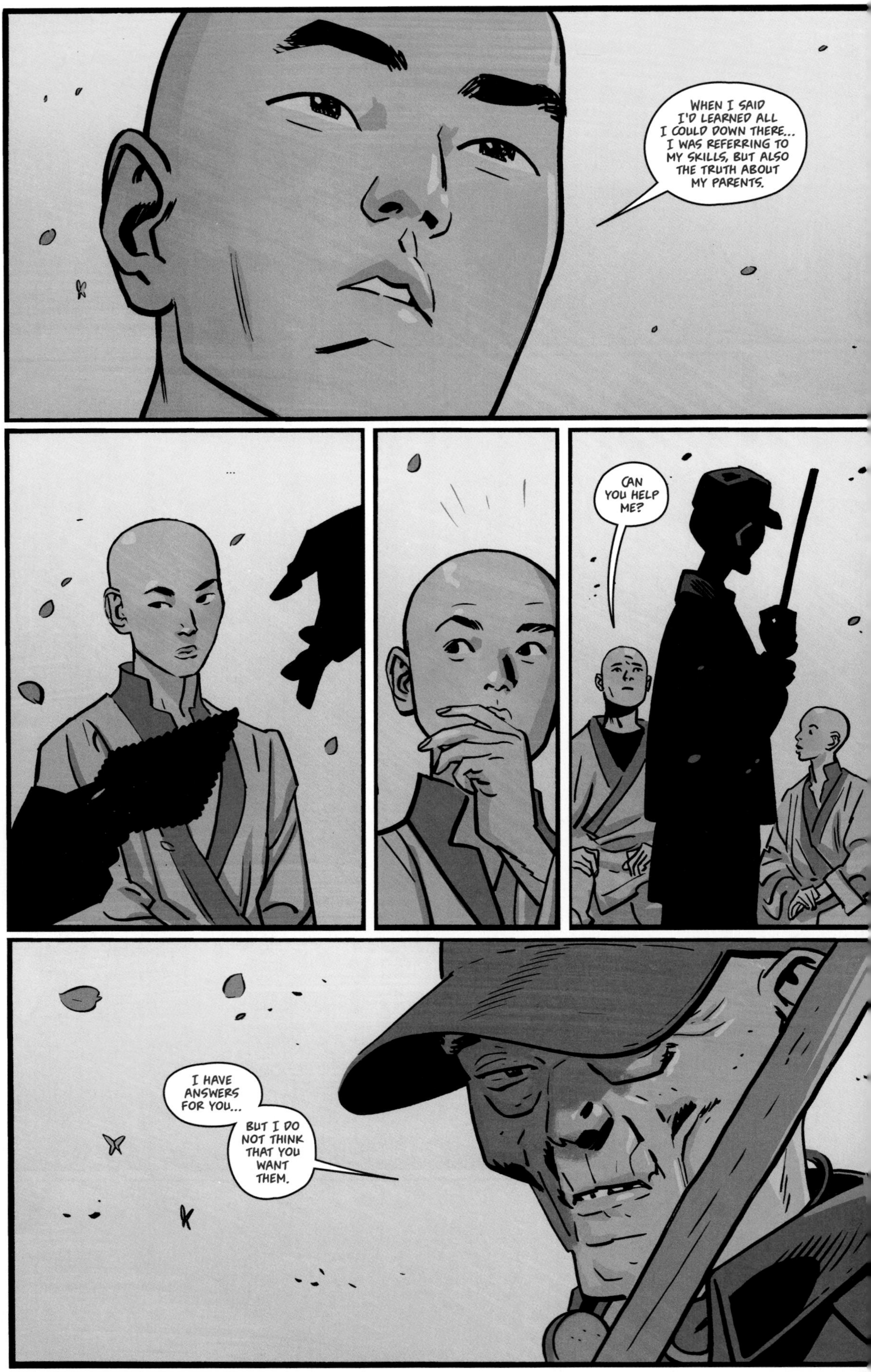
WHEN I SAID I'D LEARNED ALL I COULD DOWN THERE... I WAS REFERRING TO MY SKILLS, BUT ALSO THE TRUTH ABOUT MY PARENTS.
...
CAN YOU HELP ME?
I HAVE ANSWERS FOR YOU...
BUT I DO NOT THINK THAT YOU WANT THEM.

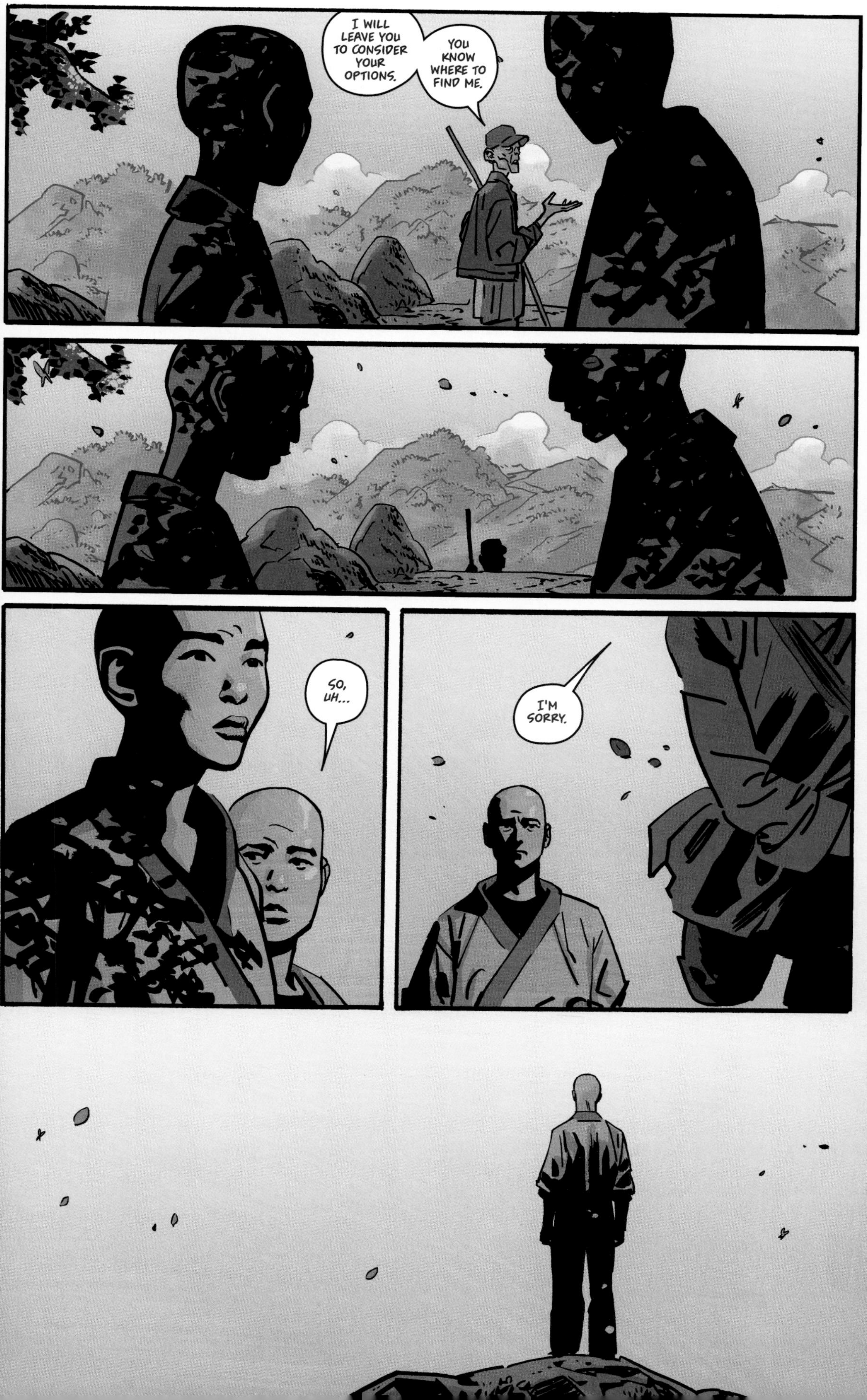
I WILL LEAVE YOU TO CONSIDER YOUR OPTIONS.
YOU KNOW WHERE TO FIND ME.
SO, UH...
I'M SORRY.

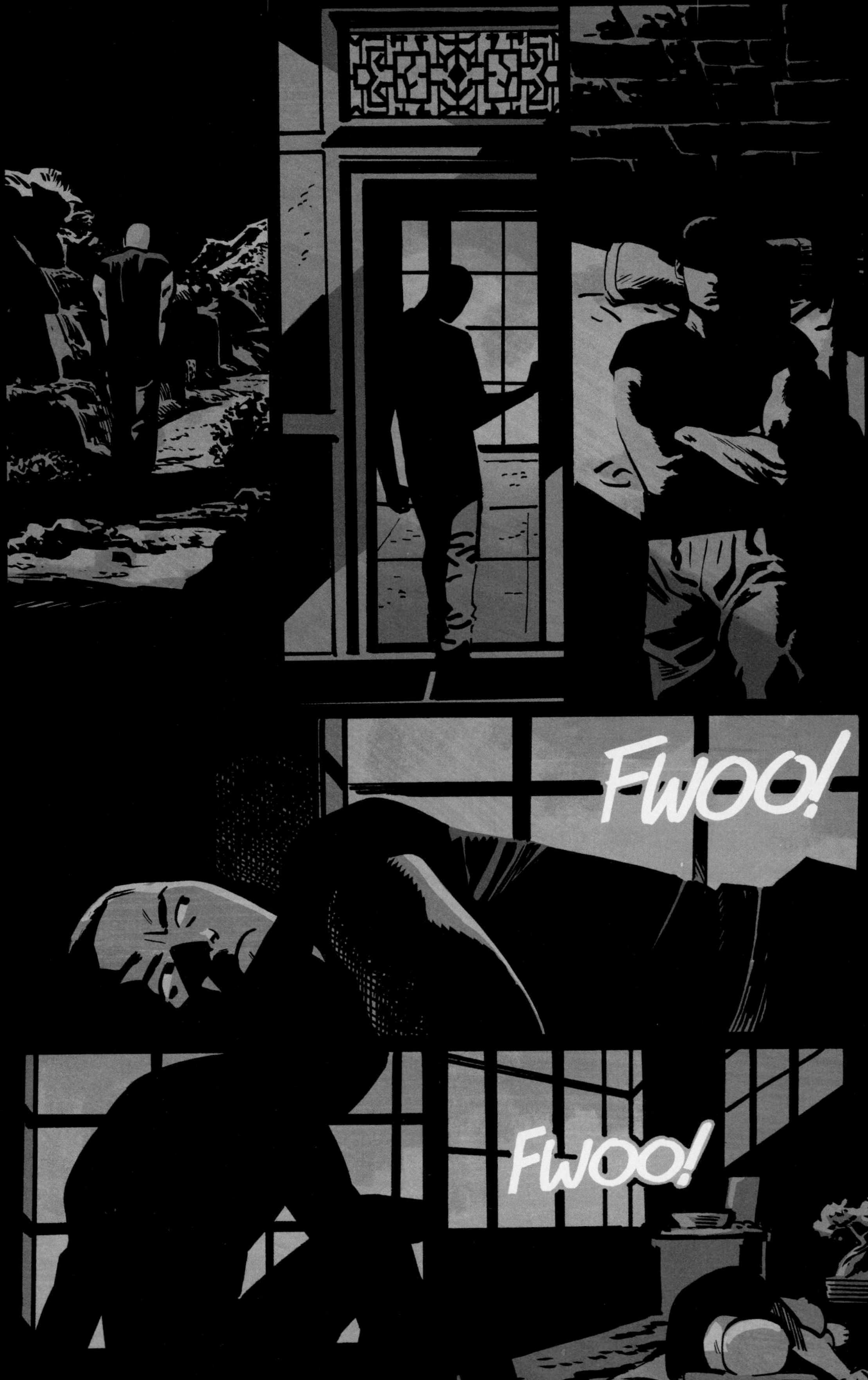
FWOO!
FWOO!

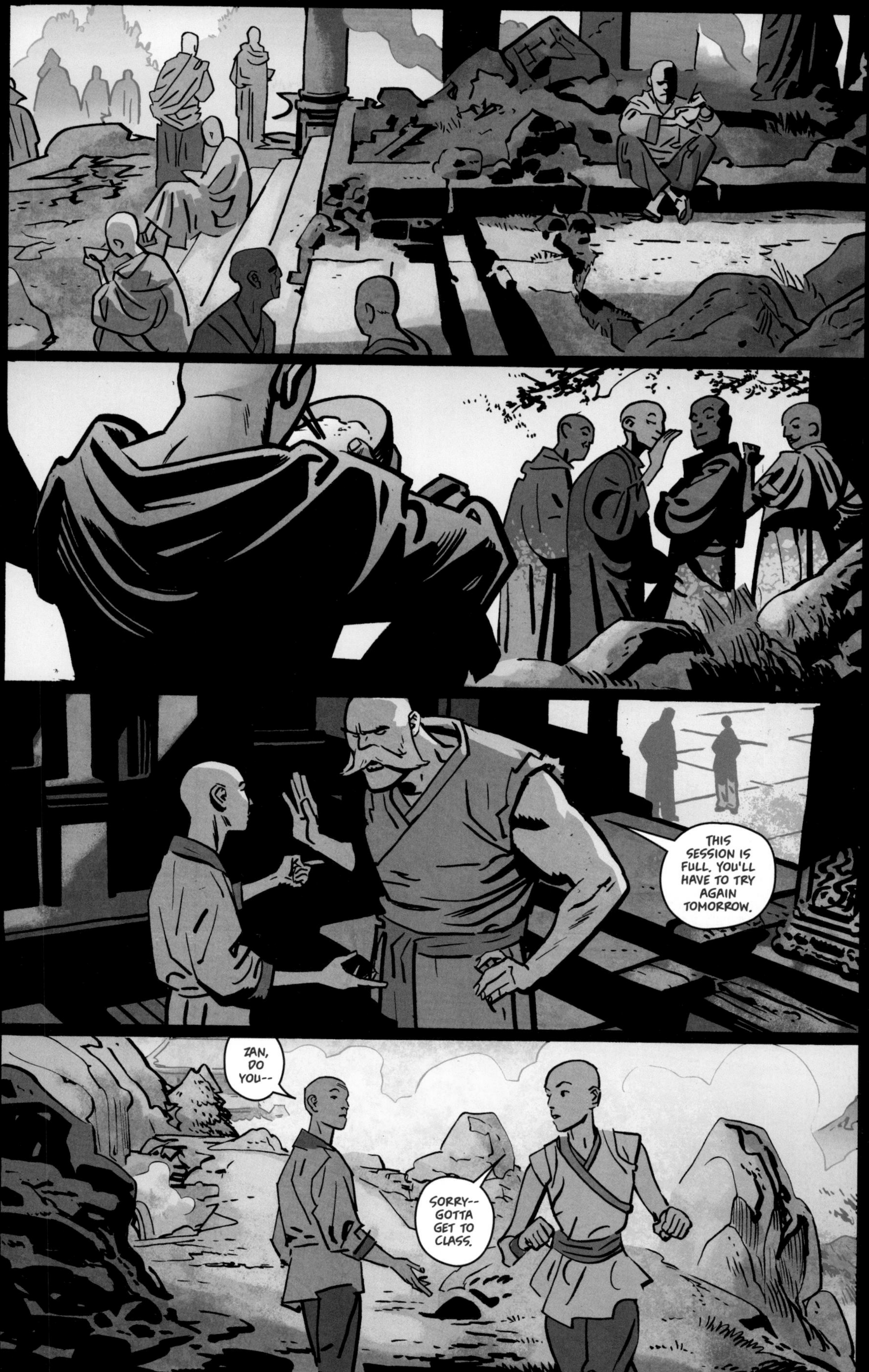
THIS SESSION IS FULL. YOU'LL HAVE TO TRY AGAIN TOMORROW.
ZAN, DO YOU--
SORRY-- GOTTA GET TO CLASS.

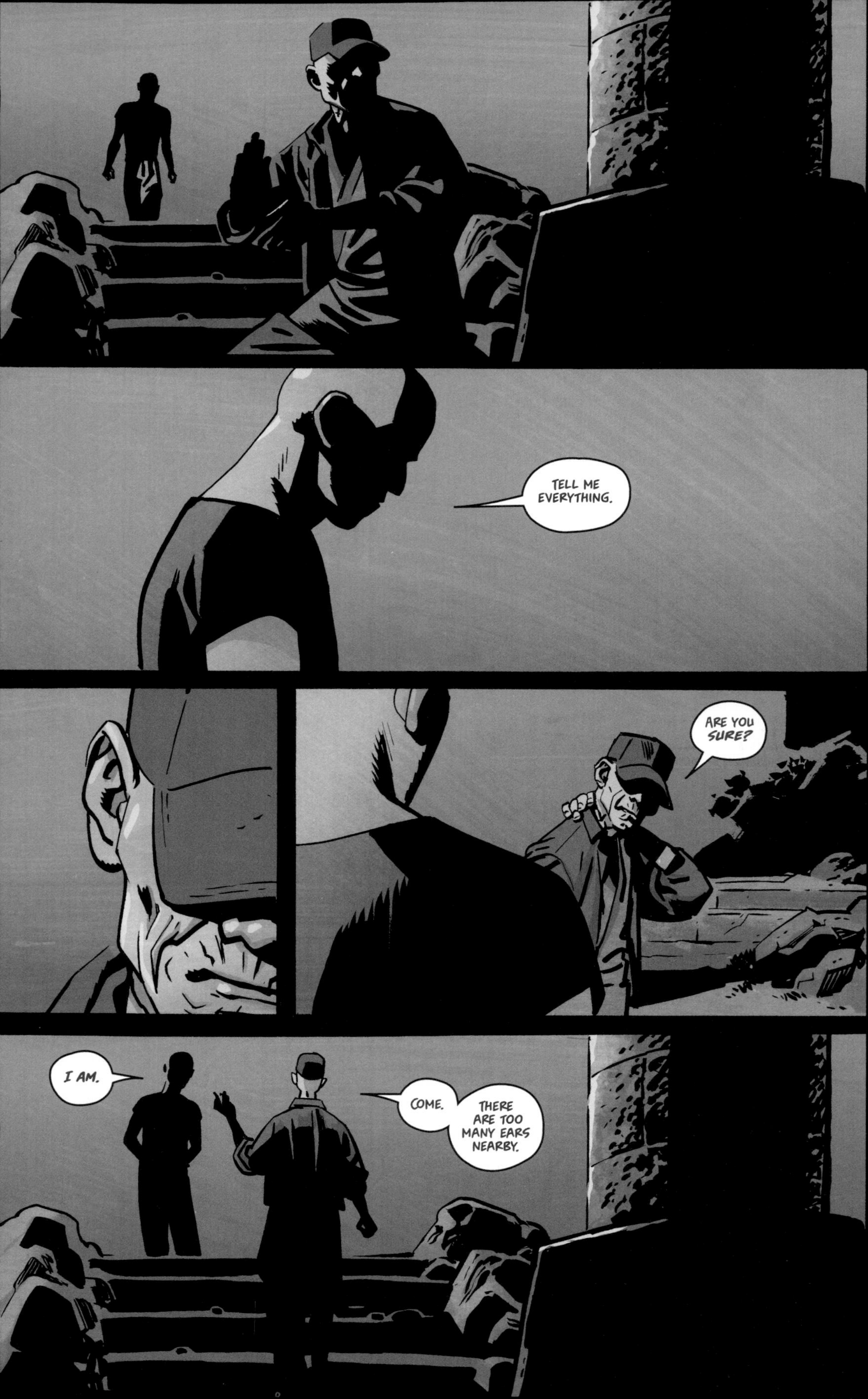
TELL ME EVERYTHING.
ARE YOU SURE?
I AM.
COME.
THERE ARE TOO MANY EARS NEARBY.

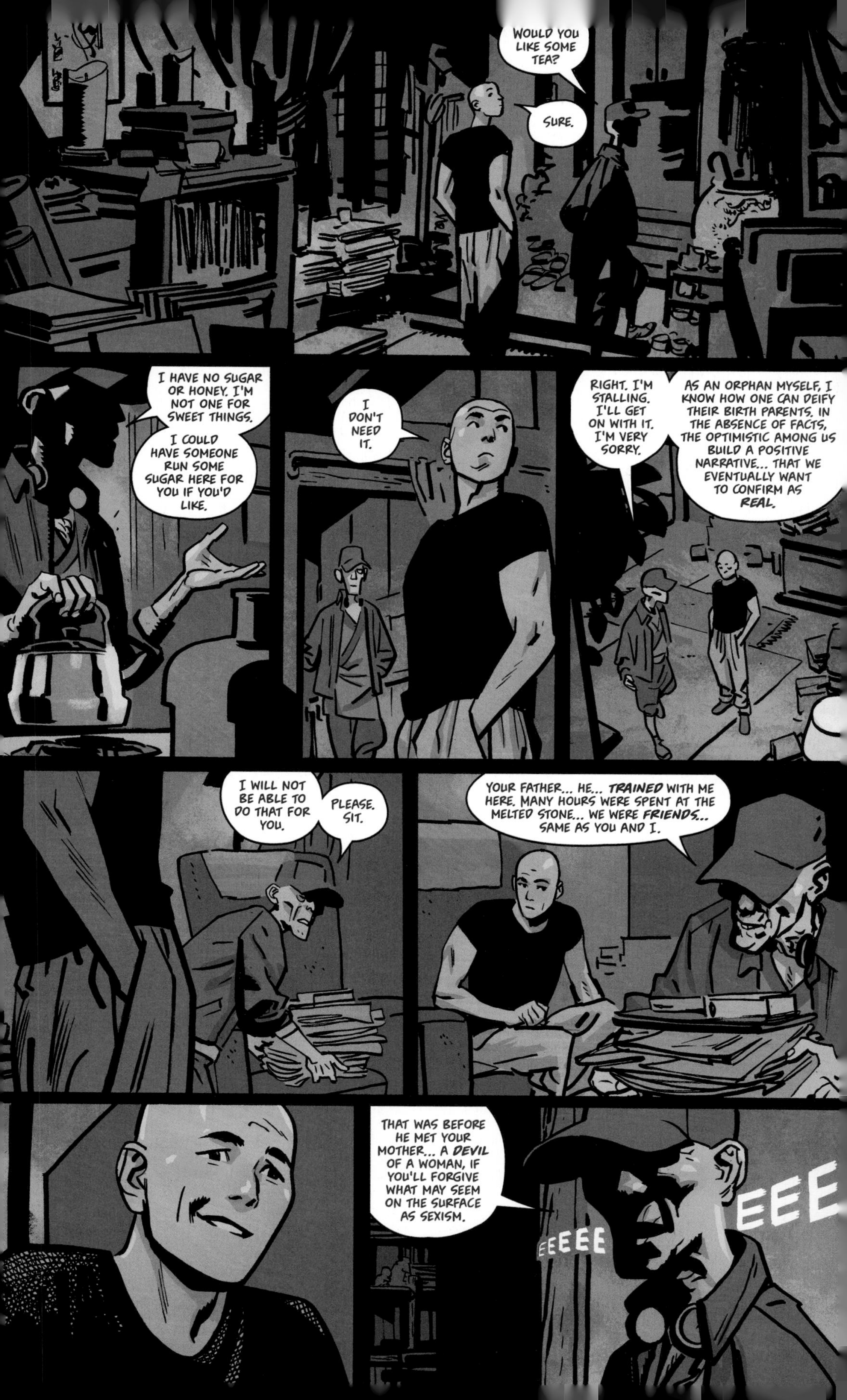
WOULD YOU LIKE SOME TEA?
SURE.
I HAVE NO SUGAR OR HONEY. I'M NOT ONE FOR SWEET THINGS.
I COULD HAVE SOMEONE RUN SOME SUGAR HERE FOR YOU IF YOU'D LIKE.
I DON'T NEED IT.
RIGHT. I'M STALLING. I'LL GET ON WITH IT. I'M VERY SORRY.
AS AN ORPHAN MYSELF, I KNOW HOW ONE CAN DEIFY THEIR BIRTH PARENTS. IN THE ABSENCE OF FACTS, THE OPTIMISTIC AMONG US BUILD A POSITIVE NARRATIVE... THAT WE EVENTUALLY WANT TO CONFIRM AS **REAL**.
I WILL NOT BE ABLE TO DO THAT FOR YOU.
PLEASE. SIT.
YOUR FATHER... HE... **TRAINED** WITH ME HERE. MANY HOURS WERE SPENT AT THE MELTED STONE... WE WERE **FRIENDS**... SAME AS YOU AND I.
THAT WAS BEFORE HE MET YOUR MOTHER... A **DEVIL** OF A WOMAN, IF YOU'LL FORGIVE WHAT MAY SEEM ON THE SURFACE AS SEXISM.
EEEEE
EEE

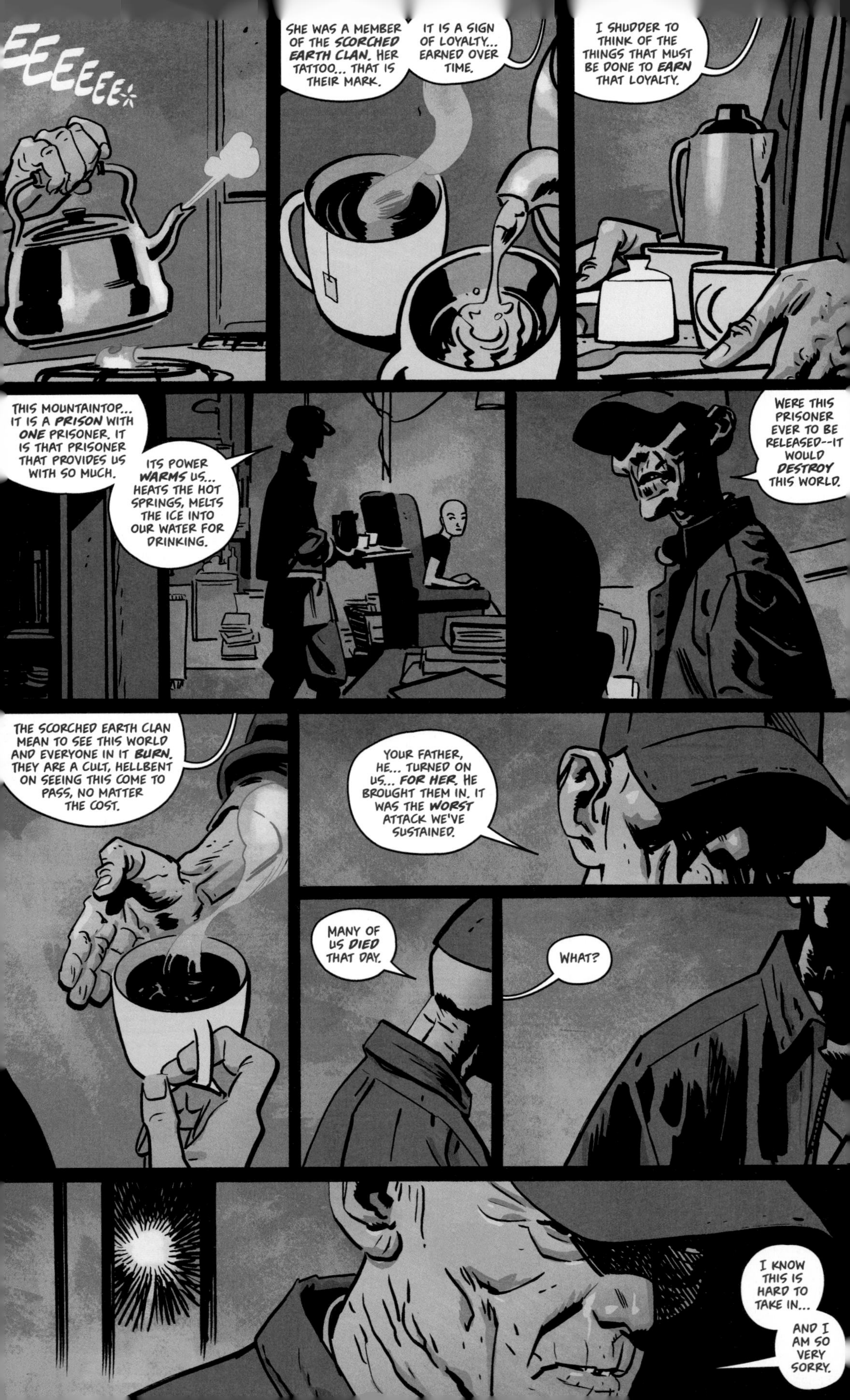
EEEEEEE
SHE WAS A MEMBER OF THE SCORCHED EARTH CLAN. HER TATTOO... THAT IS THEIR MARK.
IT IS A SIGN OF LOYALTY... EARNED OVER TIME.
I SHUDDER TO THINK OF THE THINGS THAT MUST BE DONE TO EARN THAT LOYALTY.
THIS MOUNTAINTOP... IT IS A PRISON WITH ONE PRISONER. IT IS THAT PRISONER THAT PROVIDES US WITH SO MUCH.
ITS POWER WARMS US... HEATS THE HOT SPRINGS, MELTS THE ICE INTO OUR WATER FOR DRINKING.
WERE THIS PRISONER EVER TO BE RELEASED--IT WOULD DESTROY THIS WORLD.
THE SCORCHED EARTH CLAN MEAN TO SEE THIS WORLD AND EVERYONE IN IT BURN. THEY ARE A CULT, HELLBENT ON SEEING THIS COME TO PASS, NO MATTER THE COST.
YOUR FATHER, HE... TURNED ON US... FOR HER. HE BROUGHT THEM IN. IT WAS THE WORST ATTACK WE'VE SUSTAINED.
MANY OF US DIED THAT DAY.
WHAT?
I KNOW THIS IS HARD TO TAKE IN...
AND I AM SO VERY SORRY.

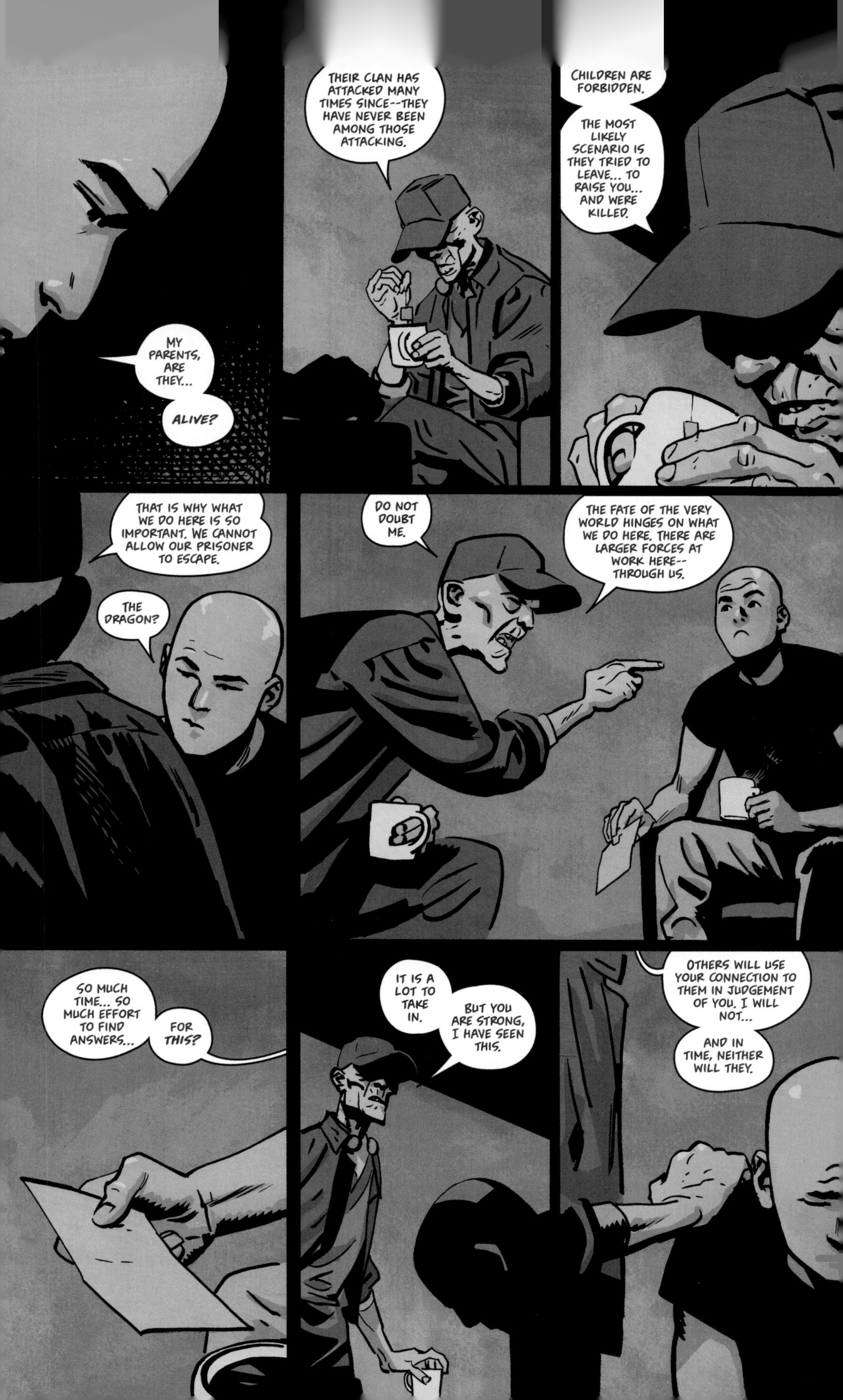

MY PARENTS, ARE THEY... ALIVE?
THEIR CLAN HAS ATTACKED MANY TIMES SINCE--THEY HAVE NEVER BEEN AMONG THOSE ATTACKING.
CHILDREN ARE FORBIDDEN.
THE MOST LIKELY SCENARIO IS THEY TRIED TO LEAVE... TO RAISE YOU... AND WERE KILLED.
THAT IS WHY WHAT WE DO HERE IS SO IMPORTANT. WE CANNOT ALLOW OUR PRISONER TO ESCAPE.
THE DRAGON?
DO NOT DOUBT ME.
THE FATE OF THE VERY WORLD HINGES ON WHAT WE DO HERE. THERE ARE LARGER FORCES AT WORK HERE--THROUGH US.
SO MUCH TIME... SO MUCH EFFORT TO FIND ANSWERS...
FOR THIS?
IT IS A LOT TO TAKE IN.
BUT YOU ARE STRONG, I HAVE SEEN THIS.
OTHERS WILL USE YOUR CONNECTION TO THEM IN JUDGEMENT OF YOU. I WILL NOT...
AND IN TIME, NEITHER WILL THEY.

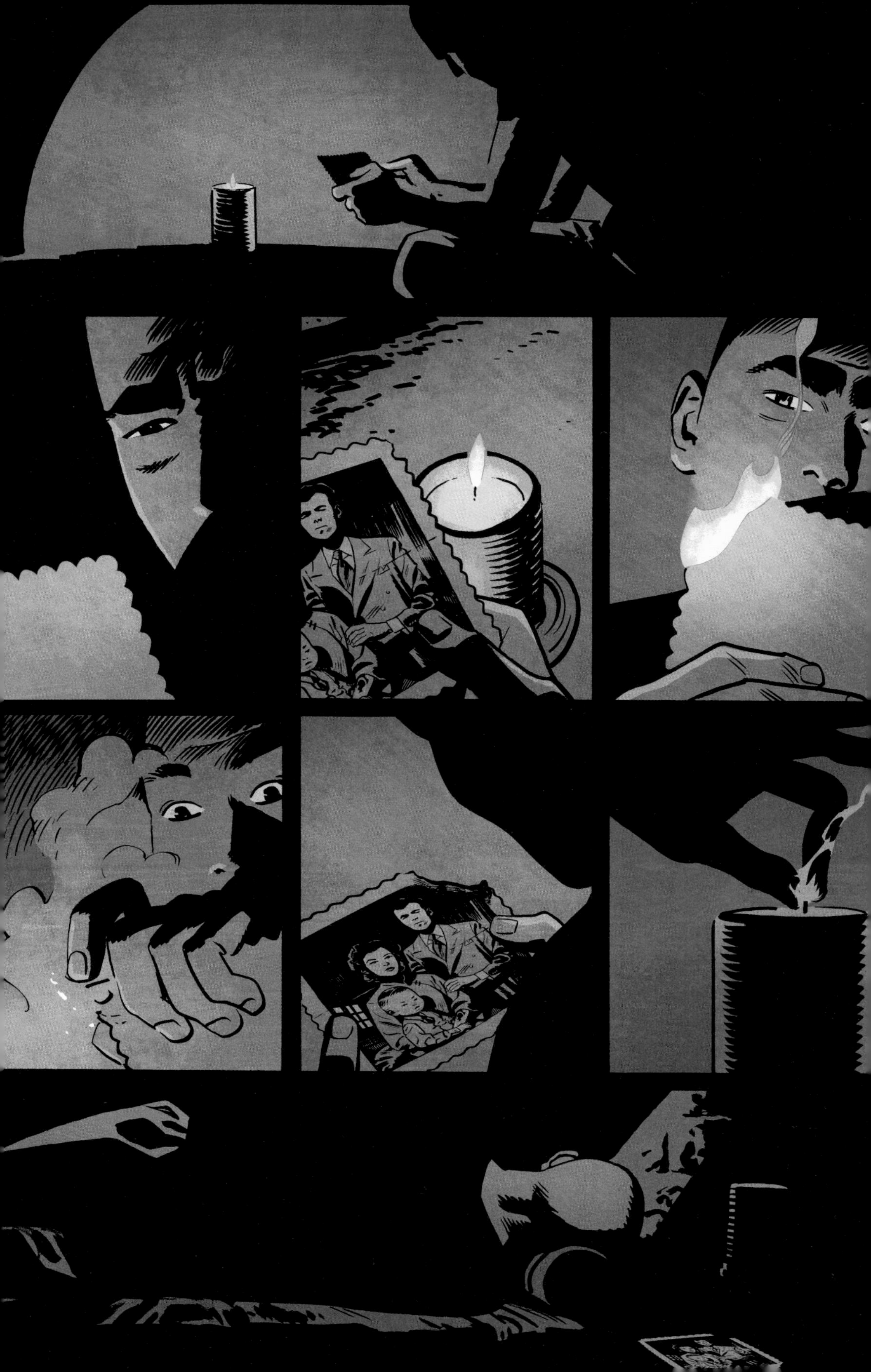

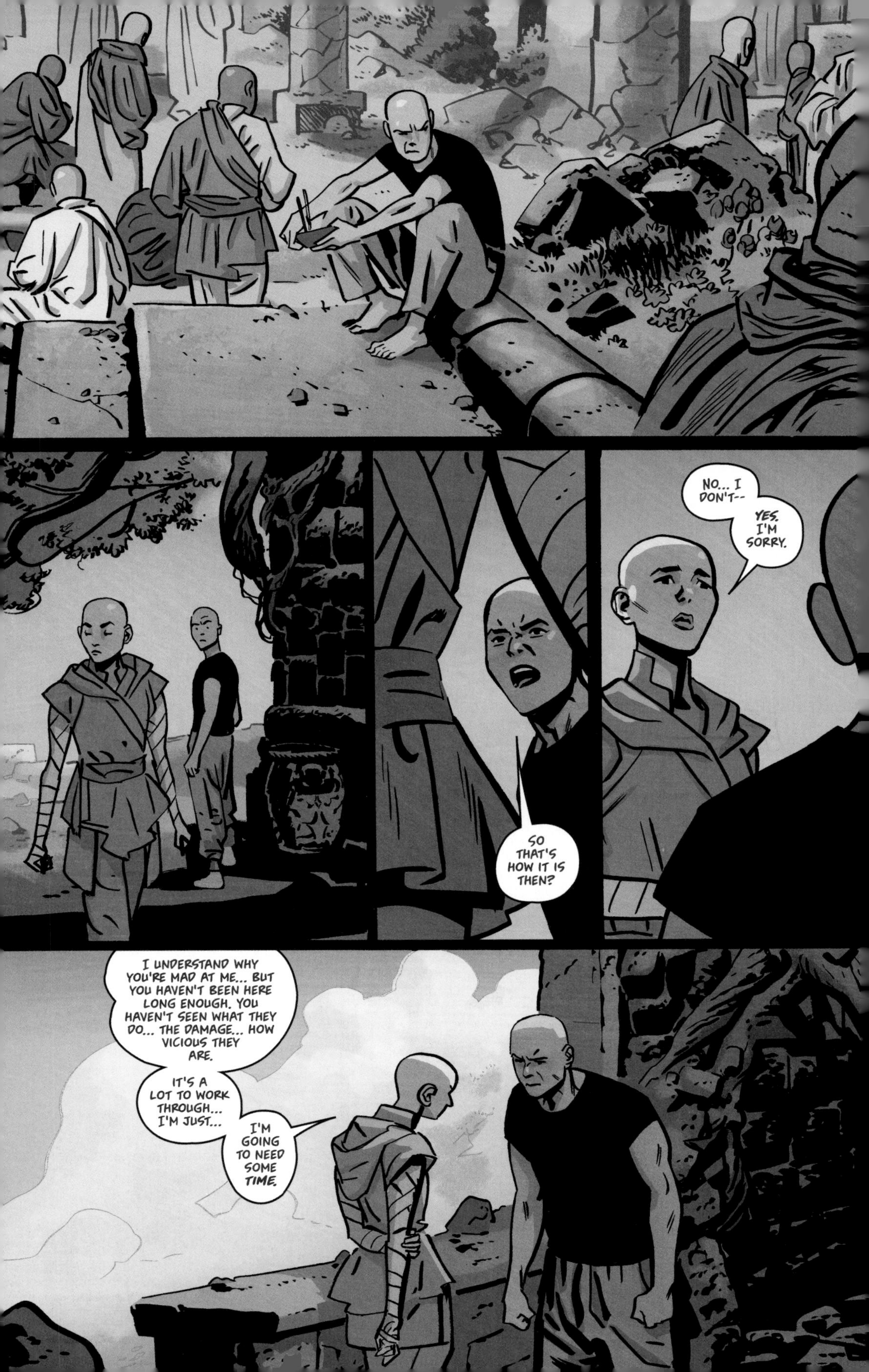
NO... I DON'T--
YES. I'M SORRY.
SO THAT'S HOW IT IS THEN?
I UNDERSTAND WHY YOU'RE MAD AT ME... BUT YOU HAVEN'T BEEN HERE LONG ENOUGH. YOU HAVEN'T SEEN WHAT THEY DO... THE DAMAGE... HOW VICIOUS THEY ARE.
IT'S A LOT TO WORK THROUGH... I'M JUST...
I'M GOING TO NEED SOME TIME.

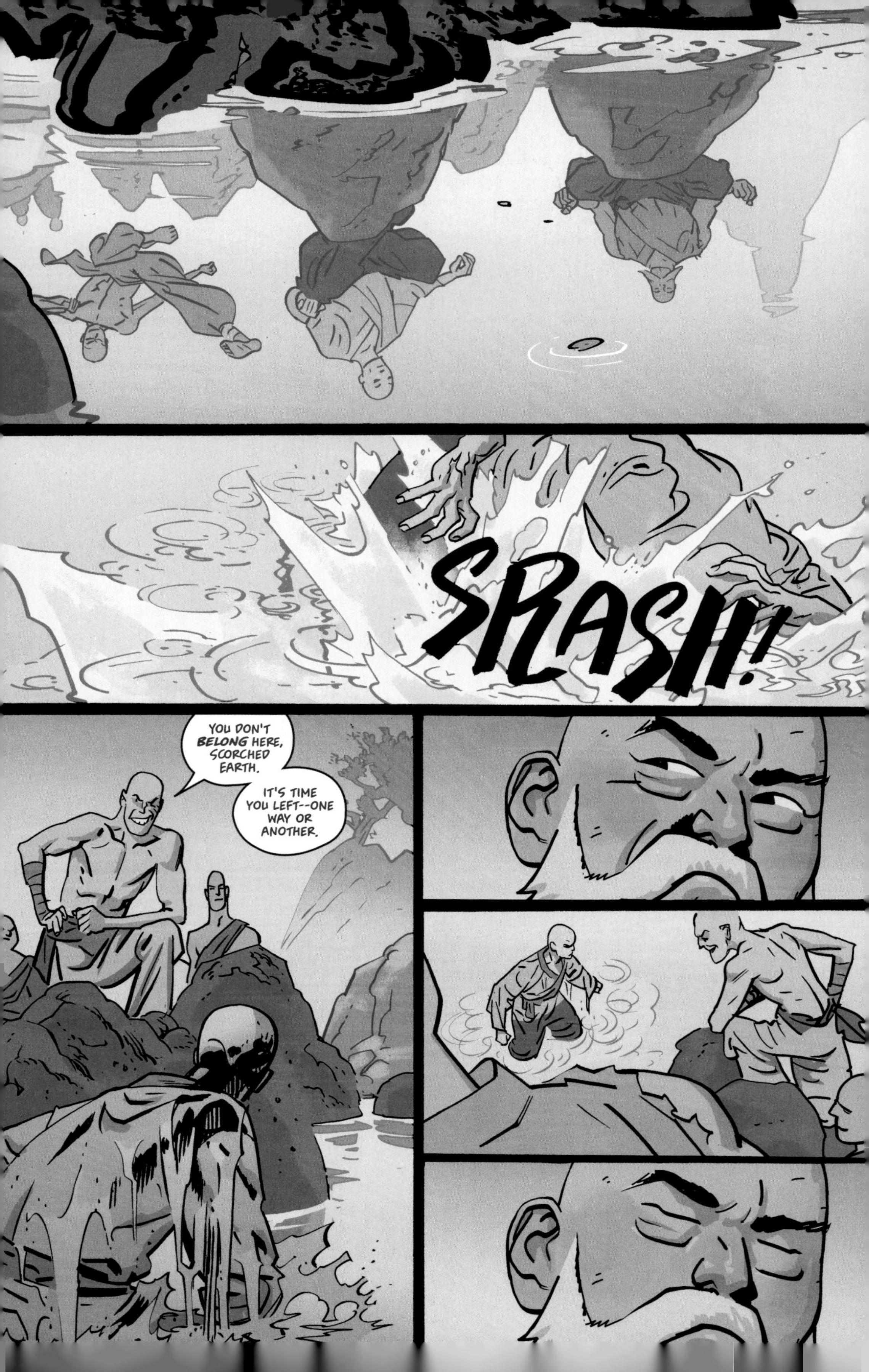
SPLASH!
YOU DON'T BELONG HERE, SCORCHED EARTH.
IT'S TIME YOU LEFT--ONE WAY OR ANOTHER.

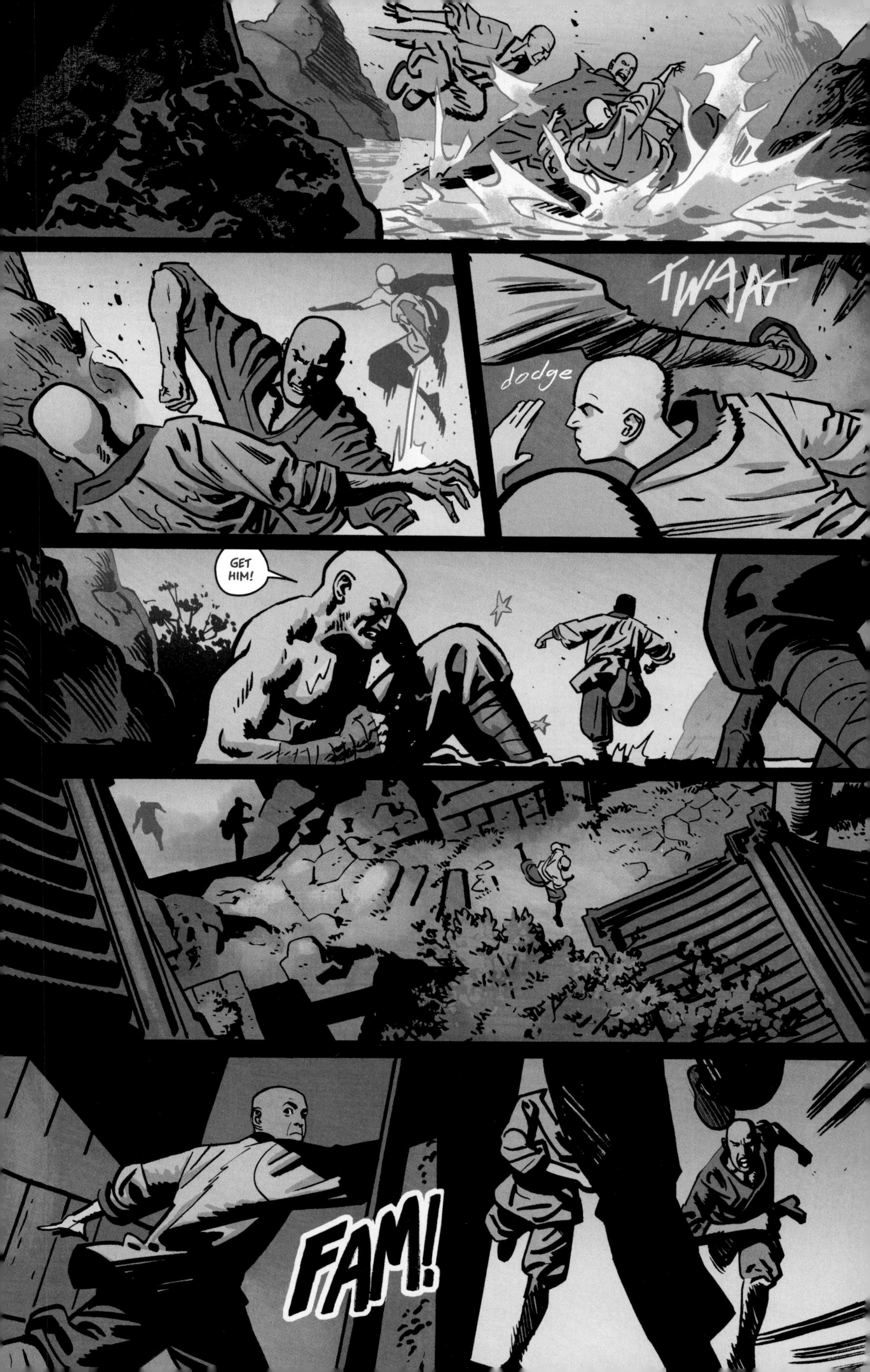
TWAAT
dodge
GET HIM!
FAM!

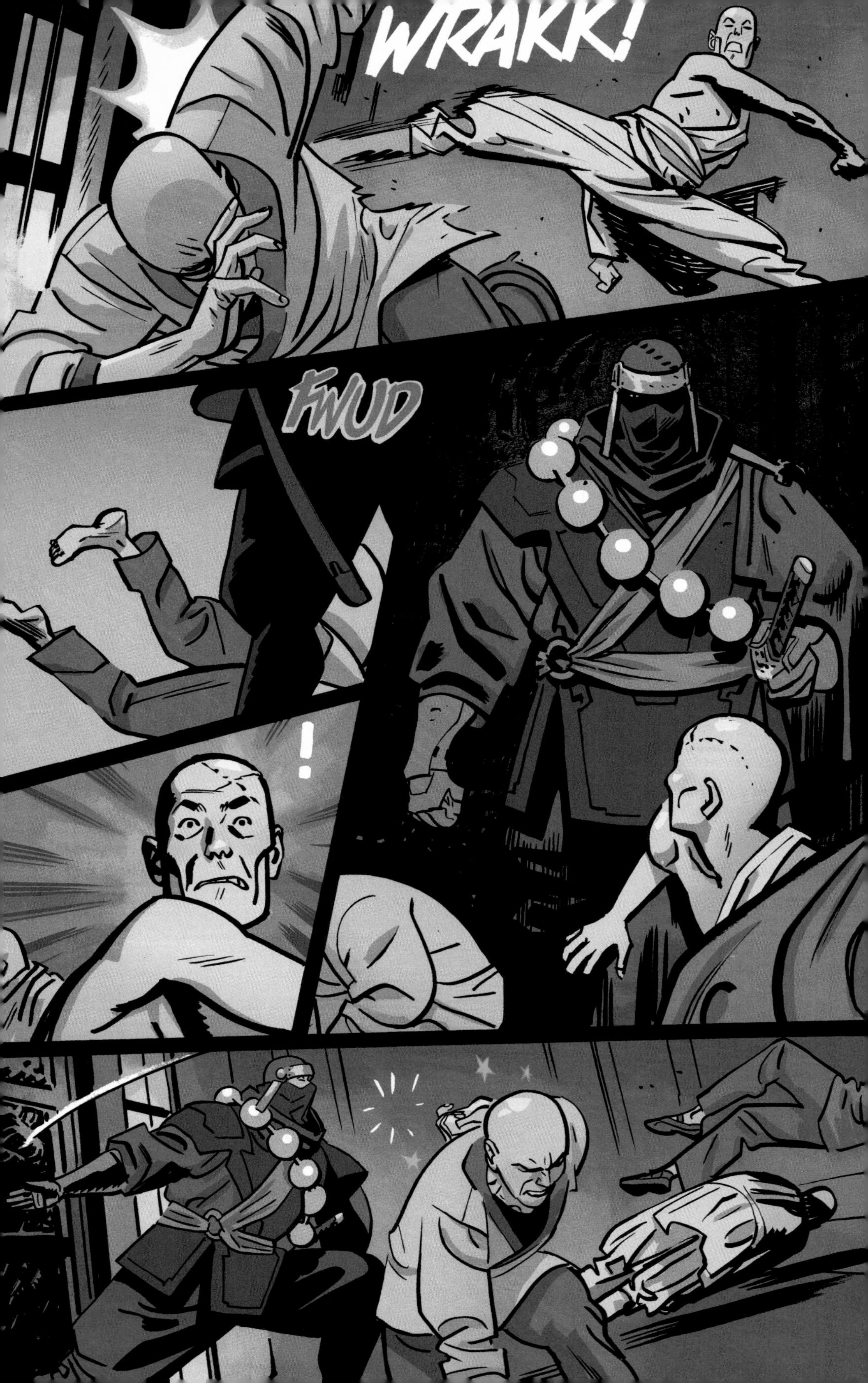
WRAKK!
FWUD
!

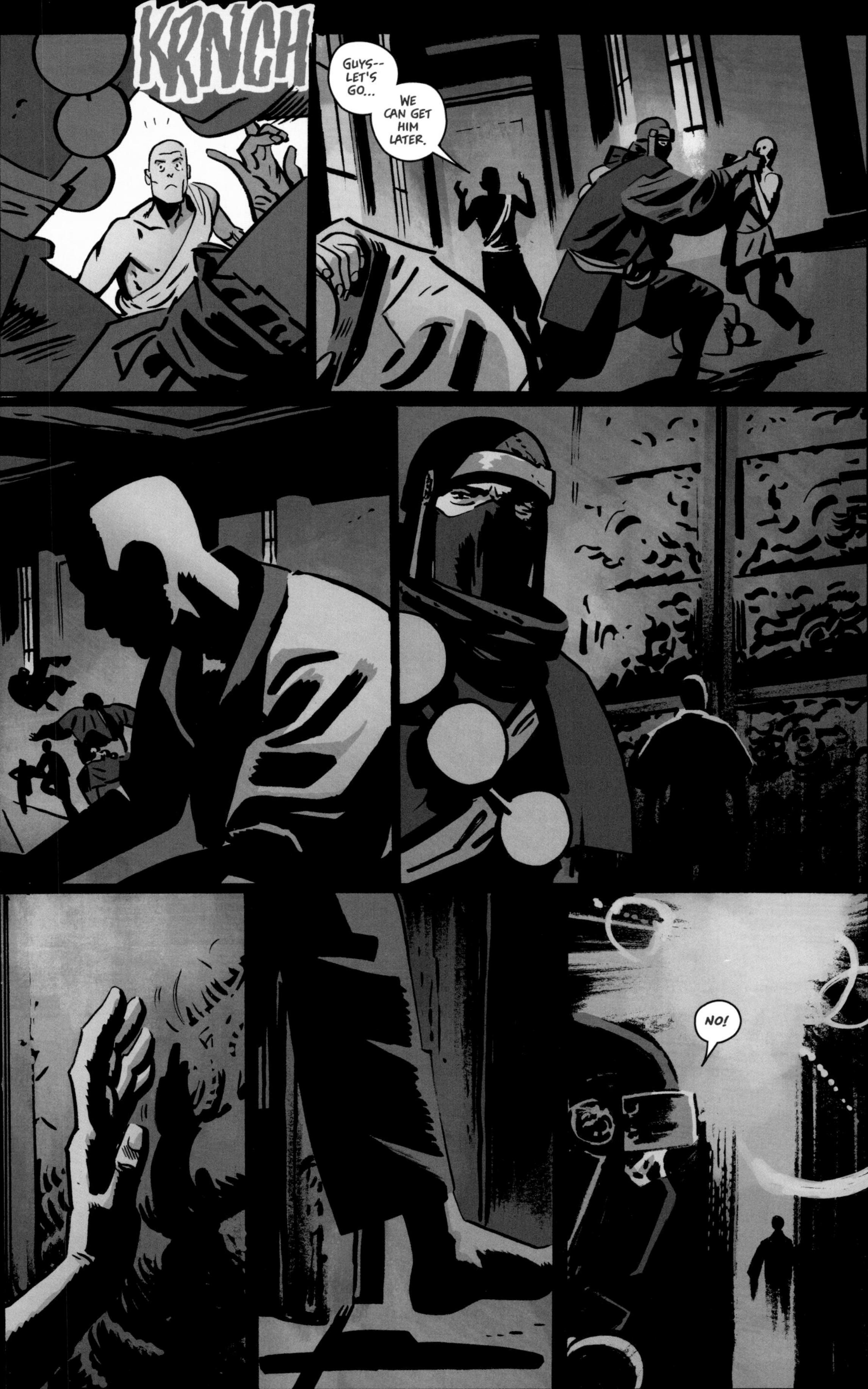
KRNCH
GUYS-- LET'S GO...
WE CAN GET HIM LATER.
NO!

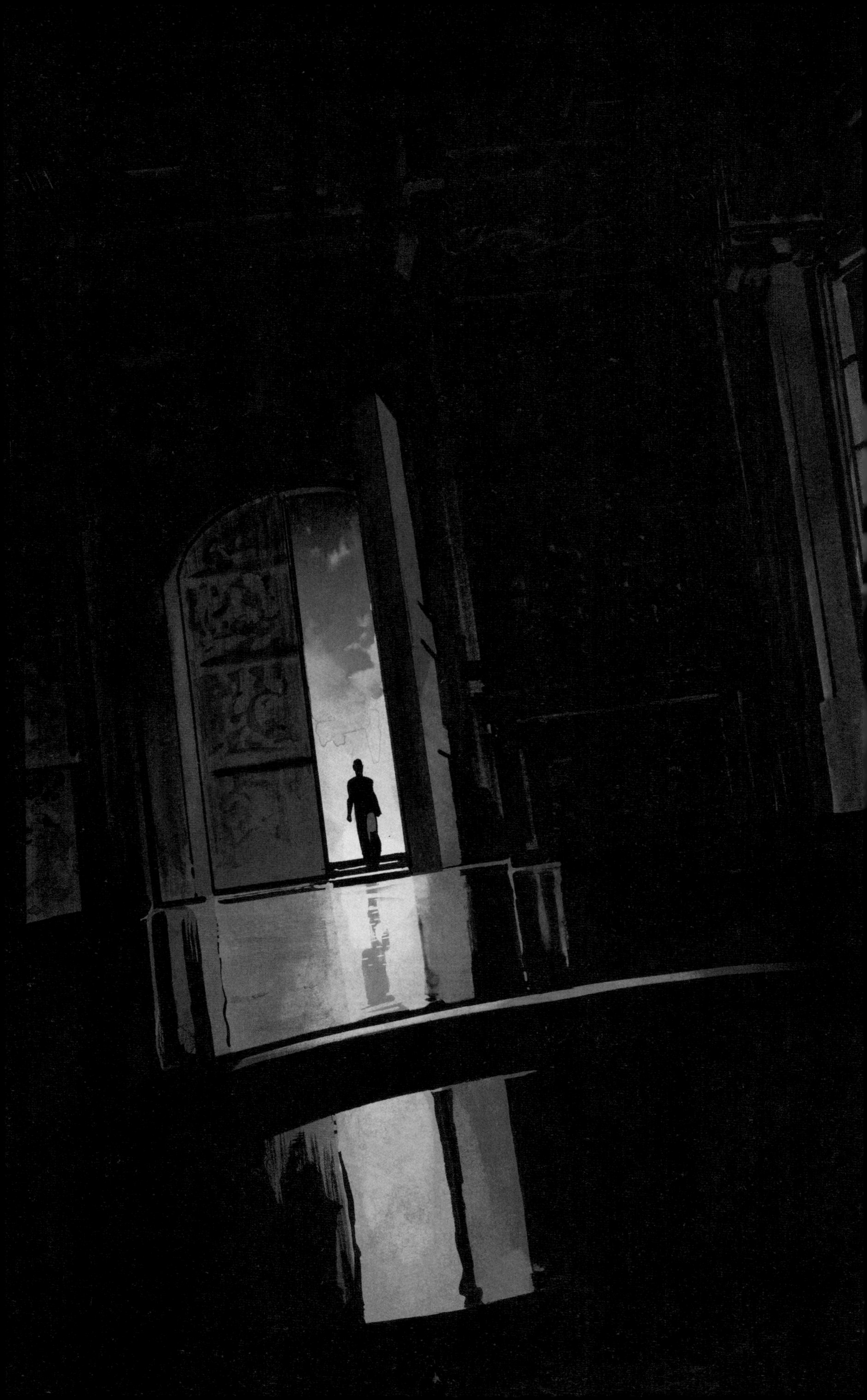

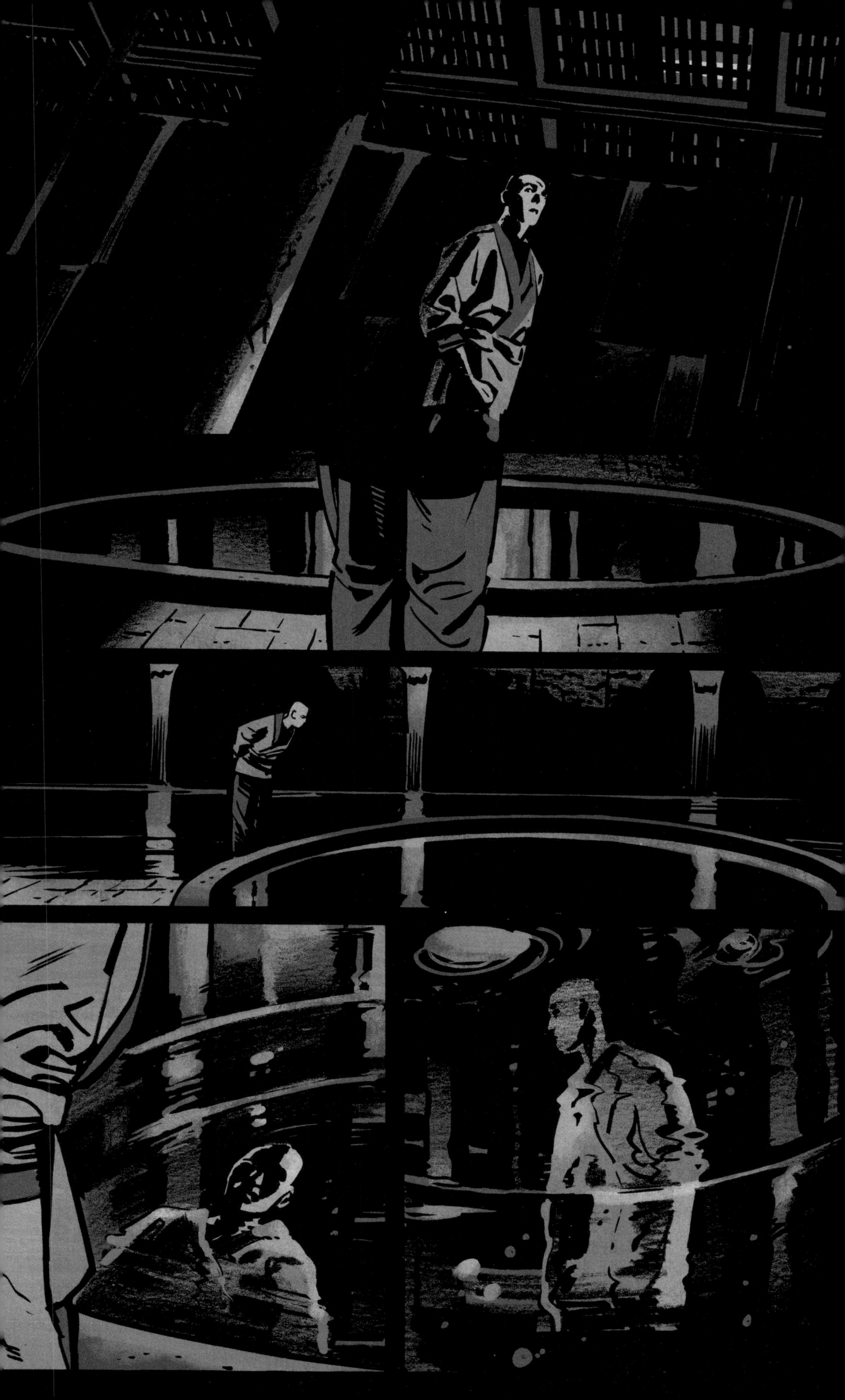

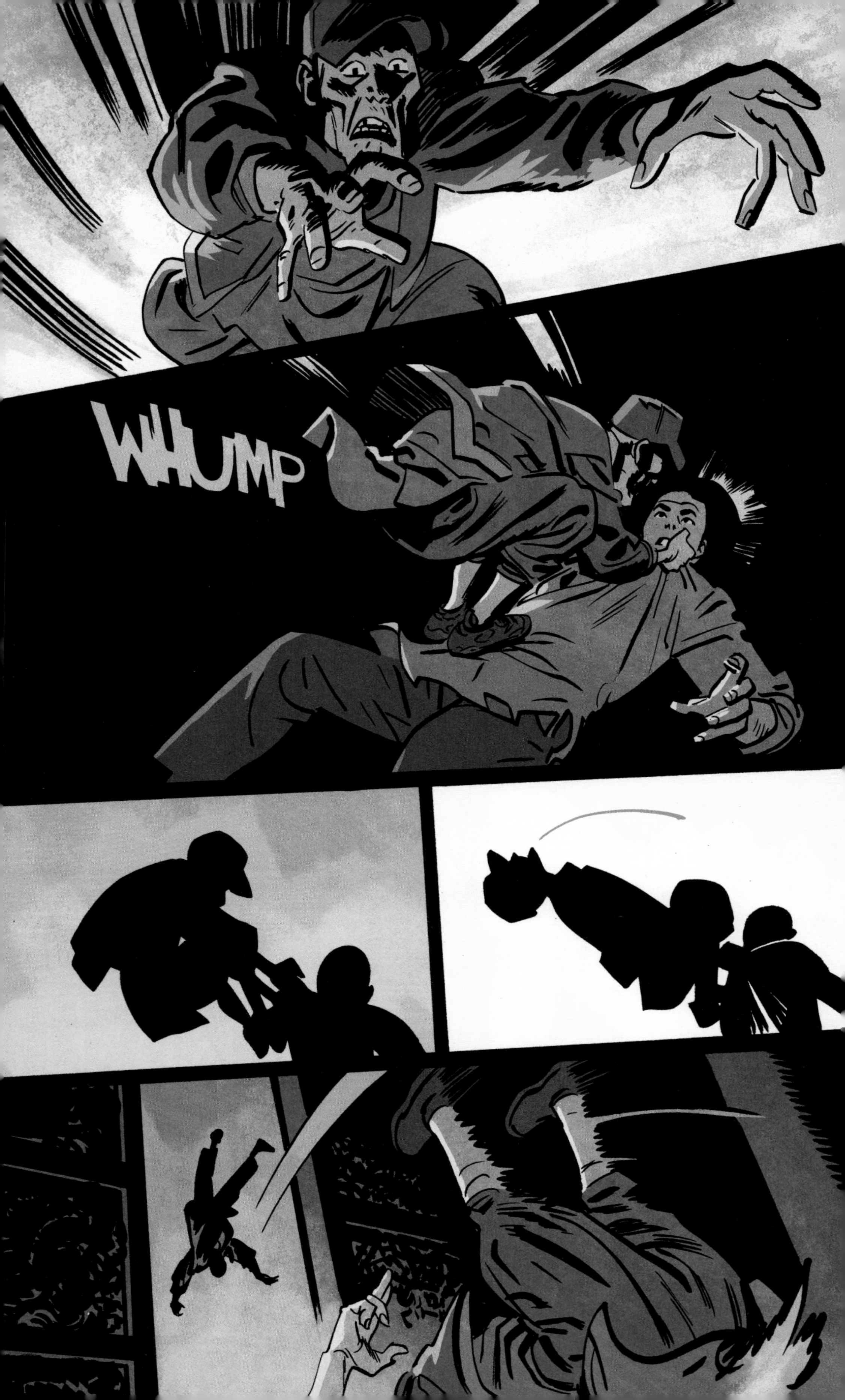
WHUMP

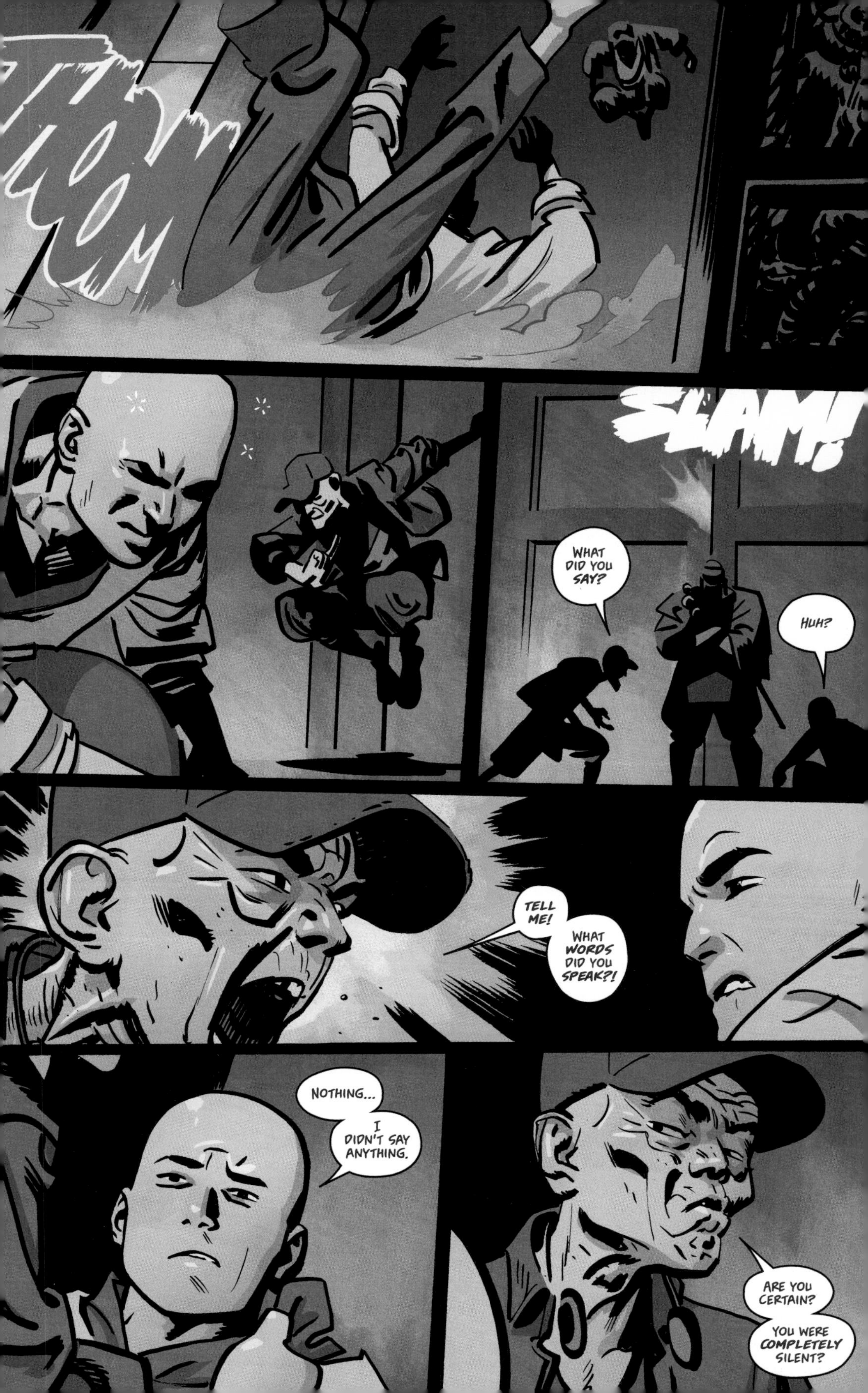
THOOM
SLAM!
WHAT DID YOU SAY?
HUH?
TELL ME!
WHAT WORDS DID YOU SPEAK?!
NOTHING...
I DIDN'T SAY ANYTHING.
ARE YOU CERTAIN?
YOU WERE COMPLETELY SILENT?

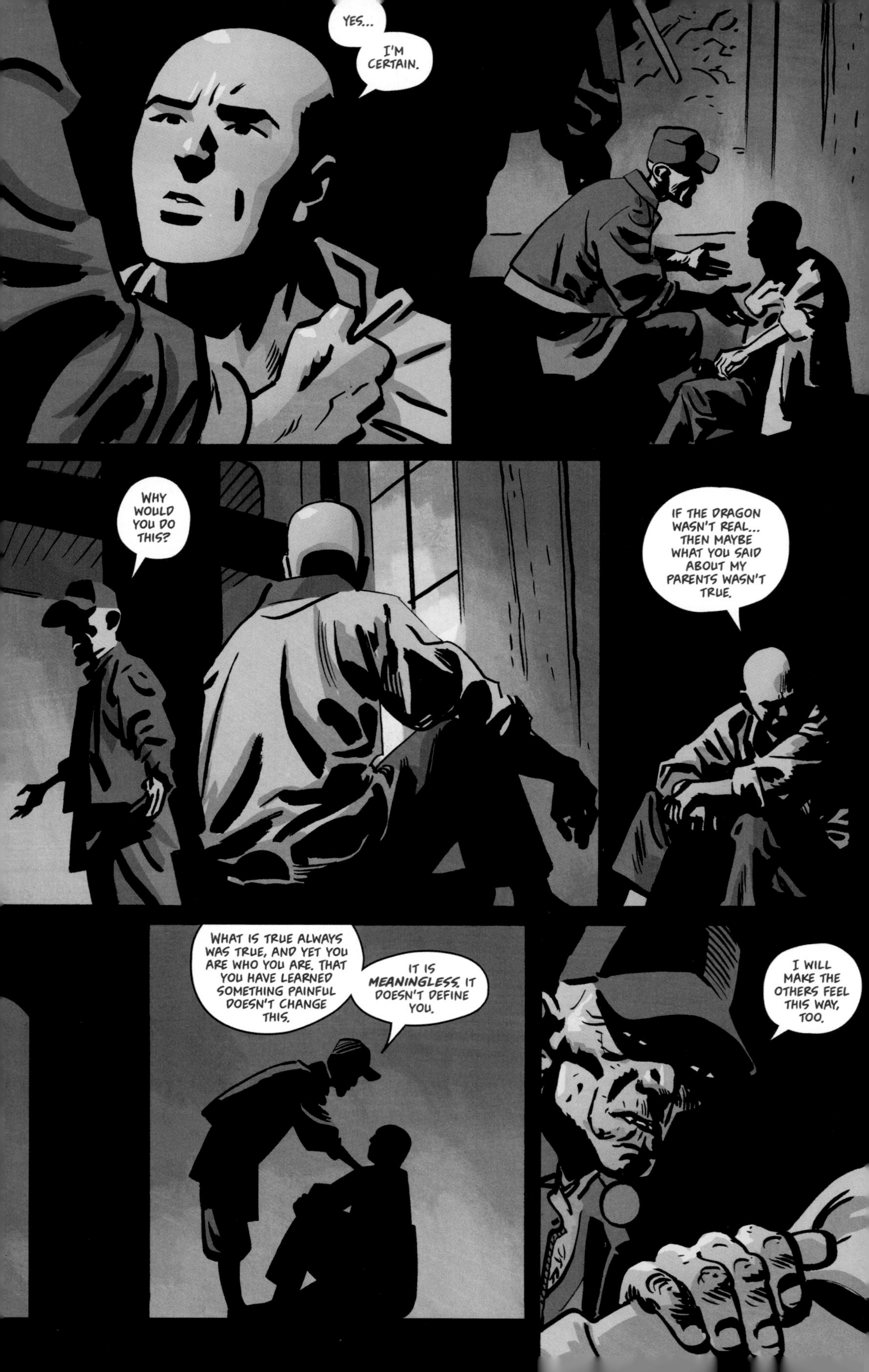
YES...
I'M CERTAIN.
WHY WOULD YOU DO THIS?
IF THE DRAGON WASN'T REAL... THEN MAYBE WHAT YOU SAID ABOUT MY PARENTS WASN'T TRUE.
WHAT IS TRUE ALWAYS WAS TRUE, AND YET YOU ARE WHO YOU ARE. THAT YOU HAVE LEARNED SOMETHING PAINFUL DOESN'T CHANGE THIS.
IT IS MEANINGLESS. IT DOESN'T DEFINE YOU.
I WILL MAKE THE OTHERS FEEL THIS WAY, TOO.

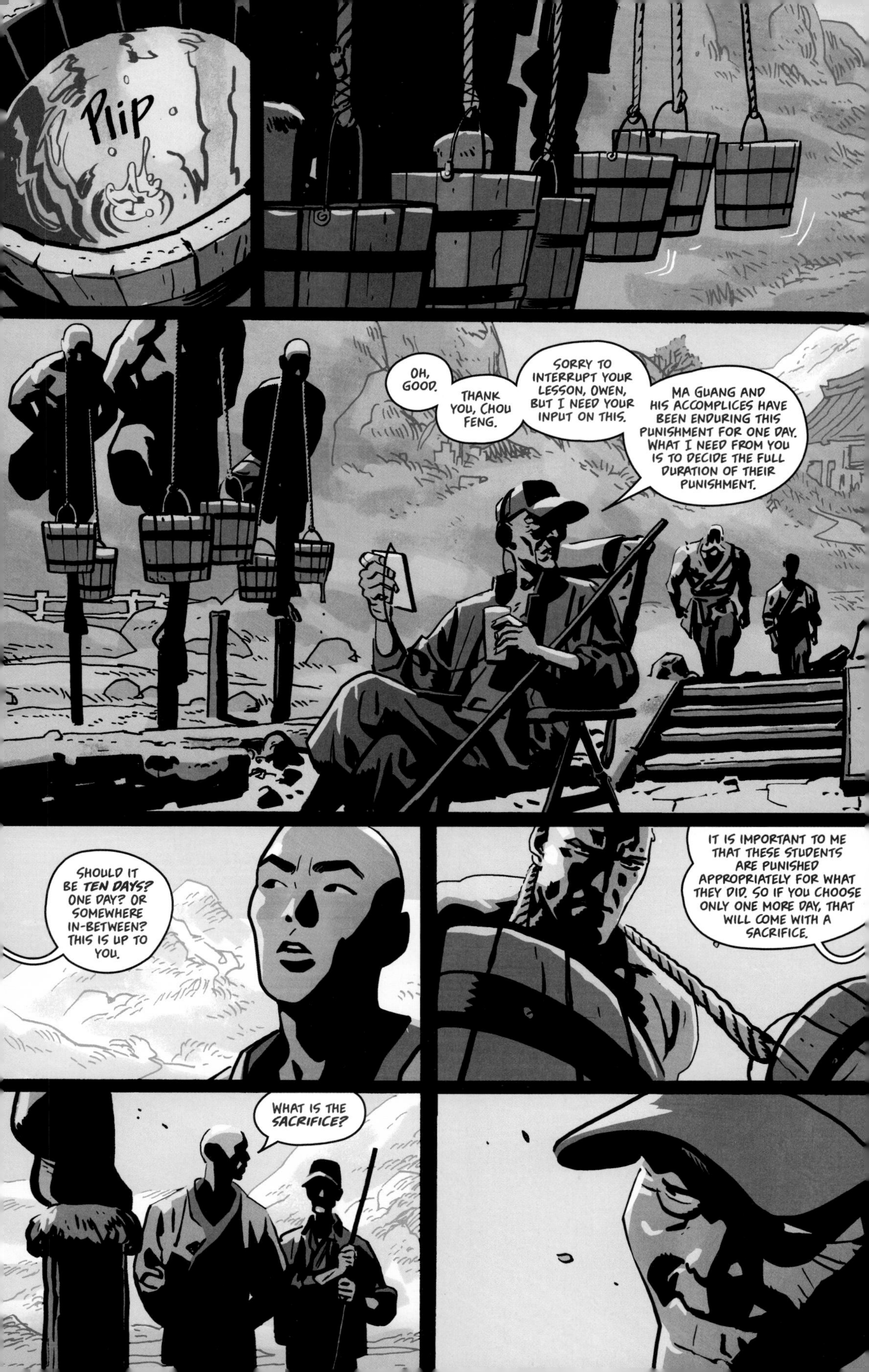
Plip
OH, GOOD.
THANK YOU, CHOU FENG.
SORRY TO INTERRUPT YOUR LESSON, OWEN, BUT I NEED YOUR INPUT ON THIS.
MA GUANG AND HIS ACCOMPLICES HAVE BEEN ENDURING THIS PUNISHMENT FOR ONE DAY. WHAT I NEED FROM YOU IS TO DECIDE THE FULL DURATION OF THEIR PUNISHMENT.
SHOULD IT BE *TEN DAYS?* ONE DAY? OR SOMEWHERE IN-BETWEEN? THIS IS UP TO YOU.
IT IS IMPORTANT TO ME THAT THESE STUDENTS ARE PUNISHED APPROPRIATELY FOR WHAT THEY DID. SO IF YOU CHOOSE ONLY ONE MORE DAY, THAT WILL COME WITH A SACRIFICE.
WHAT IS THE *SACRIFICE?*

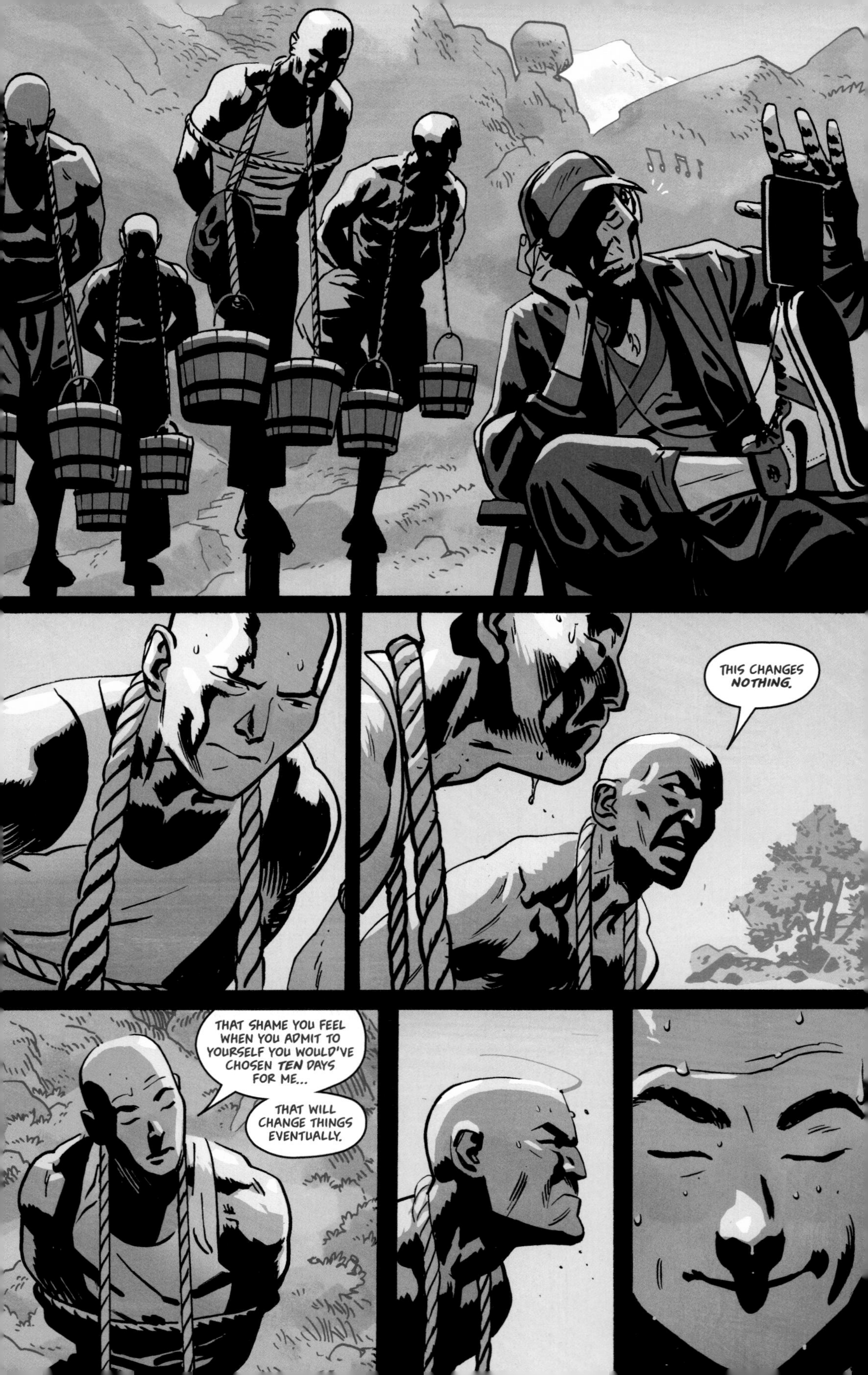
THIS CHANGES NOTHING.
THAT SHAME YOU FEEL WHEN YOU ADMIT TO YOURSELF YOU WOULD'VE CHOSEN TEN DAYS FOR ME...
THAT WILL CHANGE THINGS EVENTUALLY.

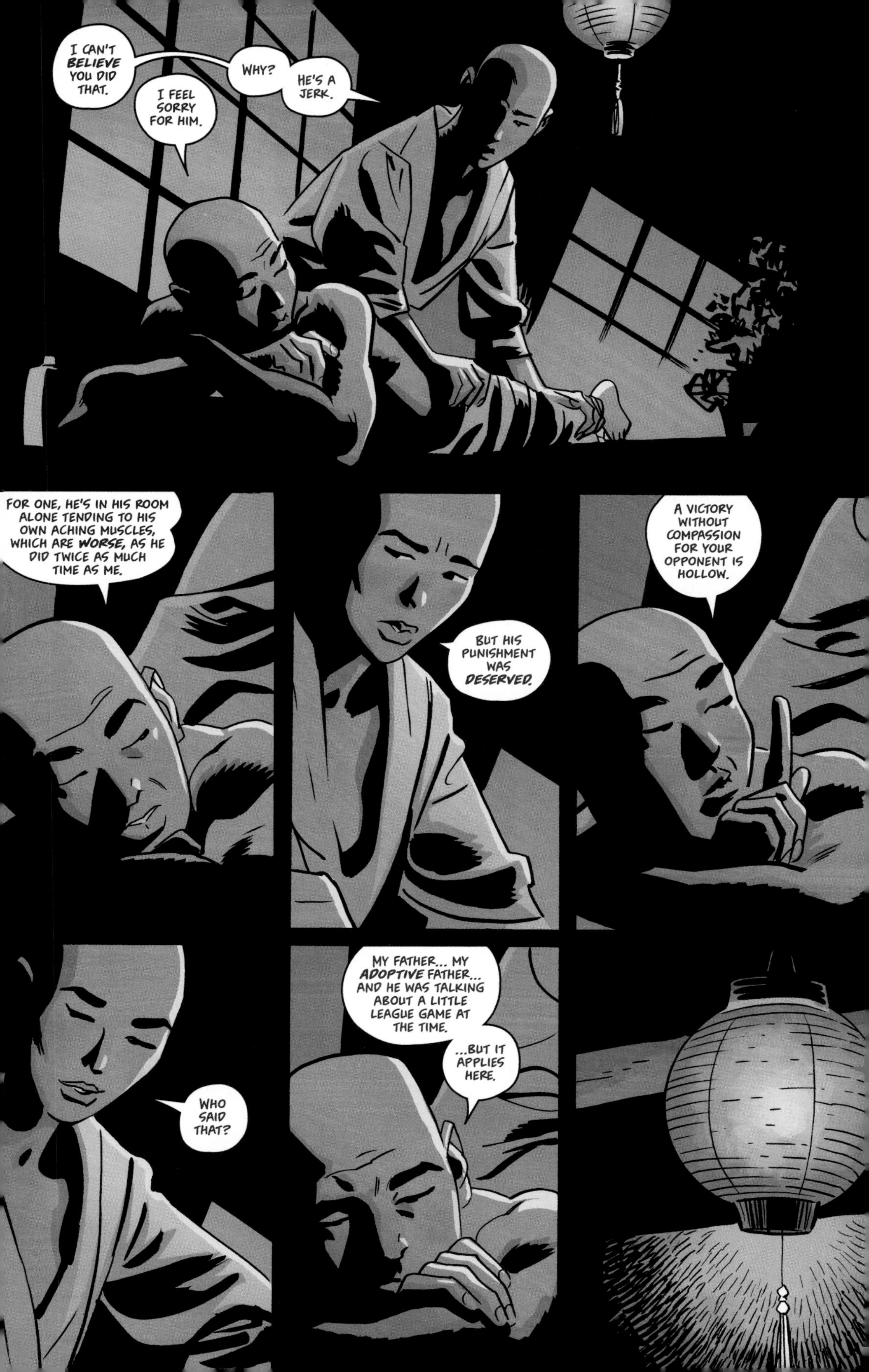
I CAN'T BELIEVE YOU DID THAT.
I FEEL SORRY FOR HIM.
WHY?
HE'S A JERK.
FOR ONE, HE'S IN HIS ROOM ALONE TENDING TO HIS OWN ACHING MUSCLES, WHICH ARE WORSE, AS HE DID TWICE AS MUCH TIME AS ME.
BUT HIS PUNISHMENT WAS DESERVED.
A VICTORY WITHOUT COMPASSION FOR YOUR OPPONENT IS HOLLOW.
WHO SAID THAT?
MY FATHER... MY ADOPTIVE FATHER... AND HE WAS TALKING ABOUT A LITTLE LEAGUE GAME AT THE TIME.
...BUT IT APPLIES HERE.

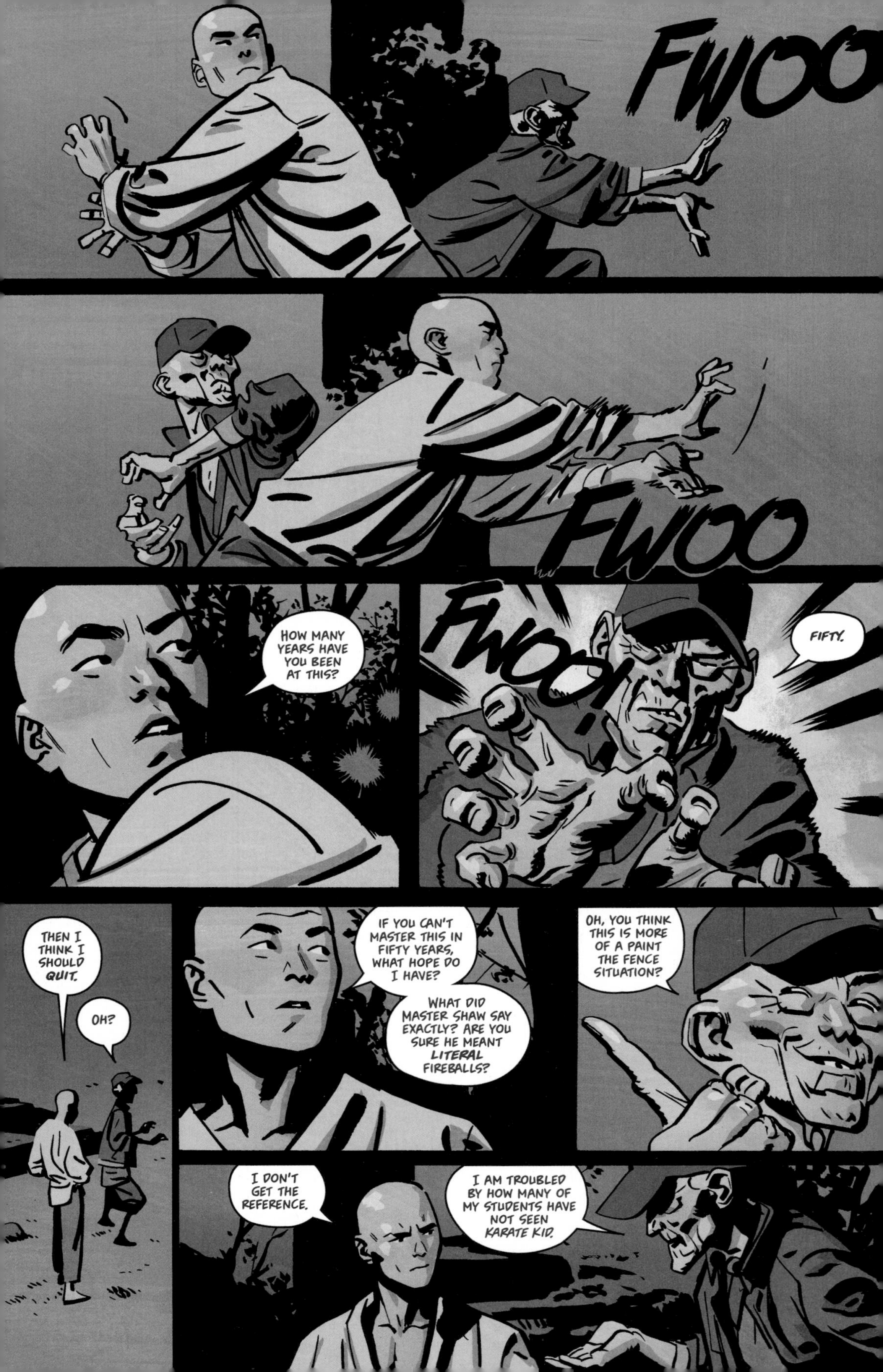
FWOO
FWOO
HOW MANY YEARS HAVE YOU BEEN AT THIS?
FWOOH
FIFTY.
THEN I THINK I SHOULD QUIT.
OH?
IF YOU CAN'T MASTER THIS IN FIFTY YEARS, WHAT HOPE DO I HAVE?
WHAT DID MASTER SHAW SAY EXACTLY? ARE YOU SURE HE MEANT LITERAL FIREBALLS?
OH, YOU THINK THIS IS MORE OF A PAINT THE FENCE SITUATION?
I DON'T GET THE REFERENCE.
I AM TROUBLED BY HOW MANY OF MY STUDENTS HAVE NOT SEEN KARATE KID.

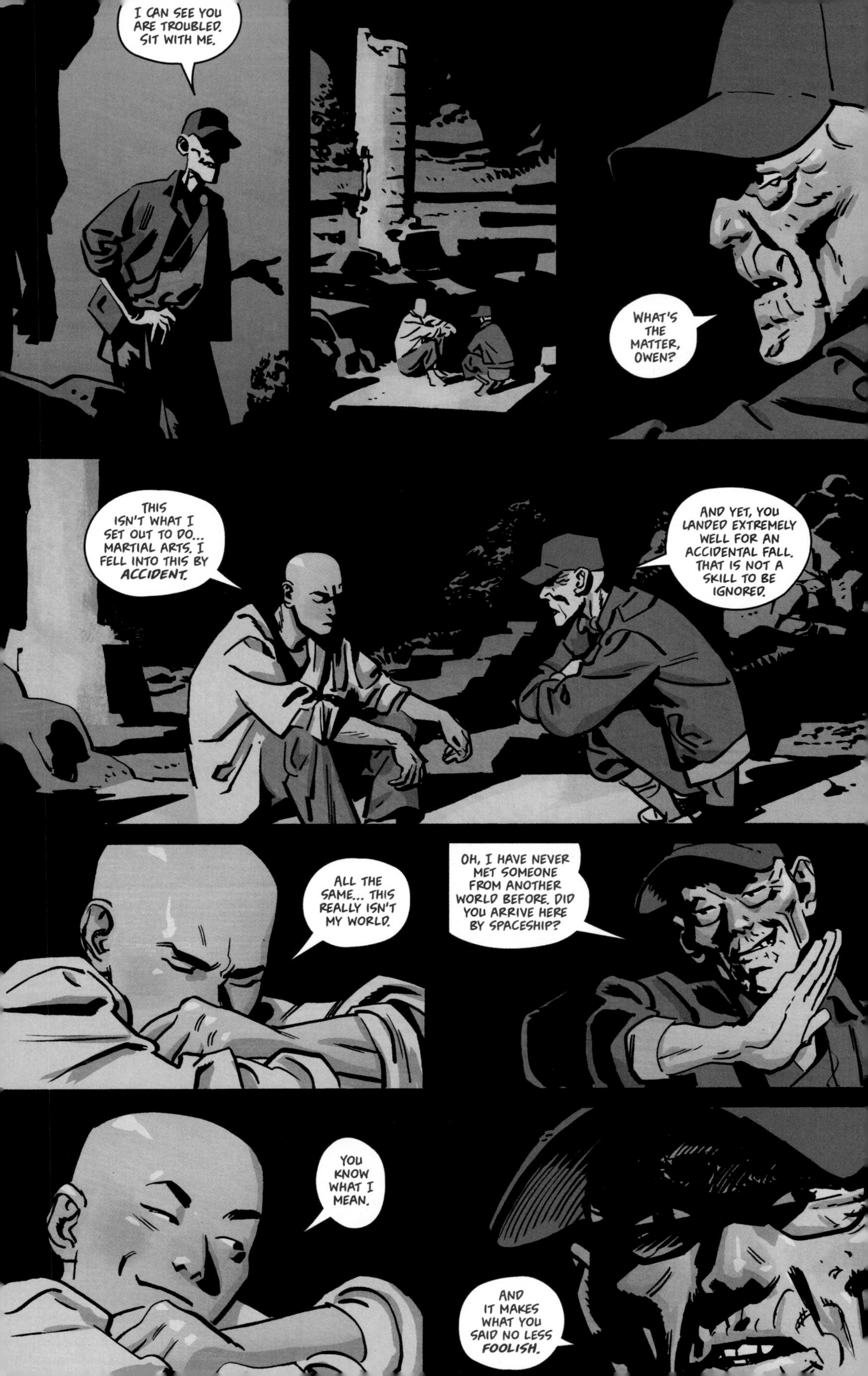
I CAN SEE YOU ARE TROUBLED. SIT WITH ME.
WHAT'S THE MATTER, OWEN?
THIS ISN'T WHAT I SET OUT TO DO... MARTIAL ARTS. I FELL INTO THIS BY ACCIDENT.
AND YET, YOU LANDED EXTREMELY WELL FOR AN ACCIDENTAL FALL. THAT IS NOT A SKILL TO BE IGNORED.
ALL THE SAME... THIS REALLY ISN'T MY WORLD.
OH, I HAVE NEVER MET SOMEONE FROM ANOTHER WORLD BEFORE. DID YOU ARRIVE HERE BY SPACESHIP?
YOU KNOW WHAT I MEAN.
AND IT MAKES WHAT YOU SAID NO LESS FOOLISH.

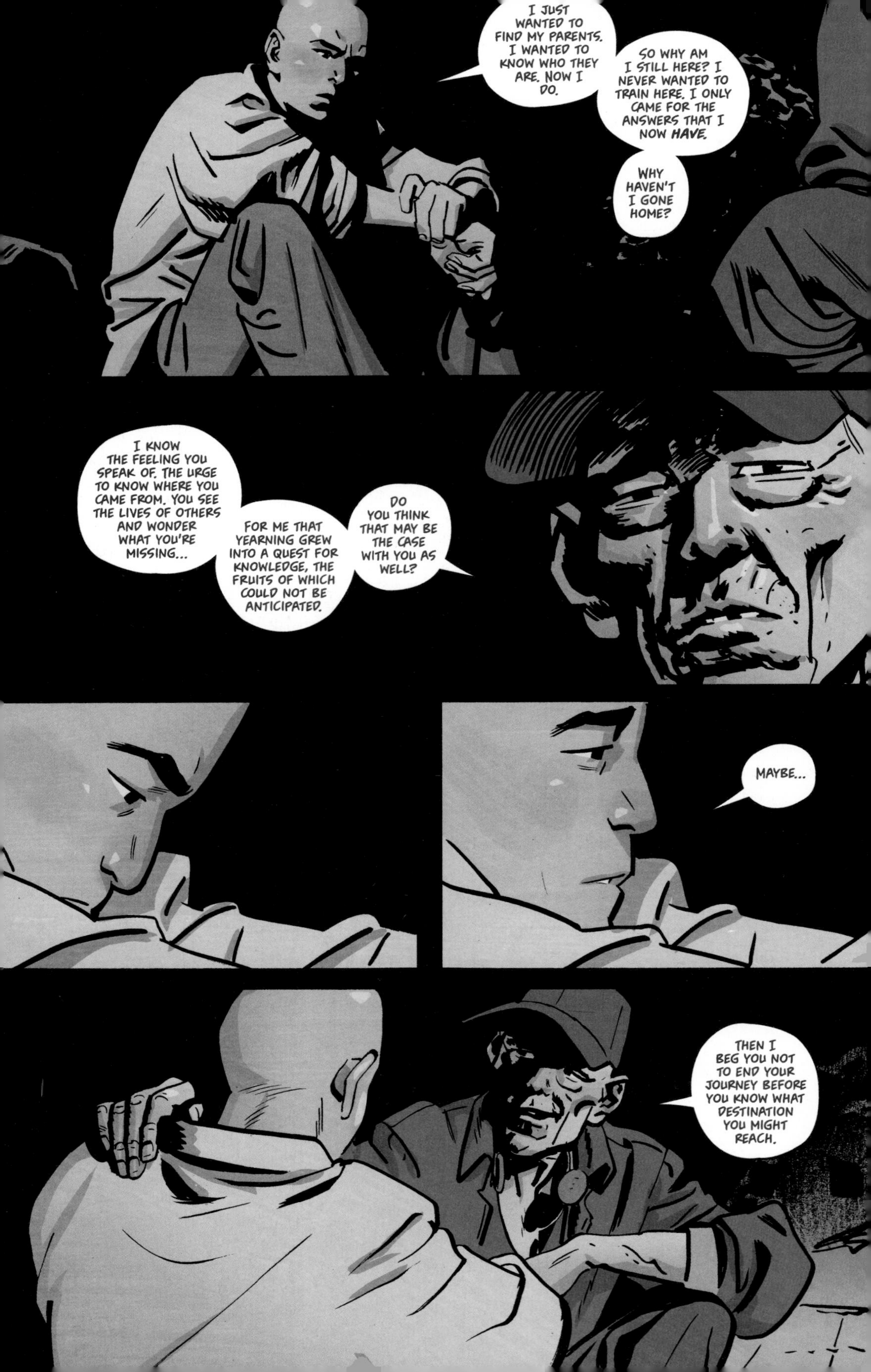
I JUST WANTED TO FIND MY PARENTS. I WANTED TO KNOW WHO THEY ARE. NOW I DO.
SO WHY AM I STILL HERE? I NEVER WANTED TO TRAIN HERE. I ONLY CAME FOR THE ANSWERS THAT I NOW *HAVE.*
WHY HAVEN'T I GONE HOME?
I KNOW THE FEELING YOU SPEAK OF. THE URGE TO KNOW WHERE YOU CAME FROM. YOU SEE THE LIVES OF OTHERS AND WONDER WHAT YOU'RE MISSING...
FOR ME THAT YEARNING GREW INTO A QUEST FOR KNOWLEDGE, THE FRUITS OF WHICH COULD NOT BE ANTICIPATED.
DO YOU THINK THAT MAY BE THE CASE WITH YOU AS WELL?
MAYBE...
THEN I BEG YOU NOT TO END YOUR JOURNEY BEFORE YOU KNOW WHAT DESTINATION YOU MIGHT REACH.

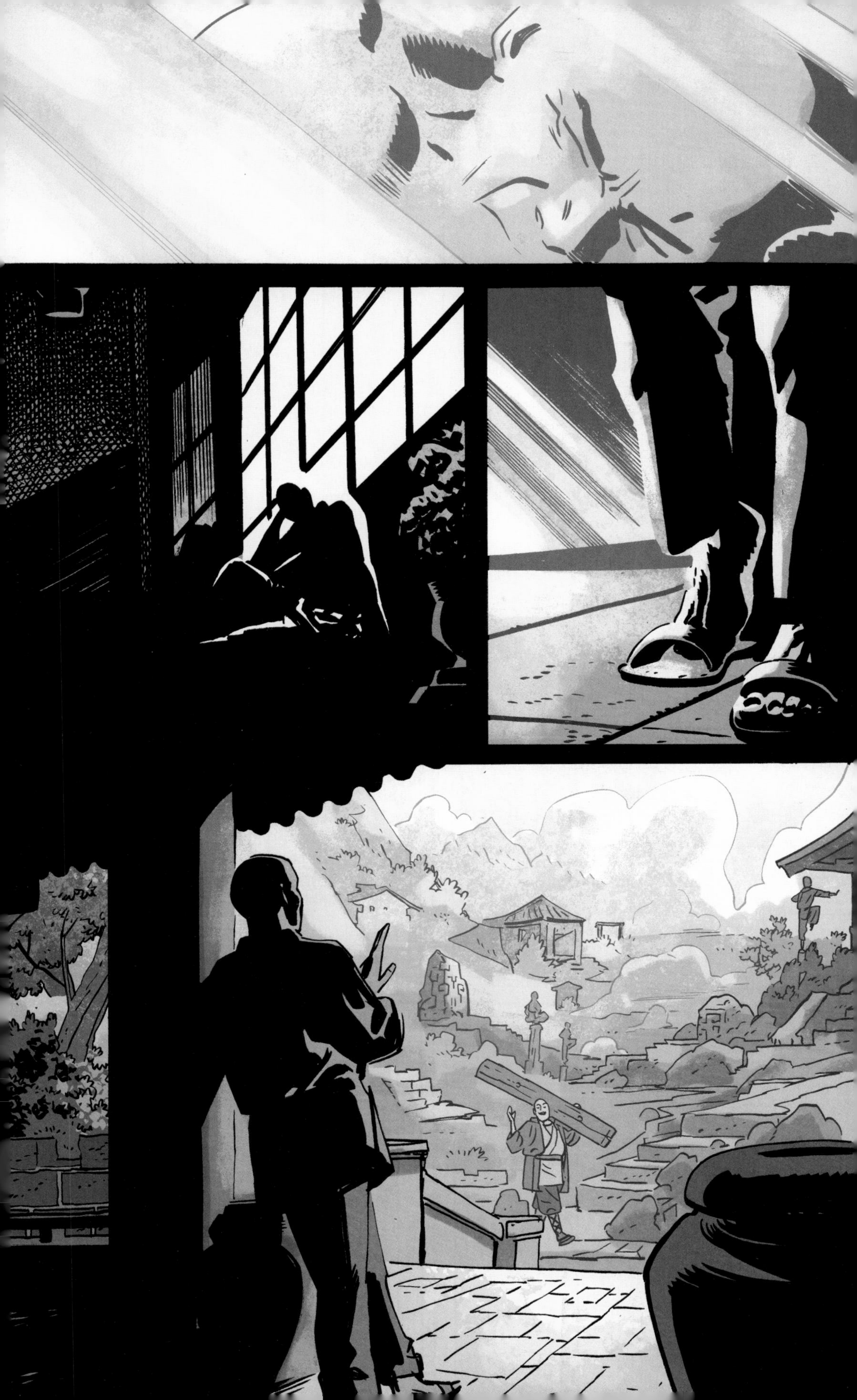

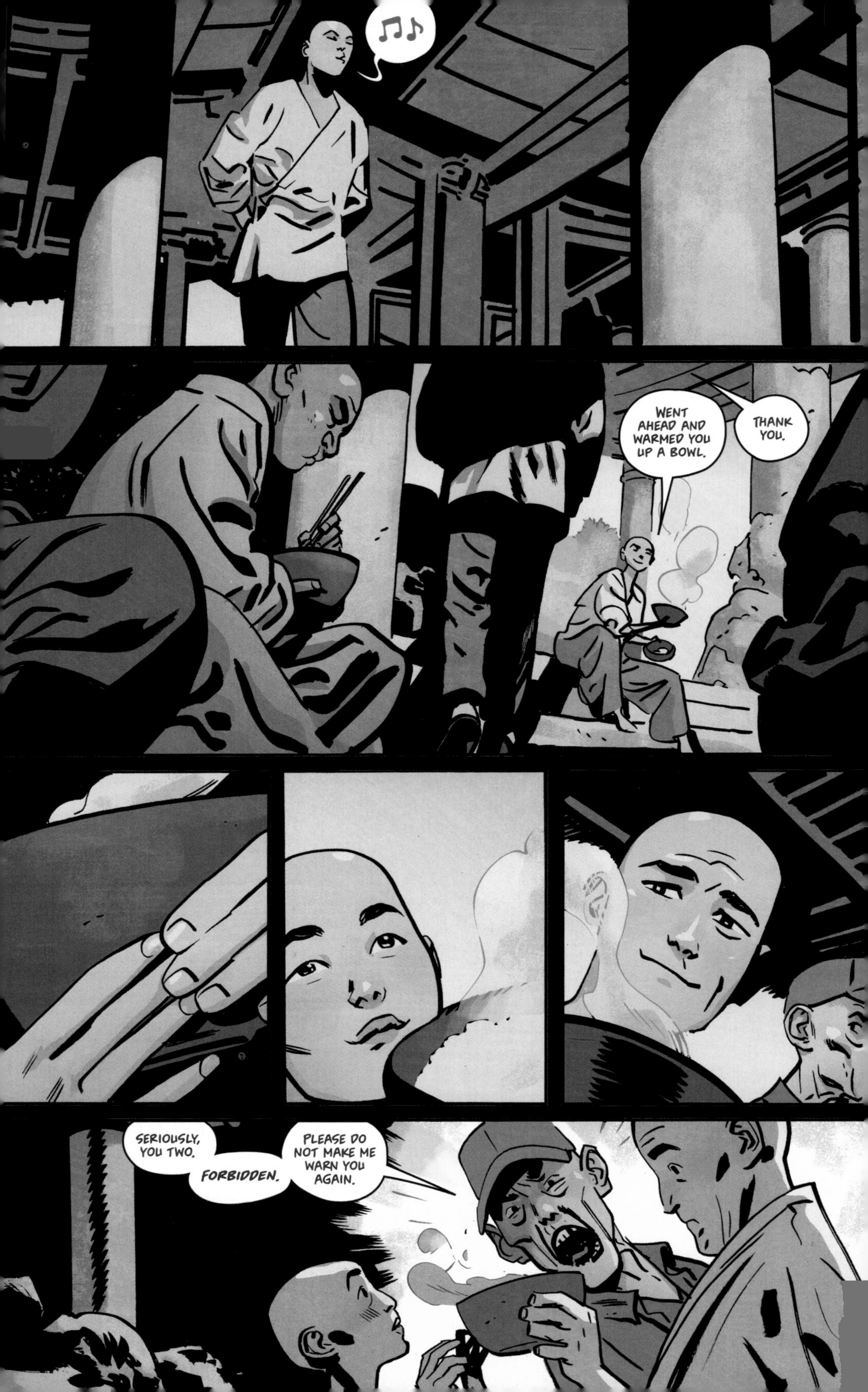
♫♪
WENT AHEAD AND WARMED YOU UP A BOWL.
THANK YOU.
SERIOUSLY, YOU TWO.
FORBIDDEN.
PLEASE DO NOT MAKE ME WARN YOU AGAIN.

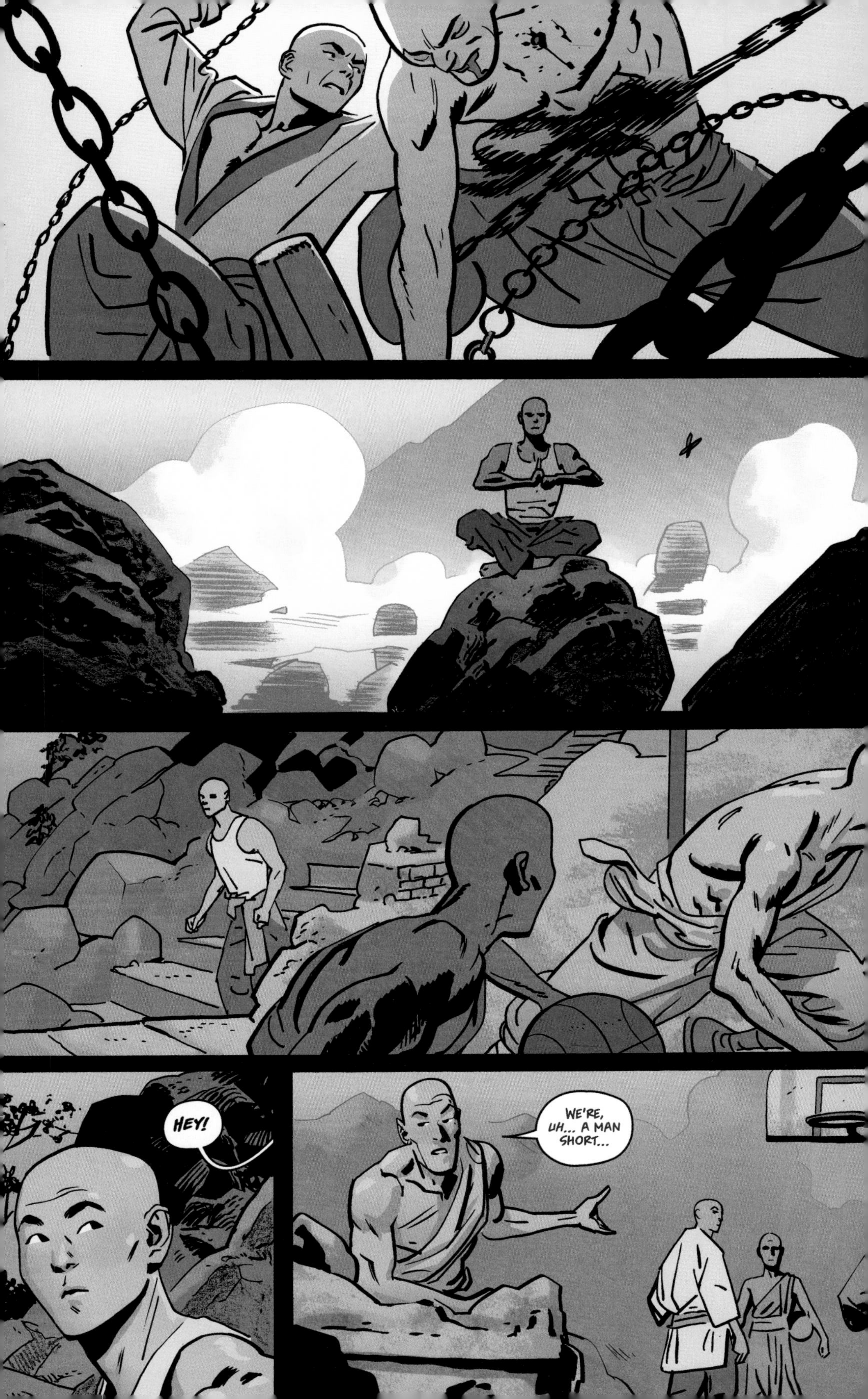
HEY!
WE'RE, UH... A MAN SHORT...

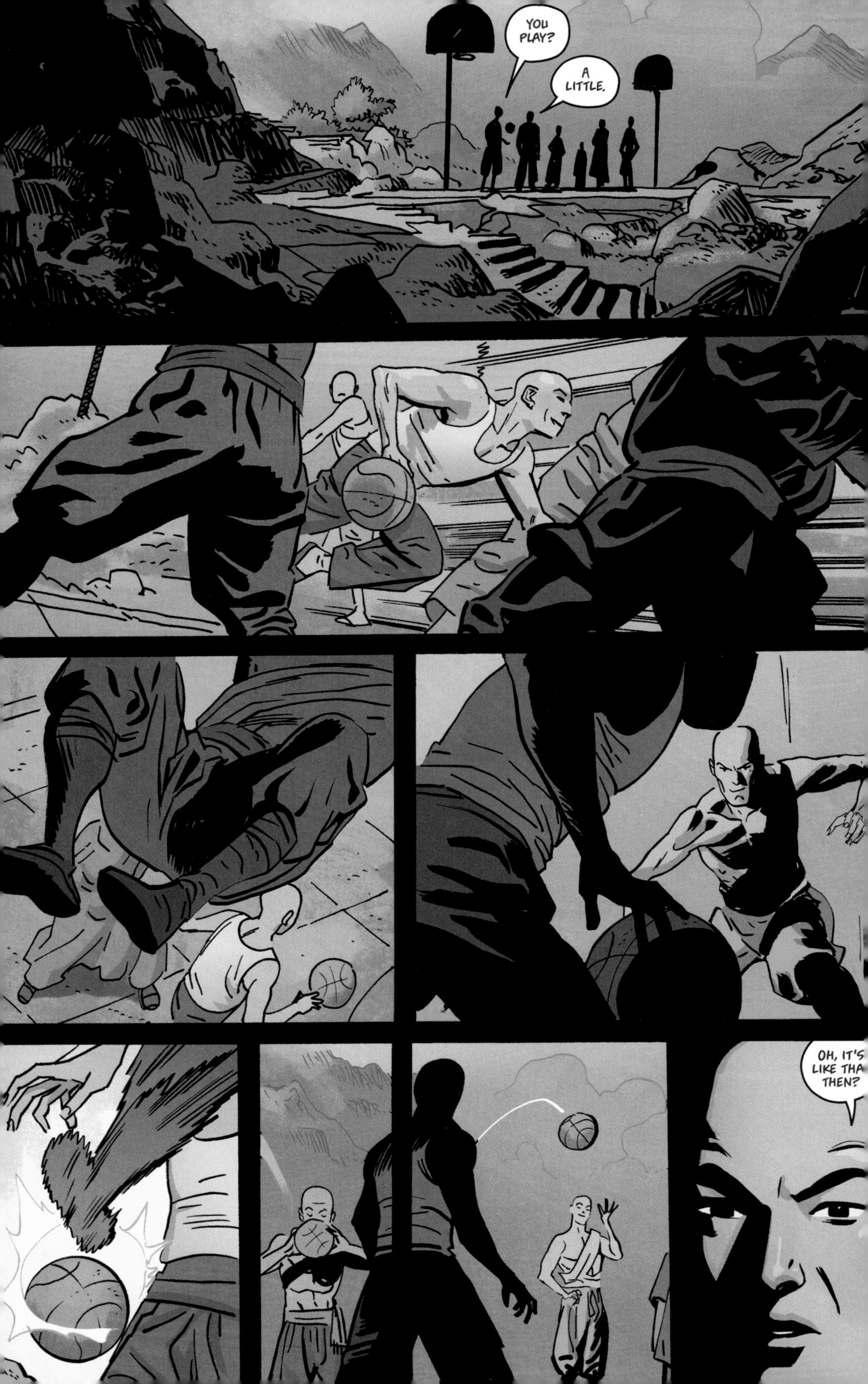
YOU PLAY?
A LITTLE.
OH, IT'S LIKE THAT THEN?

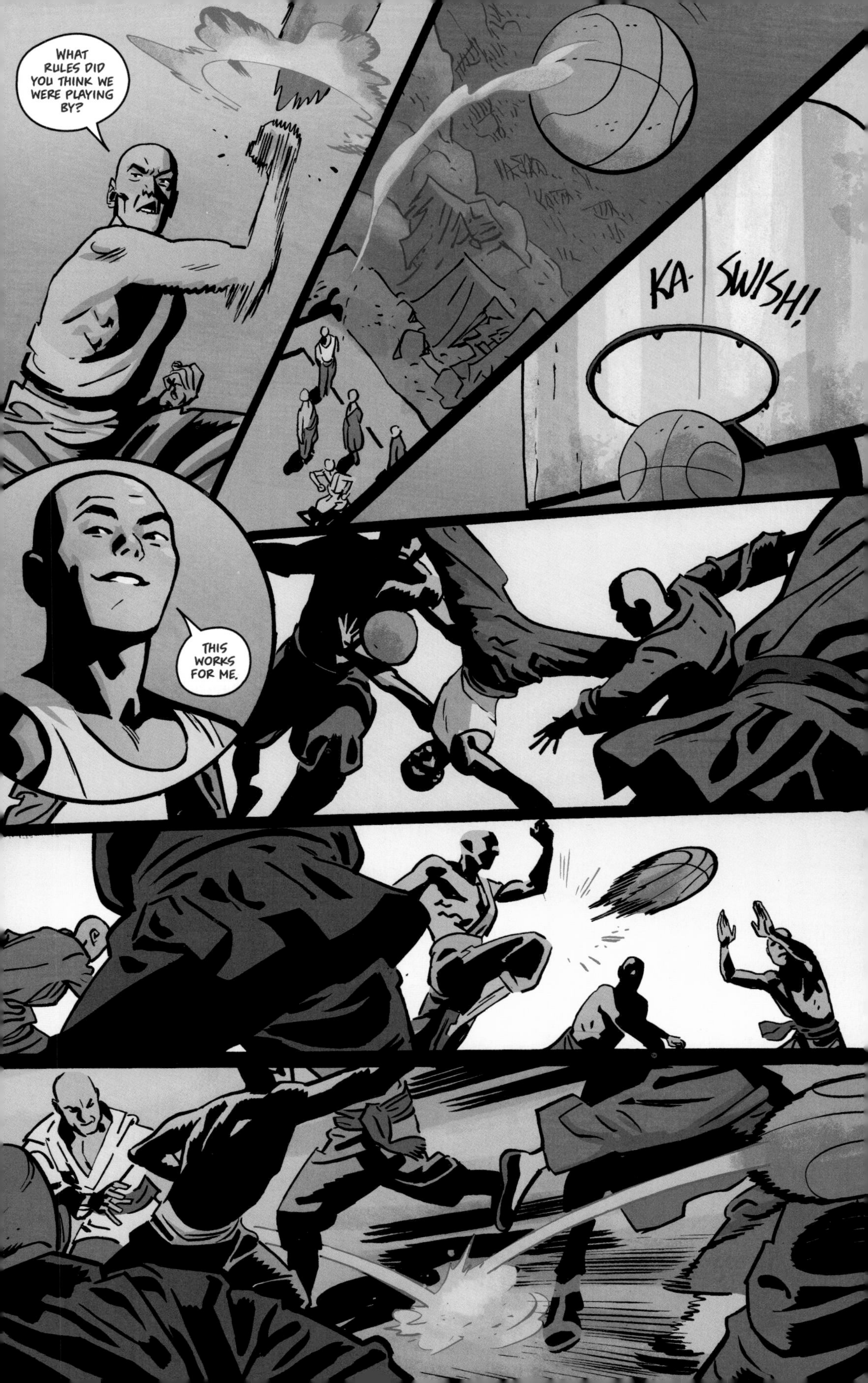
WHAT RULES DID YOU THINK WE WERE PLAYING BY?
KA-SWISH!
THIS WORKS FOR ME.

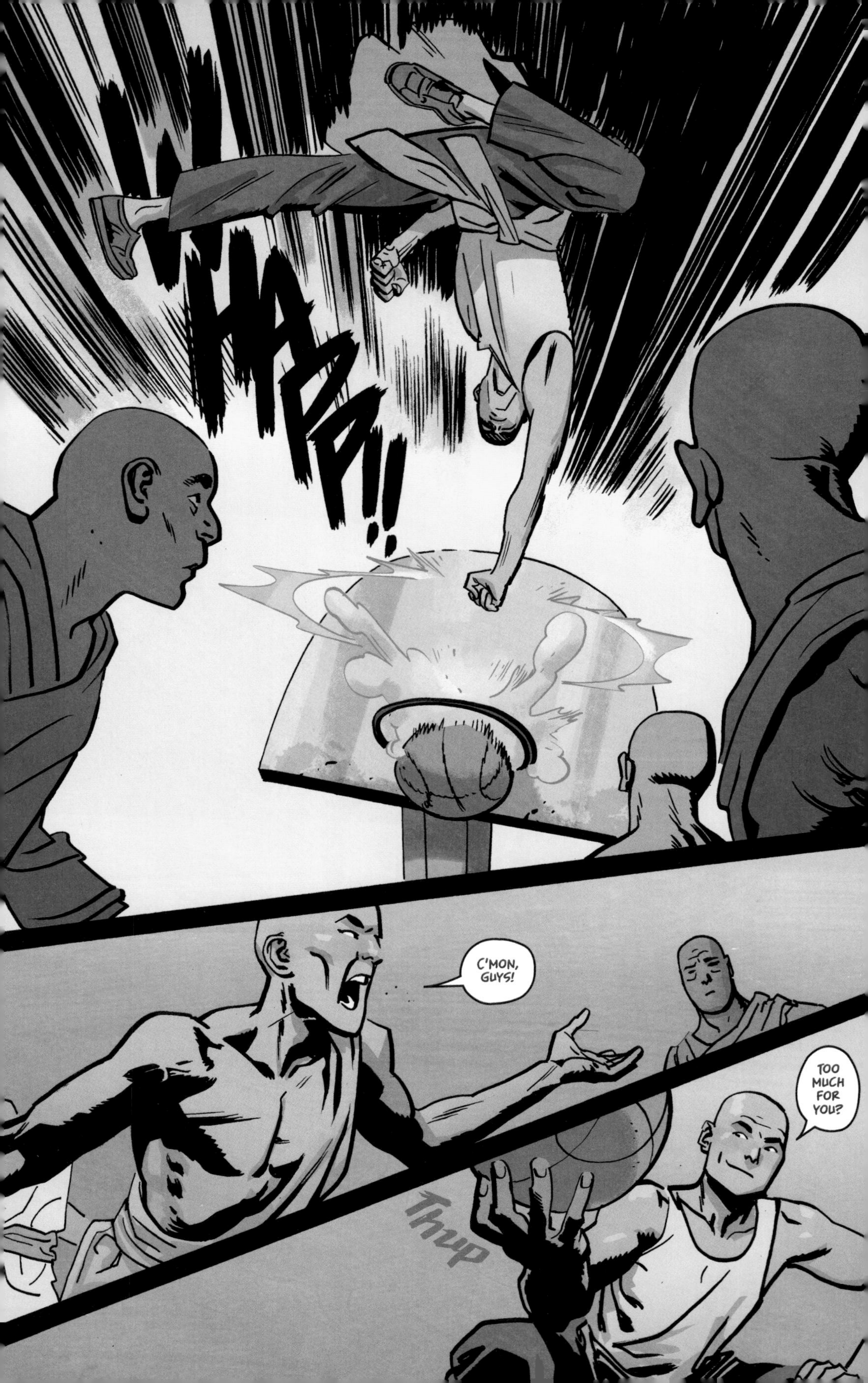
HAPP!!
C'MON, GUYS!
TOO MUCH FOR YOU?
THUP

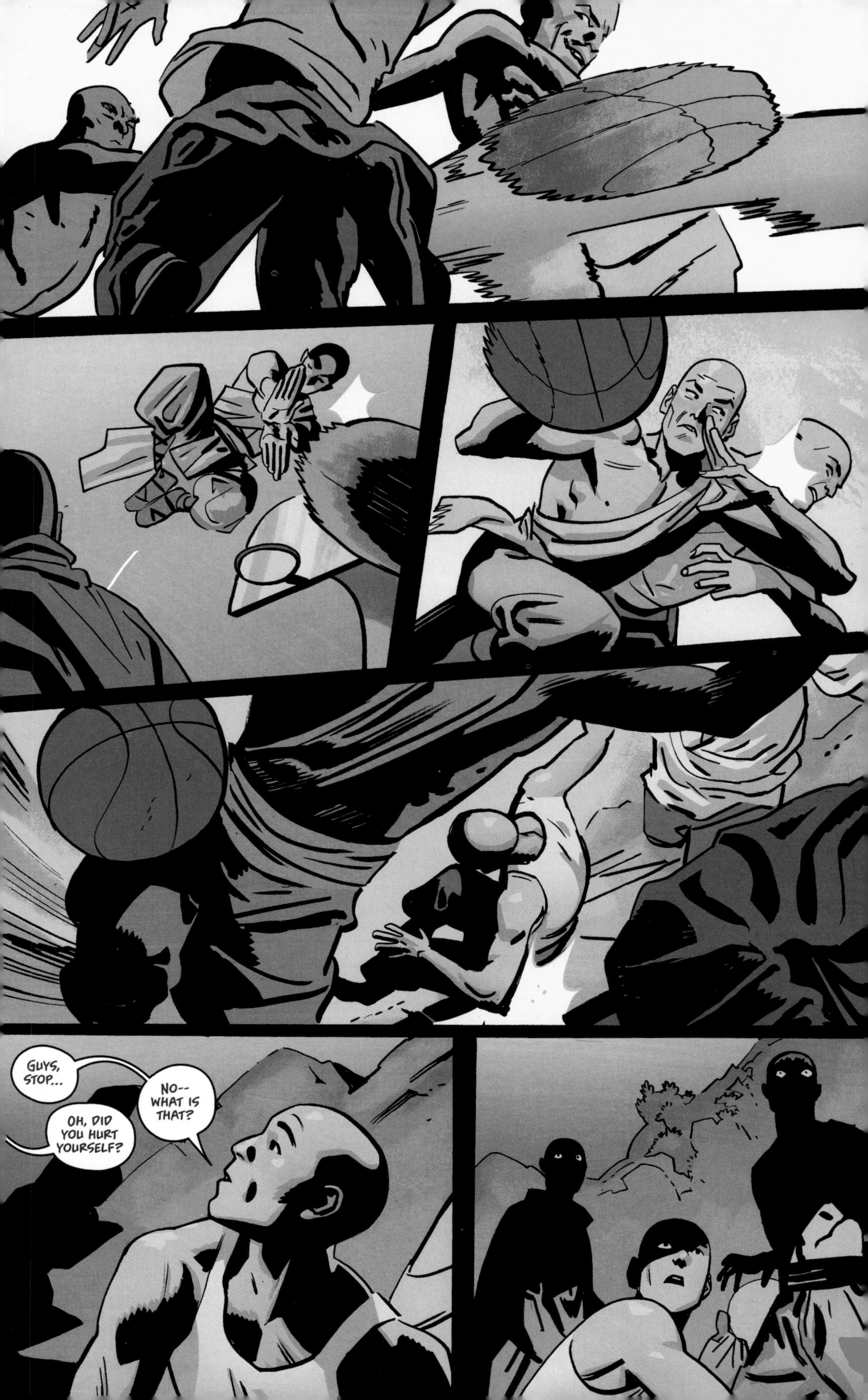
GUYS, STOP...
OH, DID YOU HURT YOURSELF?
NO-- WHAT IS THAT?

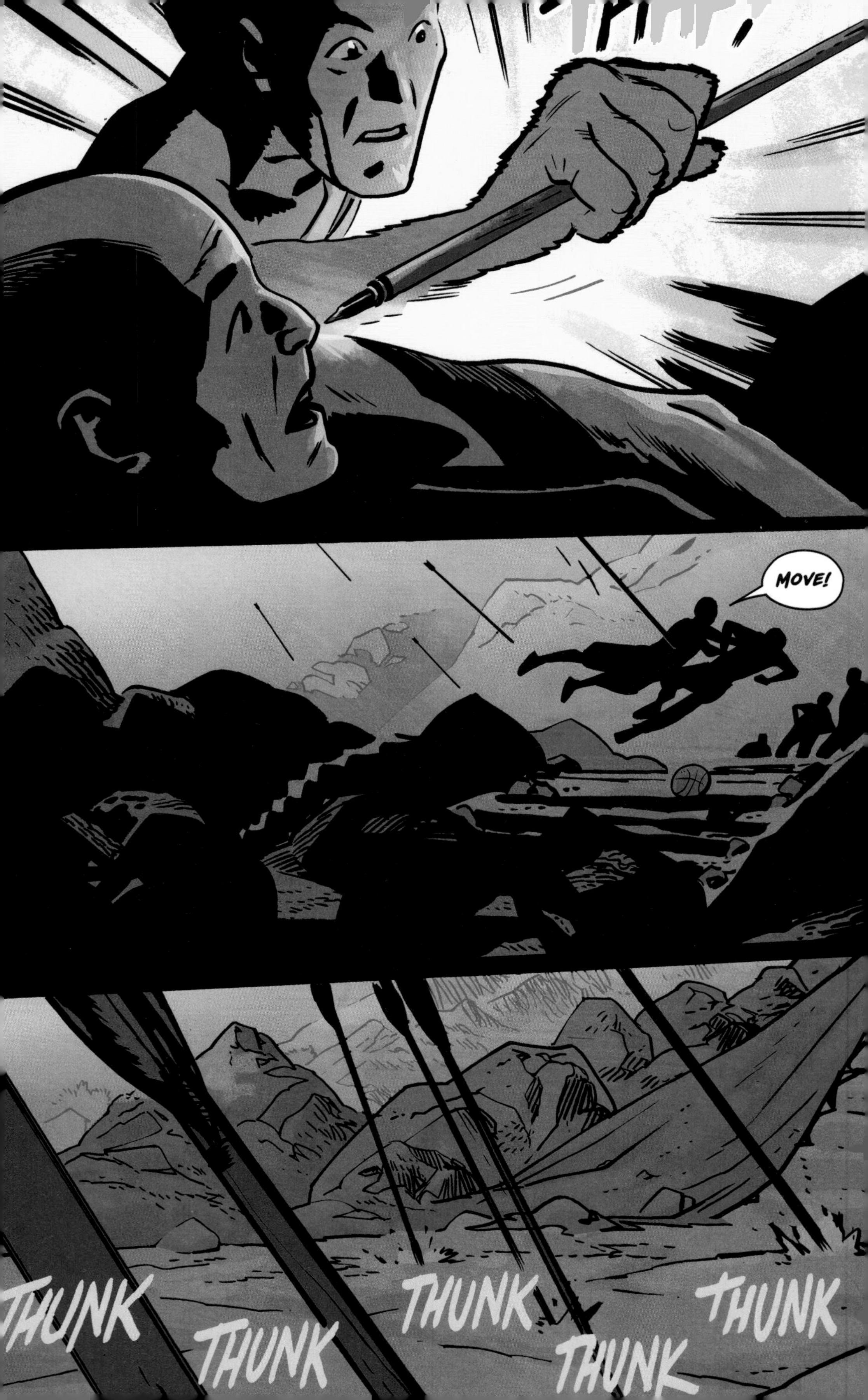
MOVE!
THUNK
THUNK
THUNK
THUNK
THUNK

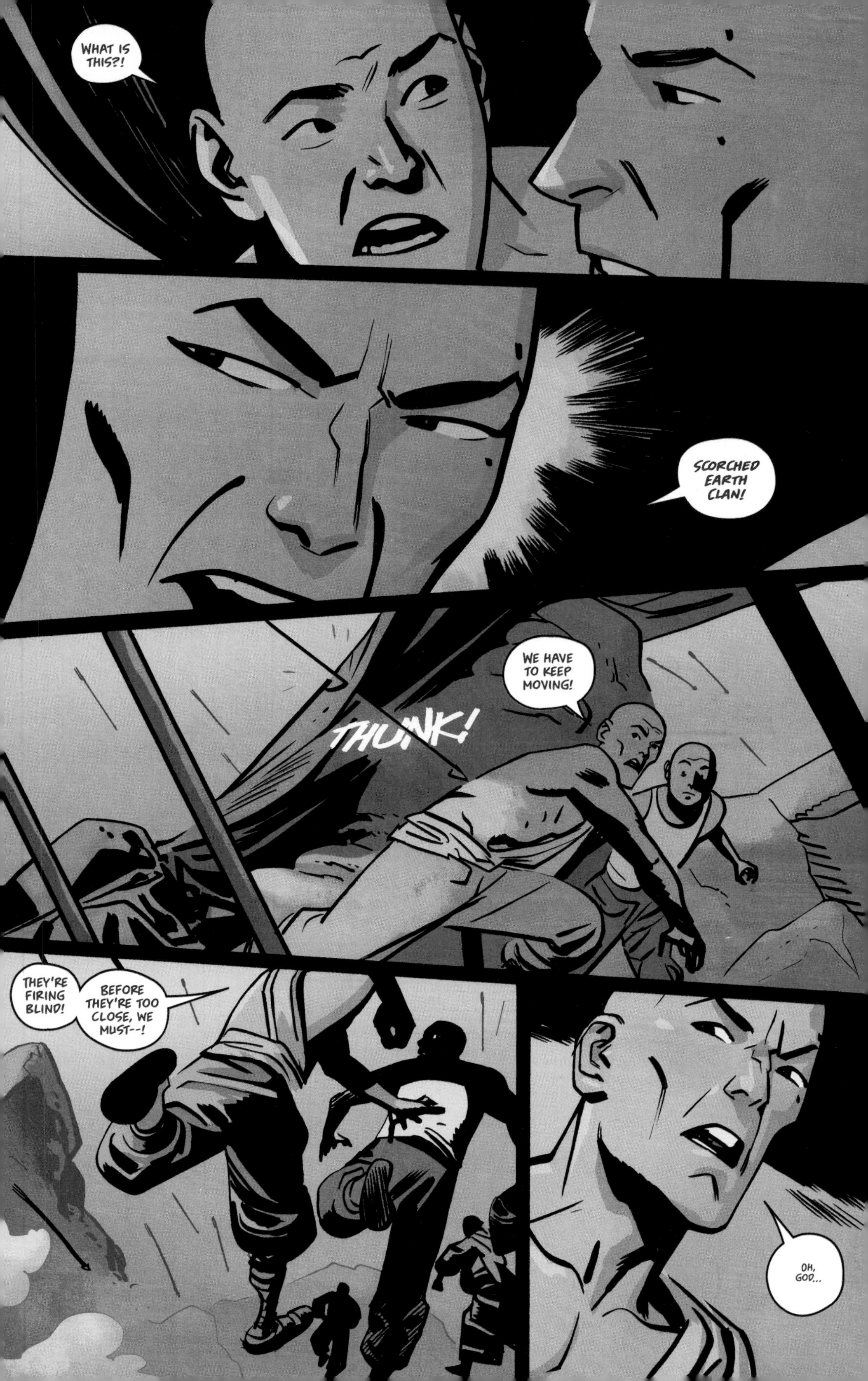
WHAT IS THIS?!
SCORCHED EARTH CLAN!
WE HAVE TO KEEP MOVING!
THUNK!
THEY'RE FIRING BLIND!
BEFORE THEY'RE TOO CLOSE, WE MUST--!
OH, GOD...

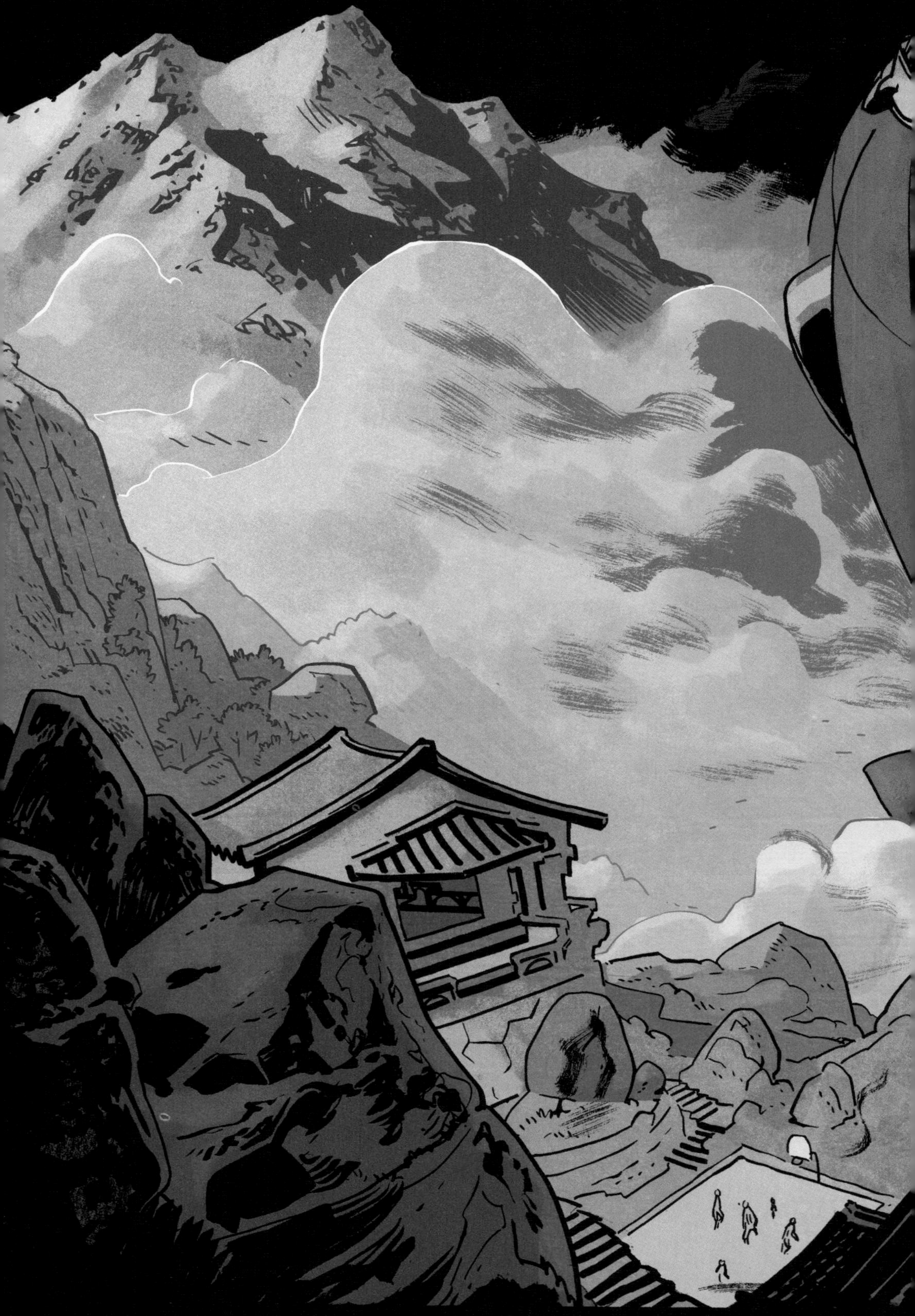

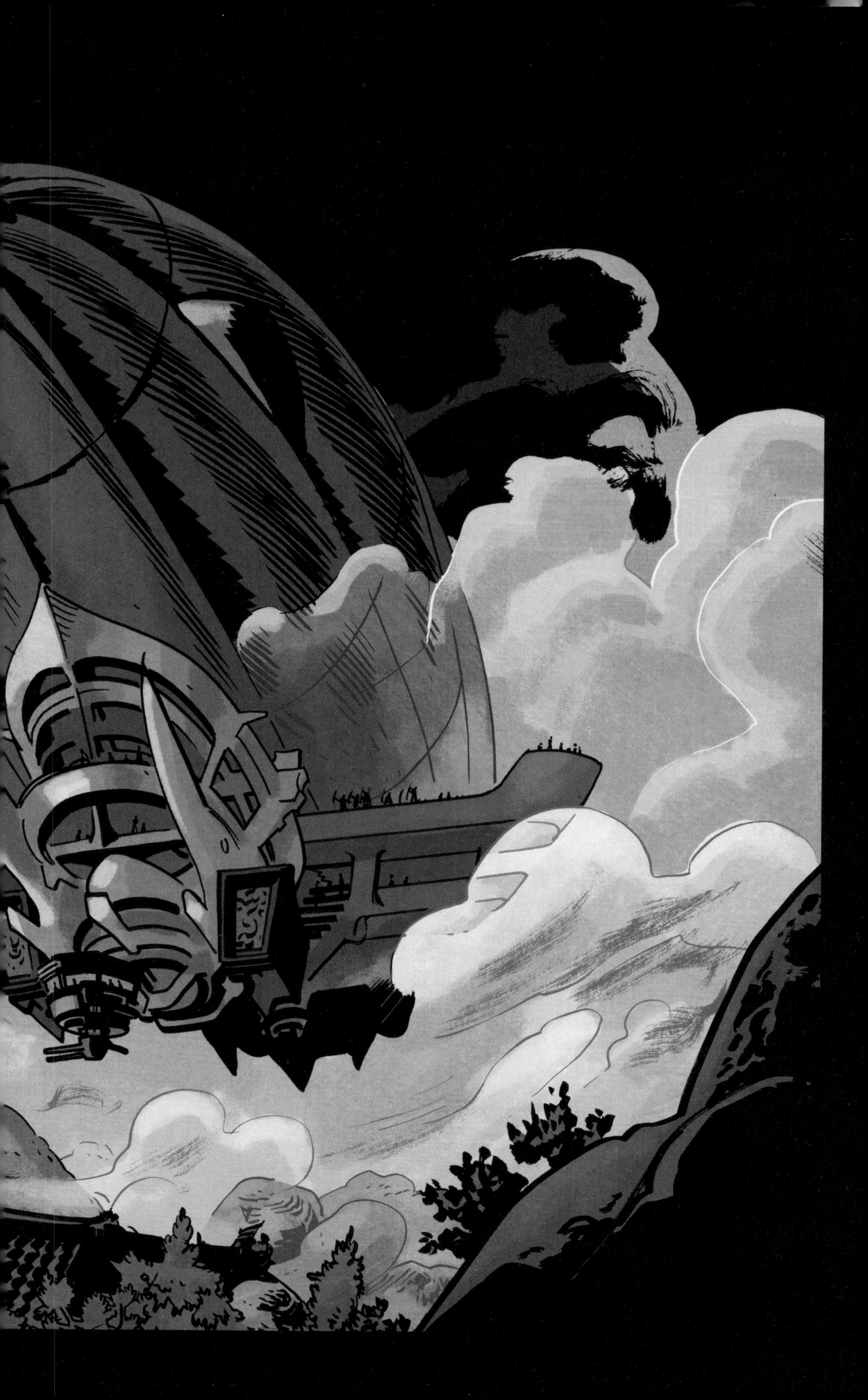

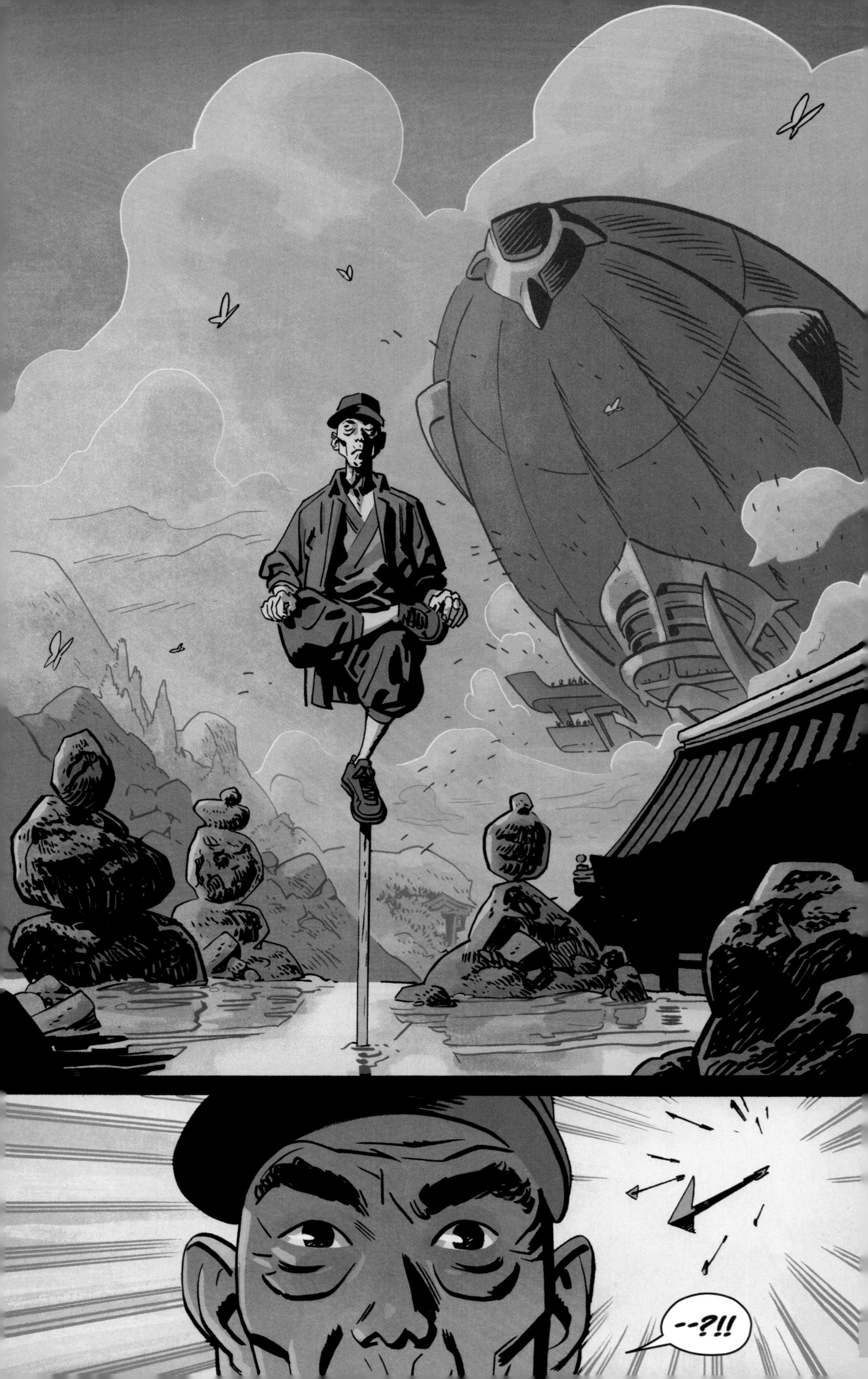
--?!!

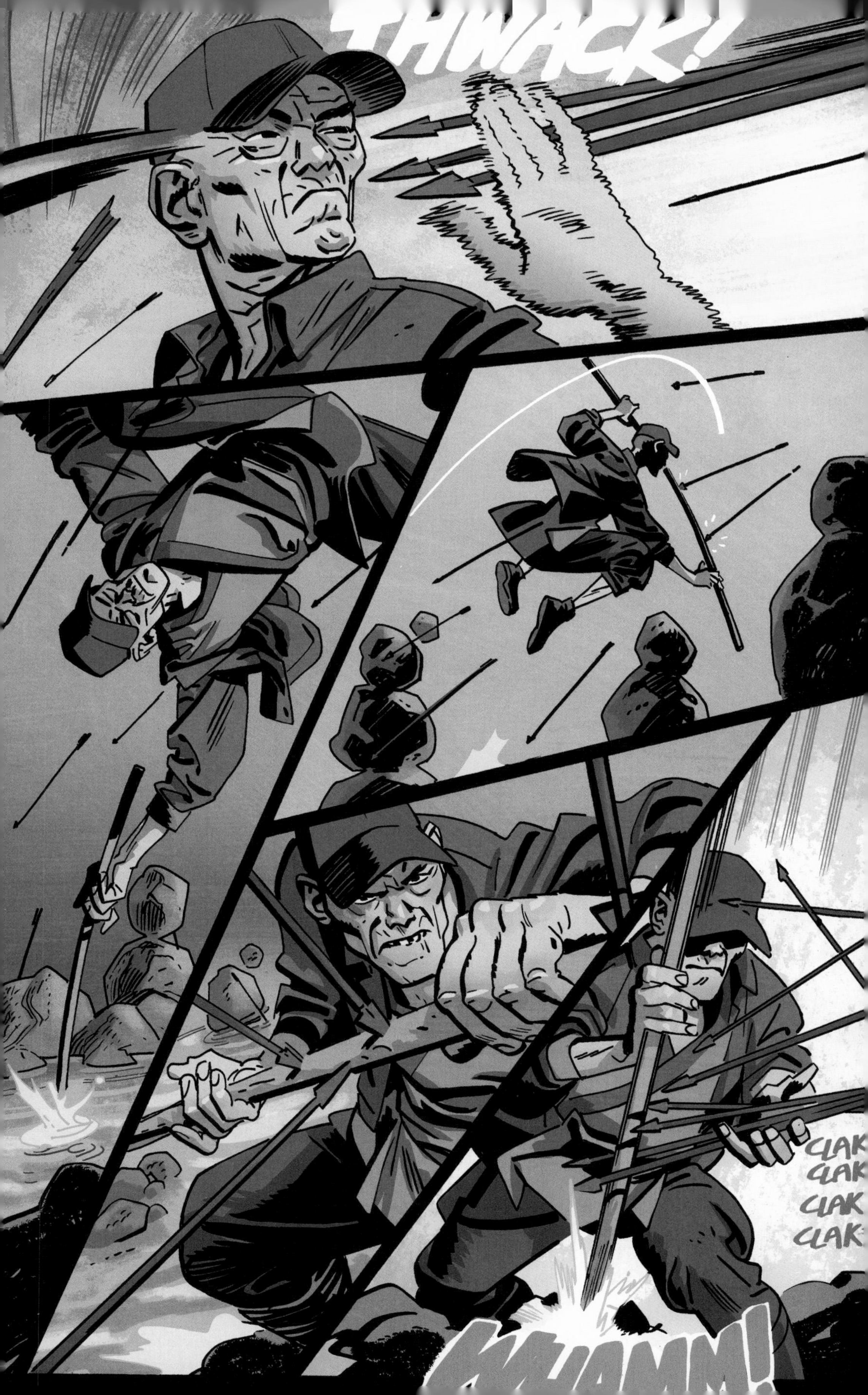
THWACK!
CLAK
CLAK
CLAK
CLAK
WHAMM!

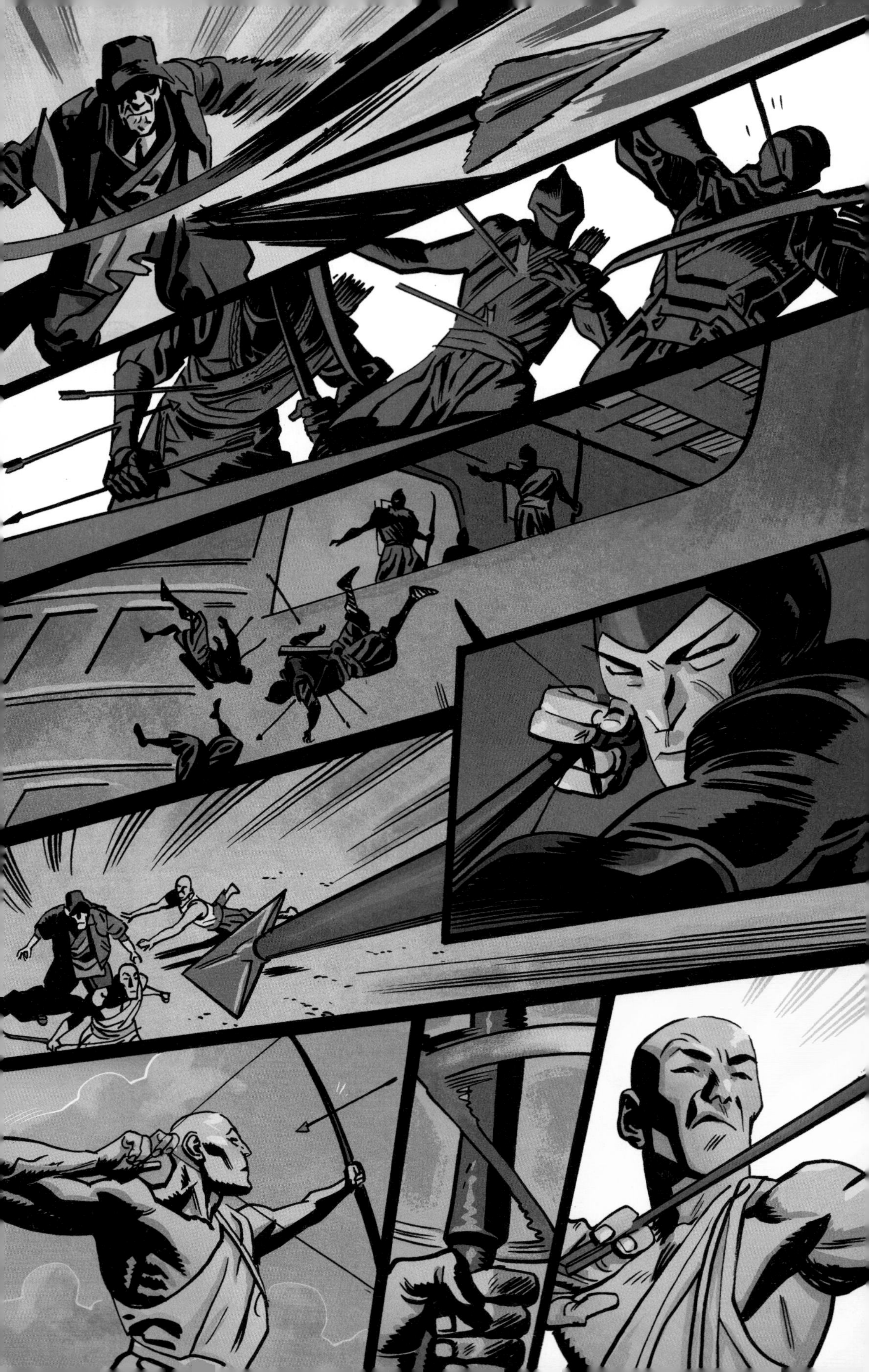

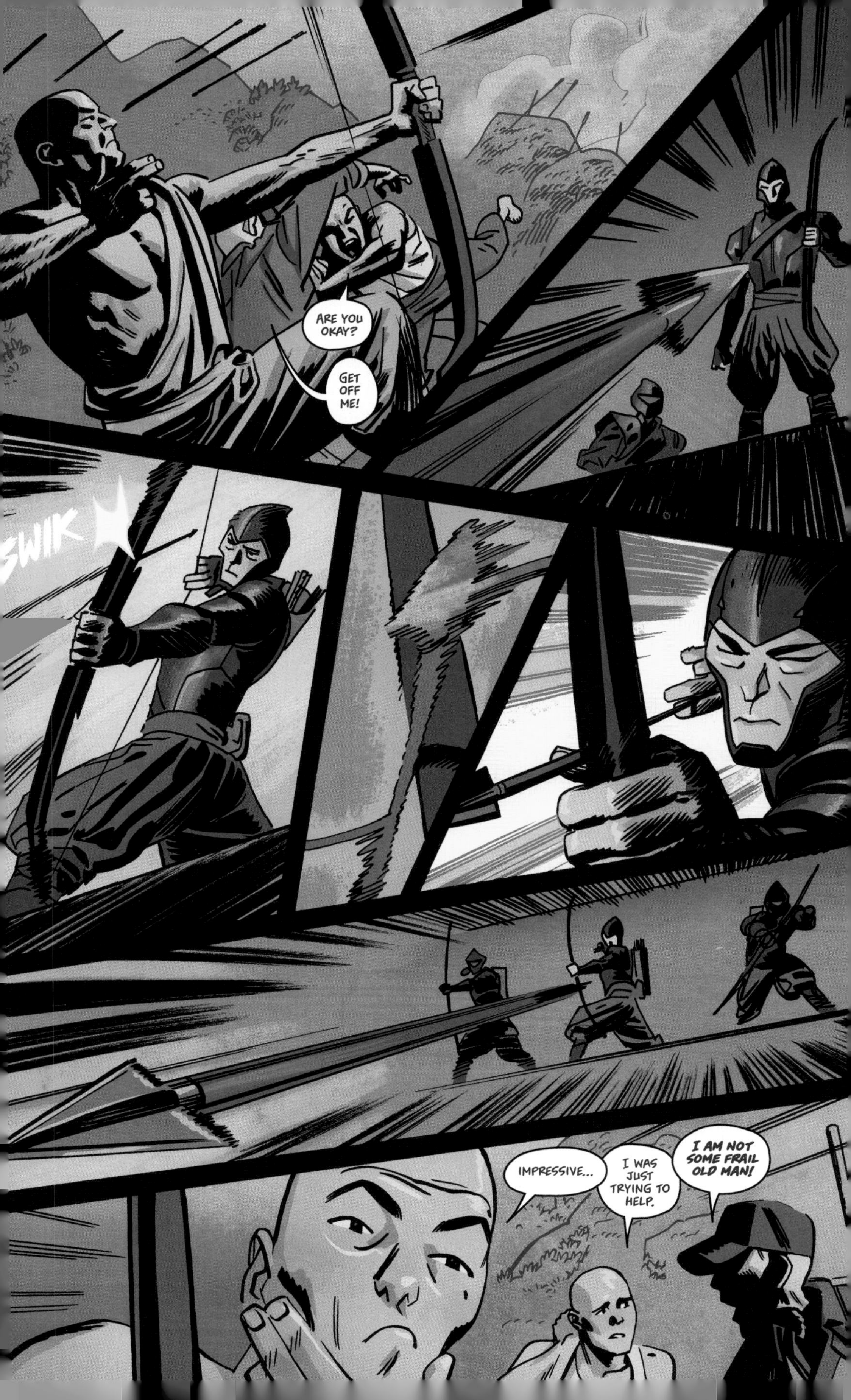
ARE YOU OKAY?
GET OFF ME!
SWIK
IMPRESSIVE...
I WAS JUST TRYING TO HELP.
I AM NOT SOME FRAIL OLD MAN!

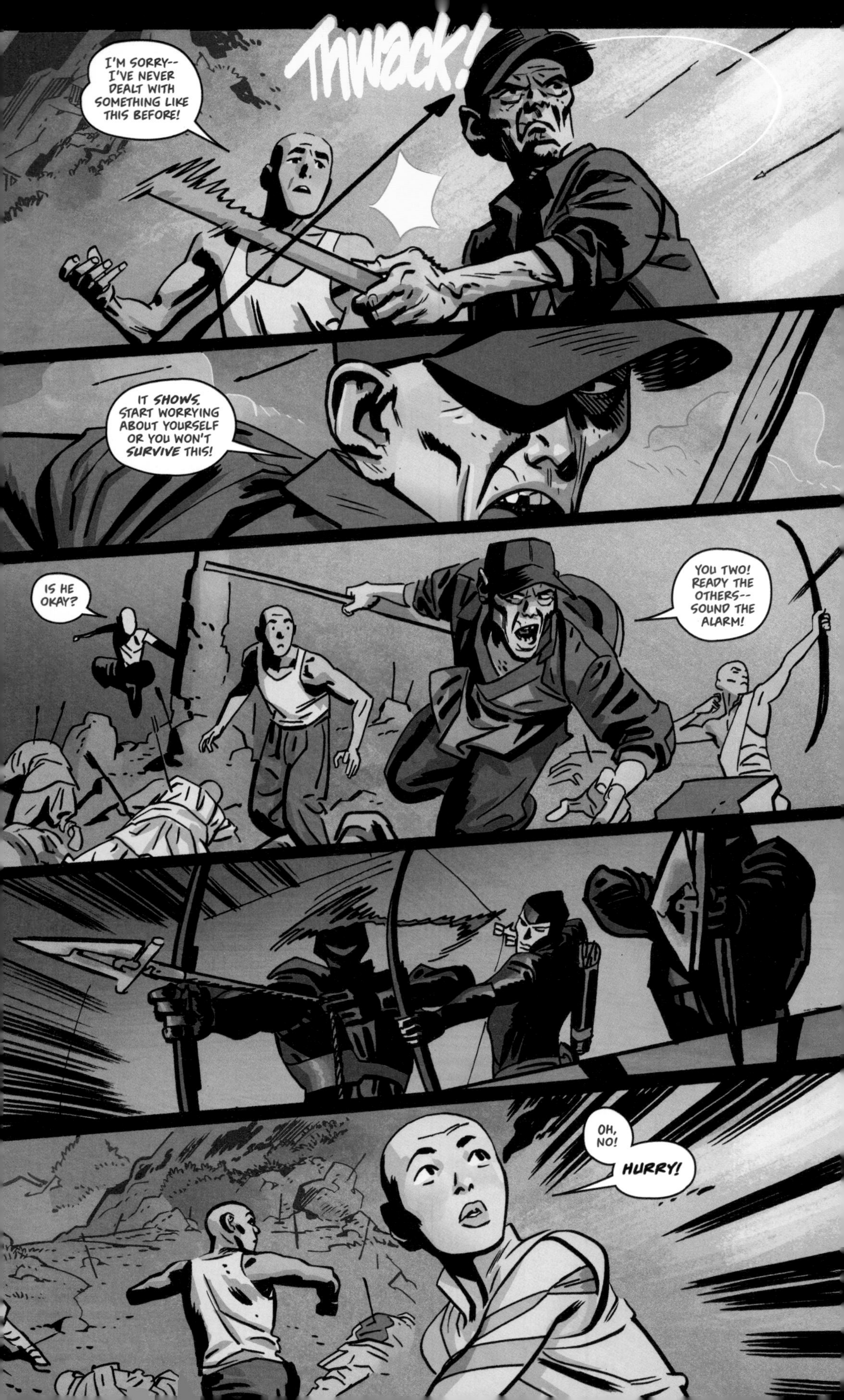
I'M SORRY-- I'VE NEVER DEALT WITH SOMETHING LIKE THIS BEFORE!
THWACK!
IT SHOWS. START WORRYING ABOUT YOURSELF OR YOU WON'T SURVIVE THIS!
IS HE OKAY?
YOU TWO! READY THE OTHERS-- SOUND THE ALARM!
OH, NO!
HURRY!

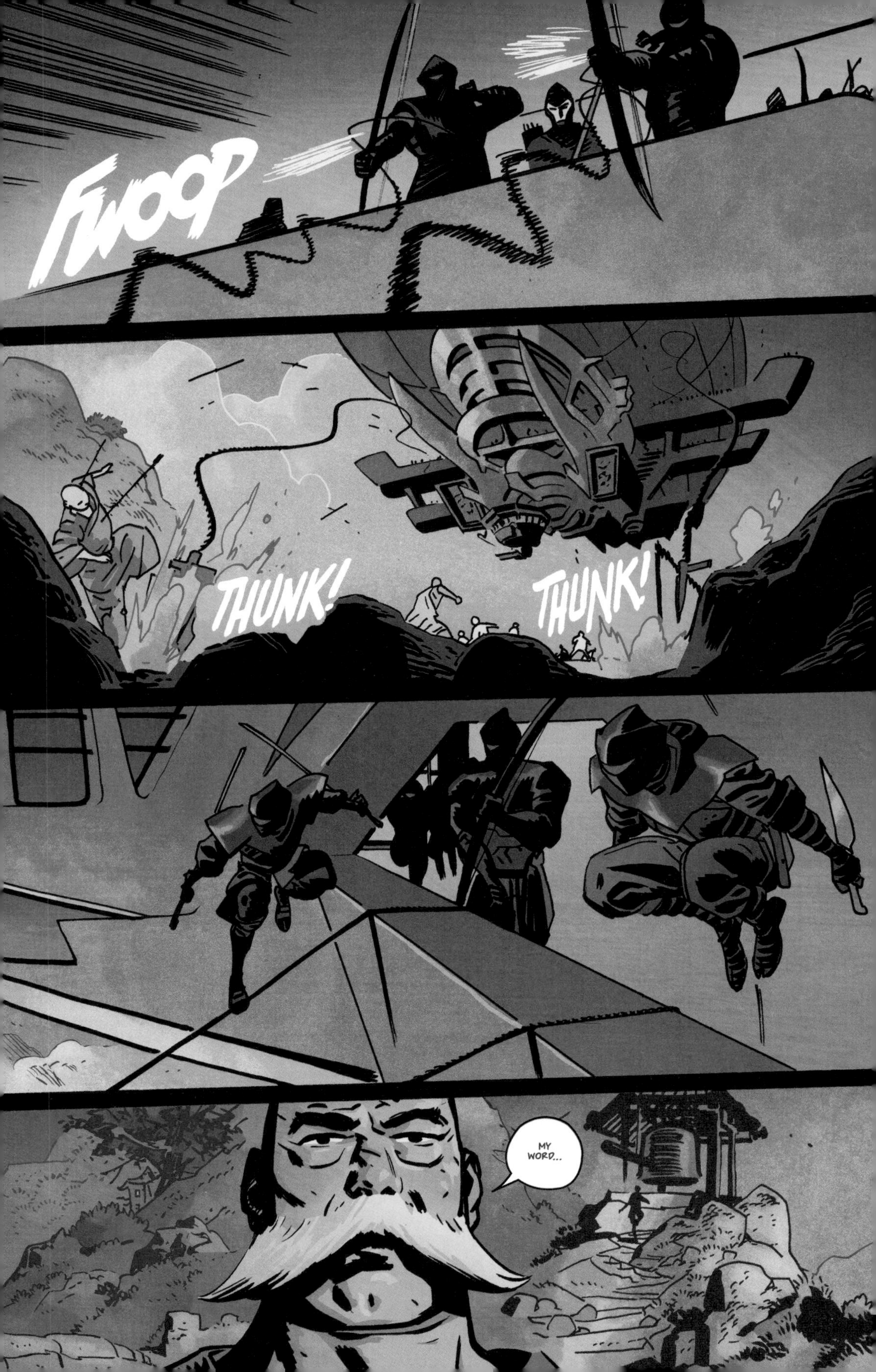
FWOOP
THUNK!
THUNK!
MY WORD...

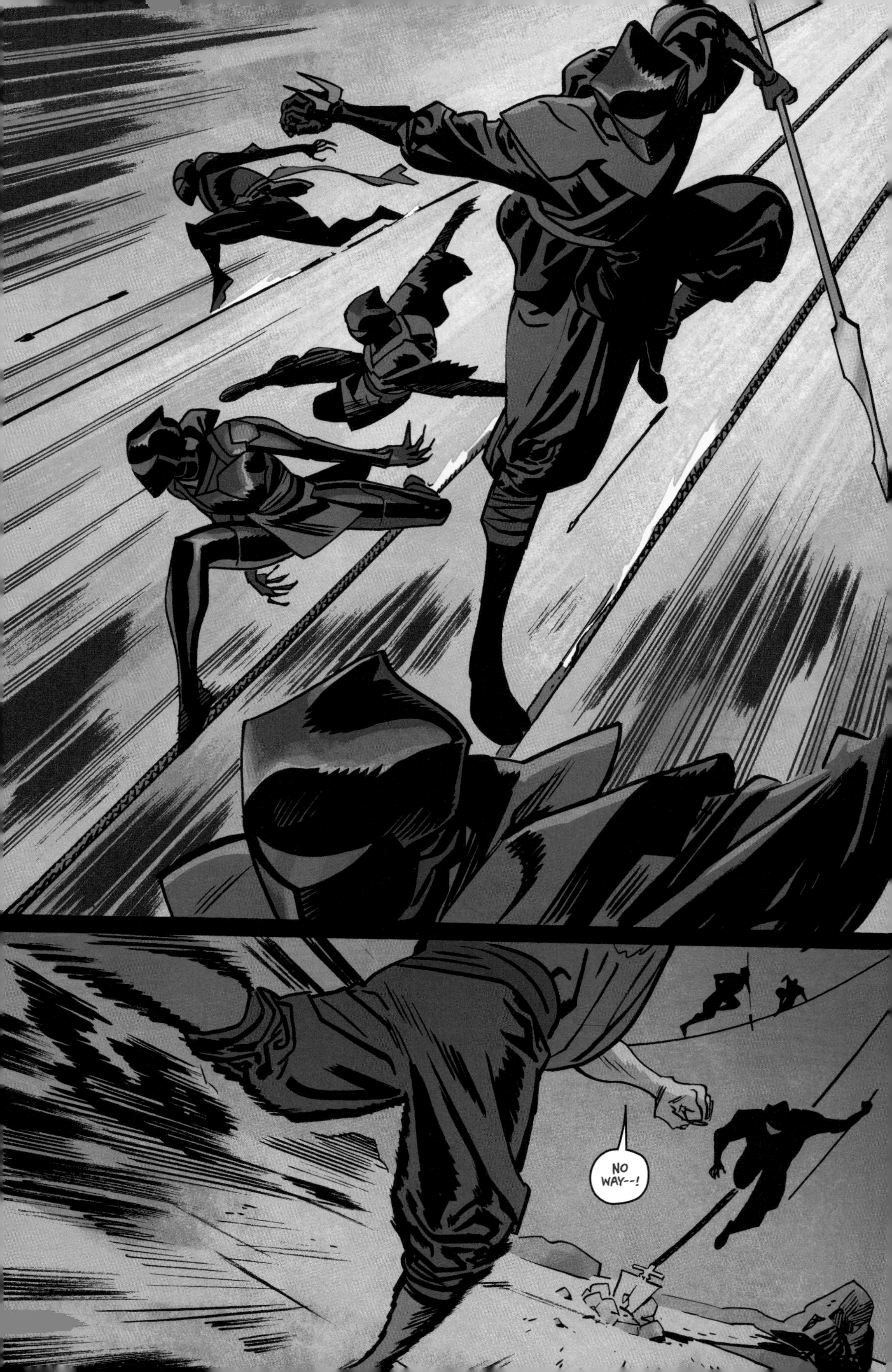
NO WAY--!

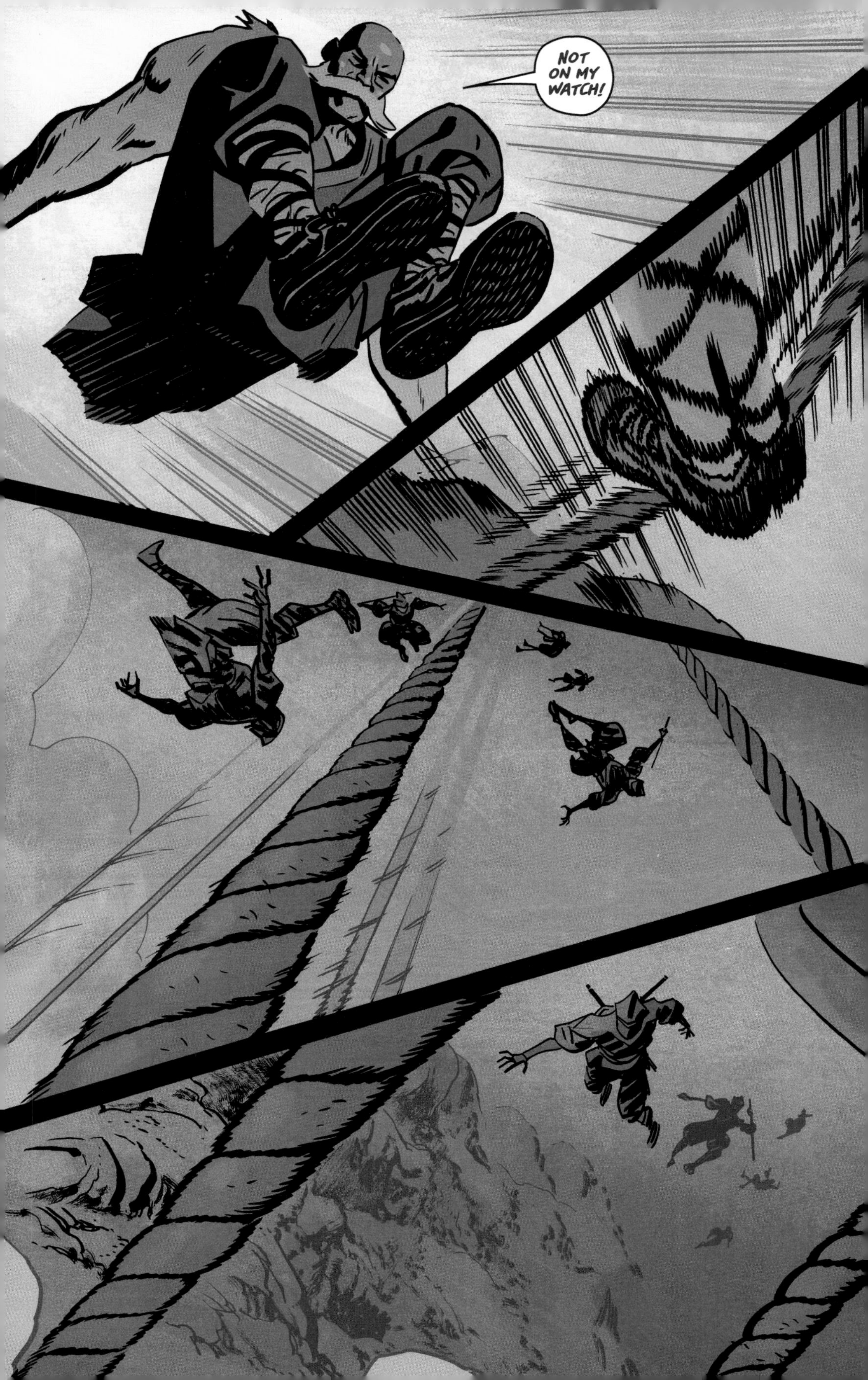
NOT ON MY WATCH!

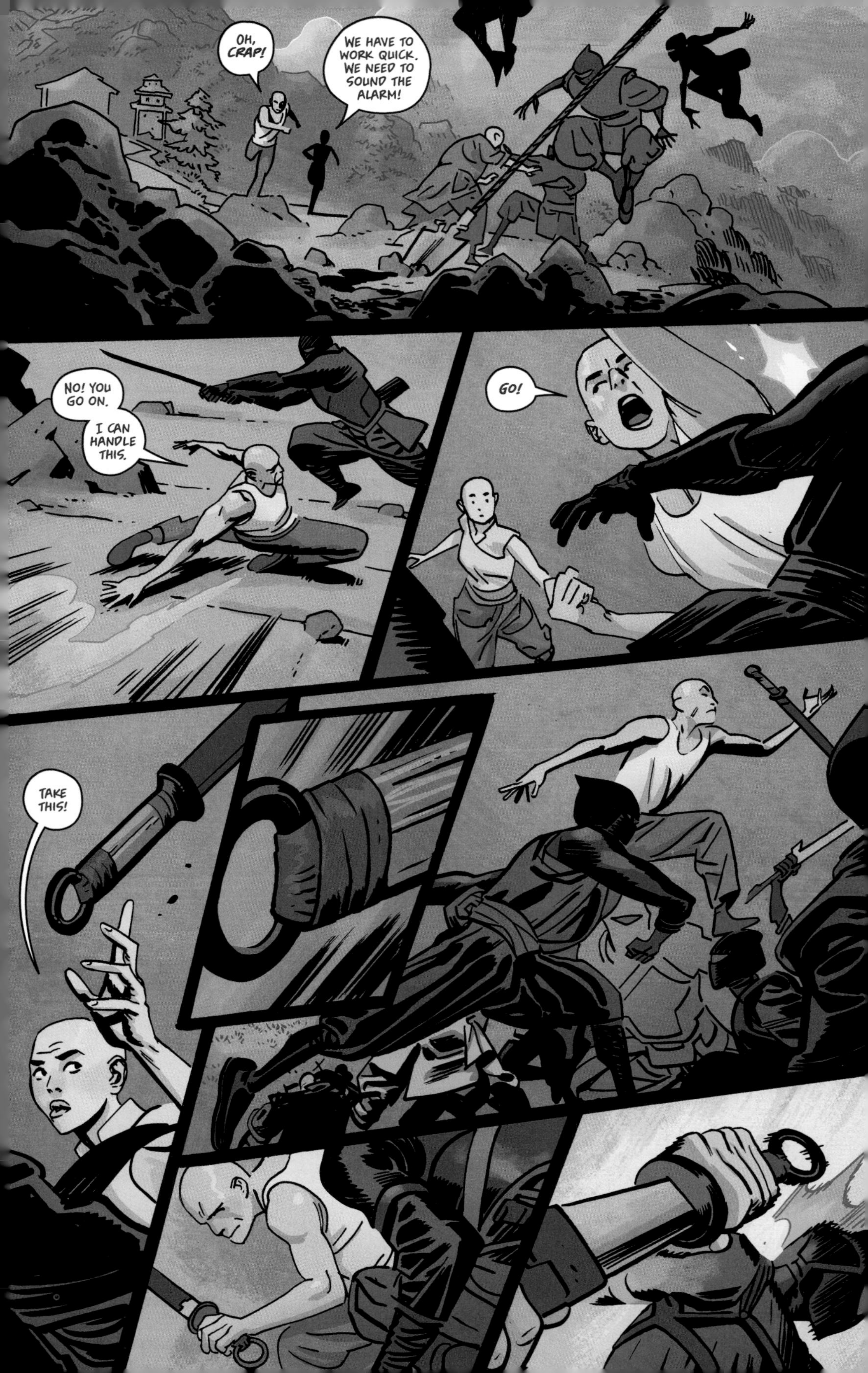
OH, CRAP!
WE HAVE TO WORK QUICK. WE NEED TO SOUND THE ALARM!
NO! YOU GO ON.
I CAN HANDLE THIS.
GO!
TAKE THIS!

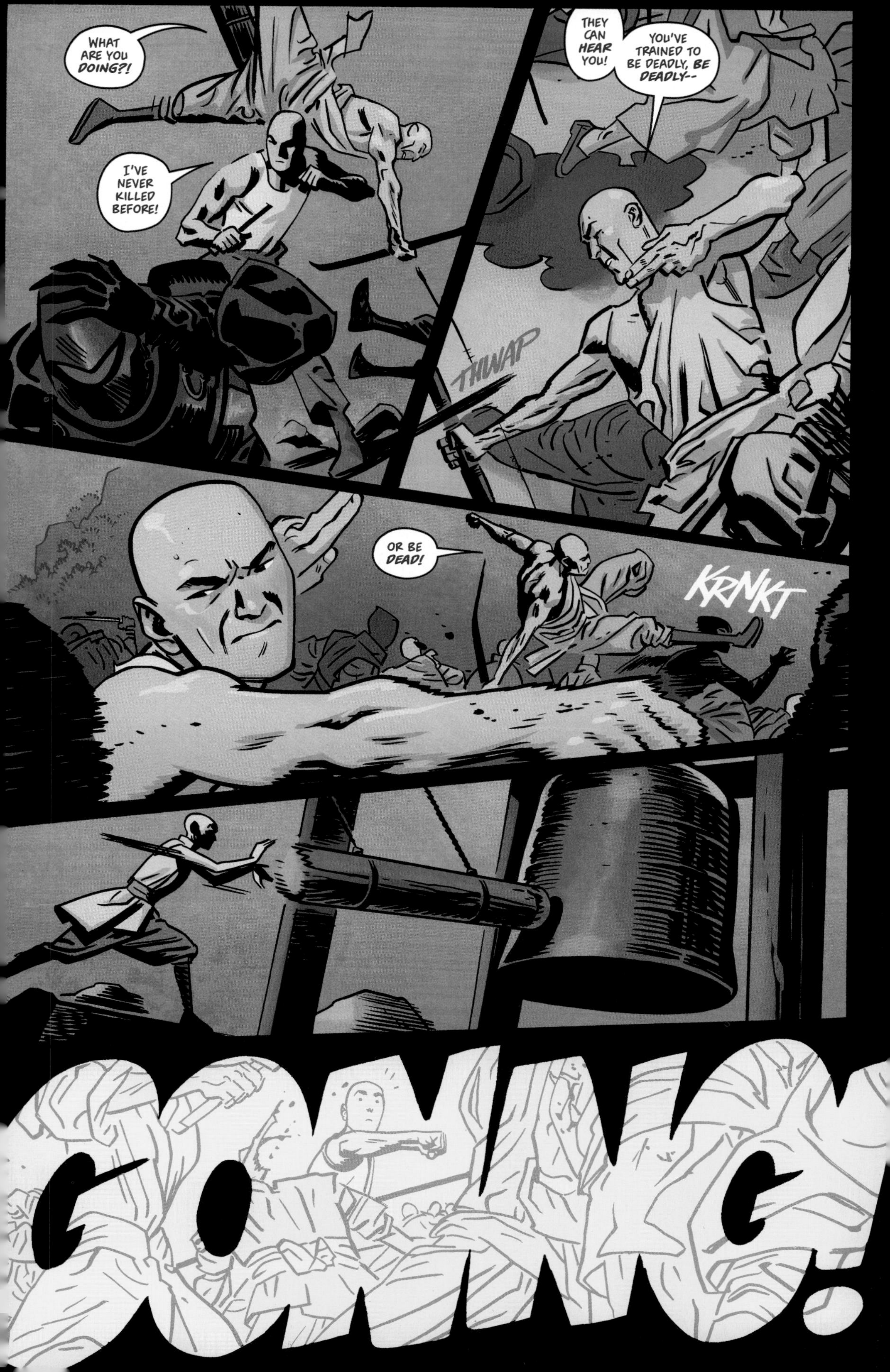
WHAT ARE YOU DOING?!
I'VE NEVER KILLED BEFORE!
THEY CAN HEAR YOU!
YOU'VE TRAINED TO BE DEADLY, BE DEADLY--
THWAP
OR BE DEAD!
KRNKT
GONNG!

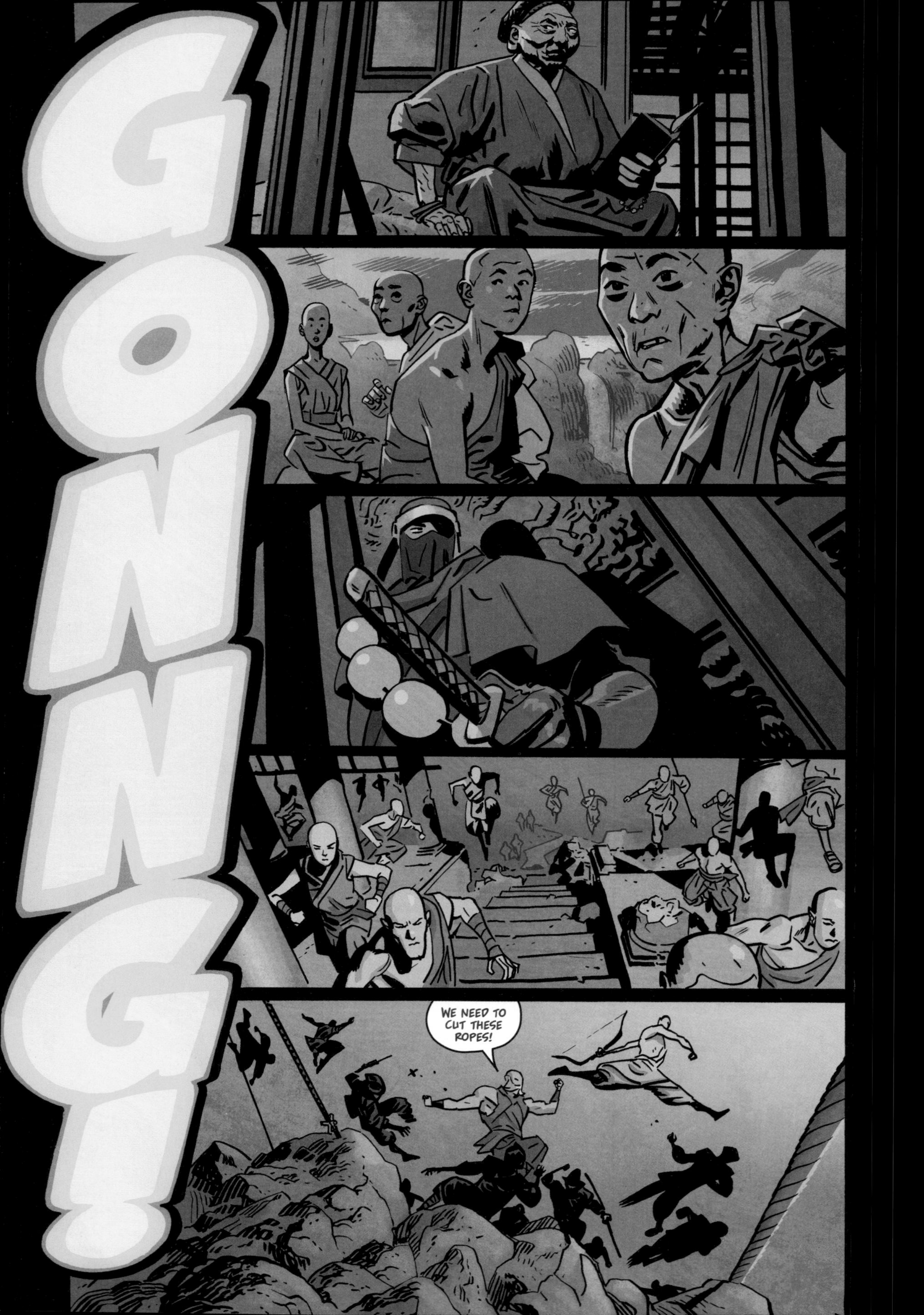
GONG!
WE NEED TO CUT THESE ROPES!

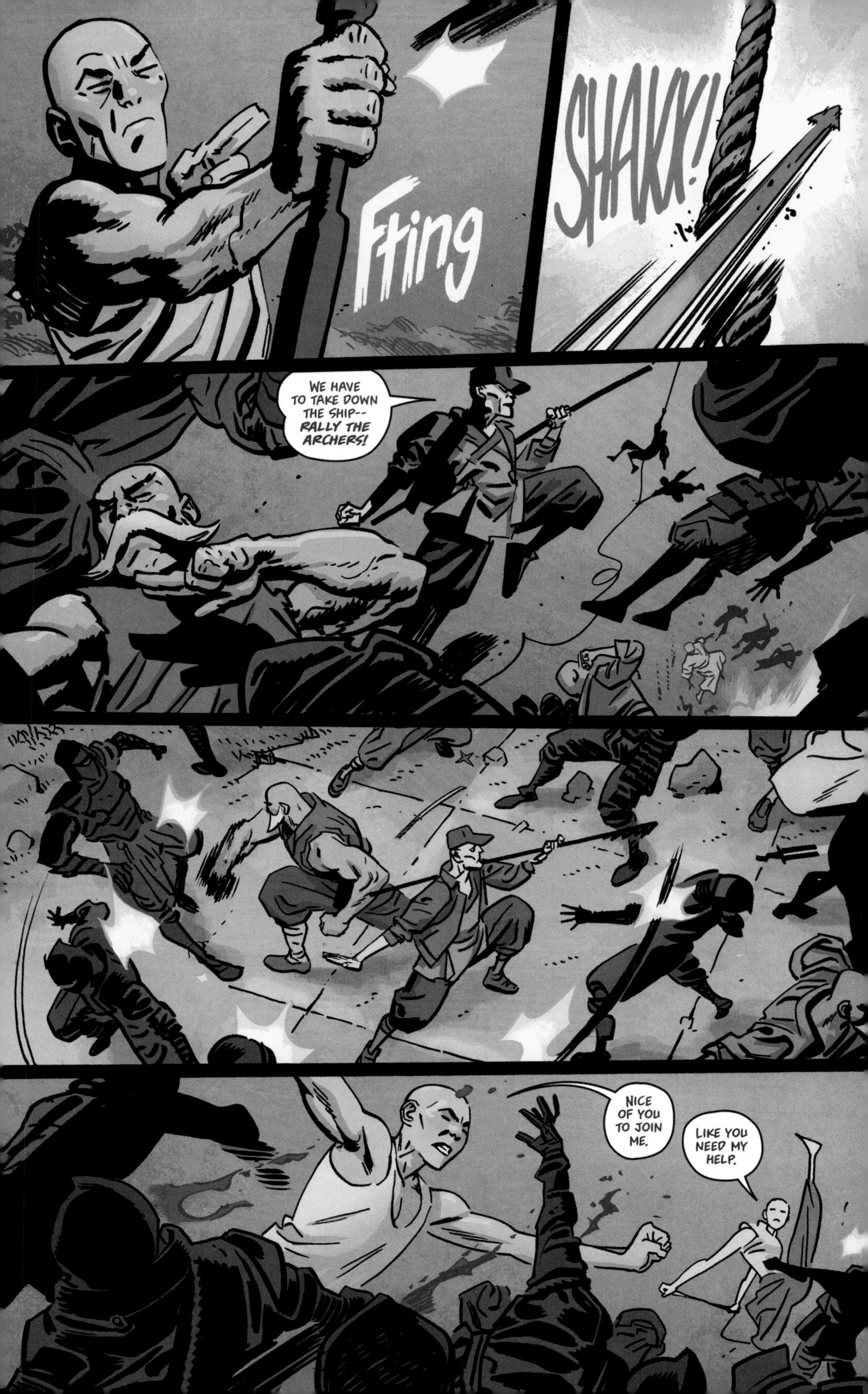
Fting
SHAKK!
WE HAVE TO TAKE DOWN THE SHIP-- RALLY THE ARCHERS!
NICE OF YOU TO JOIN ME.
LIKE YOU NEED MY HELP.

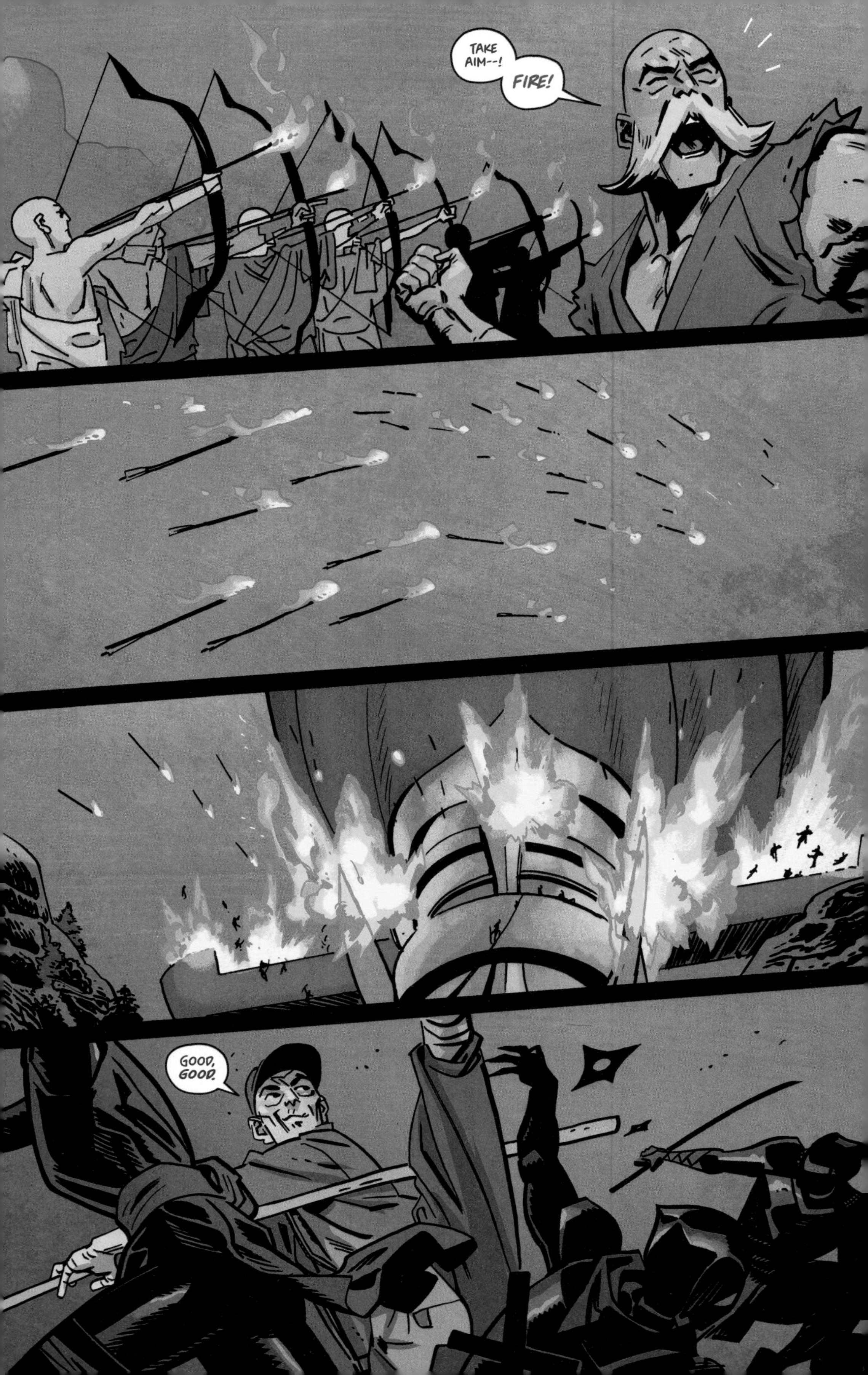
TAKE AIM--!
FIRE!
GOOD, GOOD.

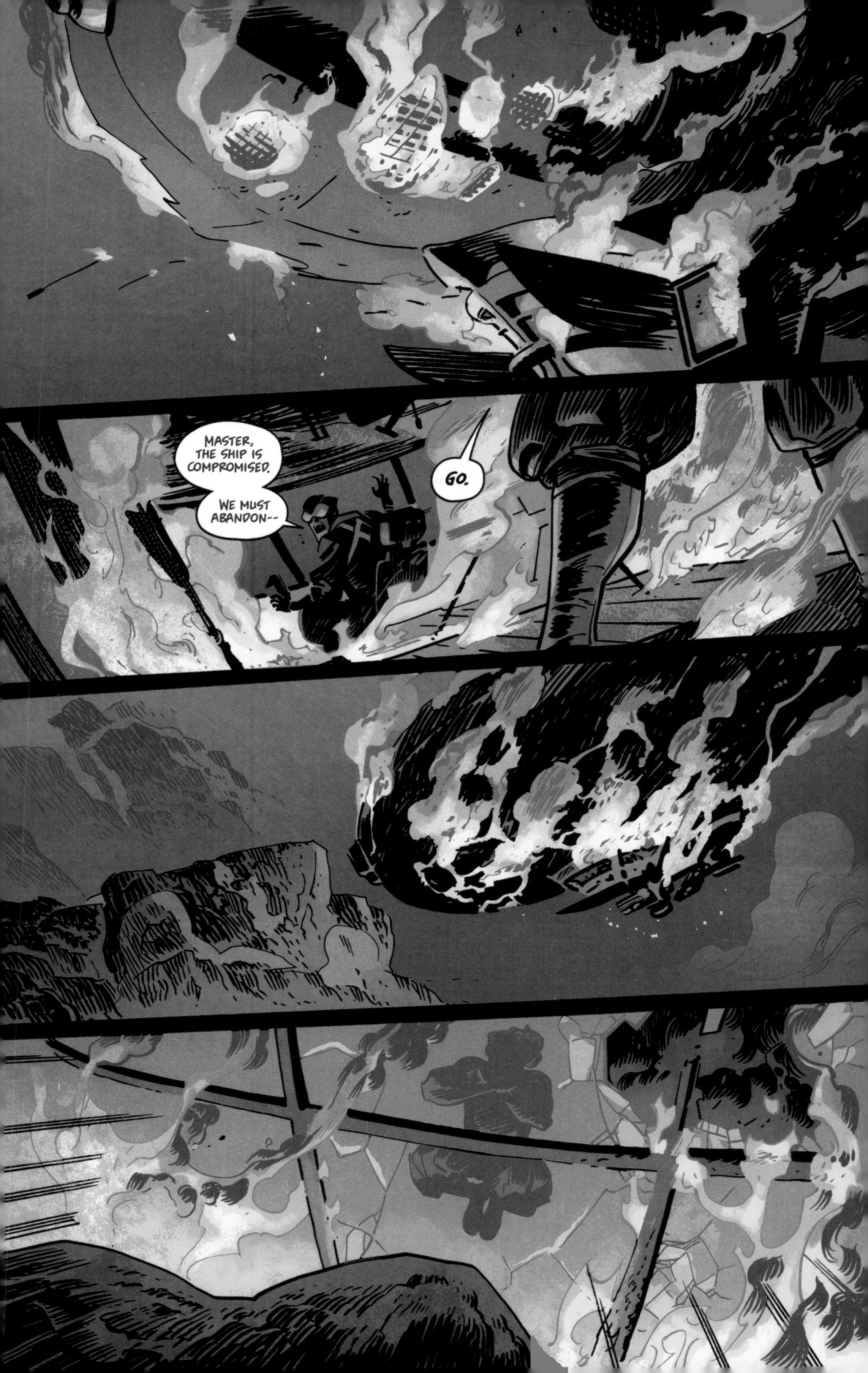
MASTER, THE SHIP IS COMPROMISED.
WE MUST ABANDON--
GO.

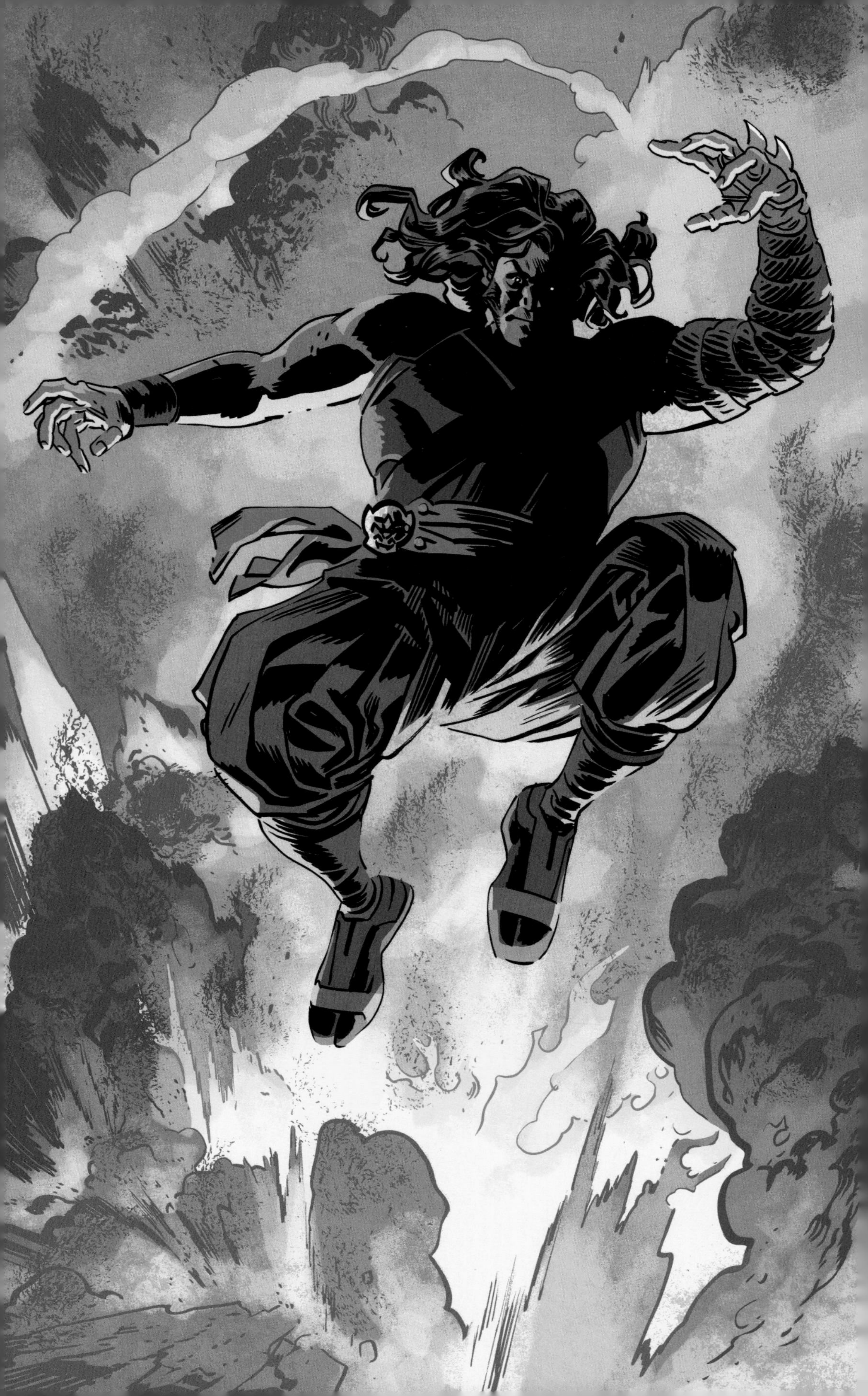

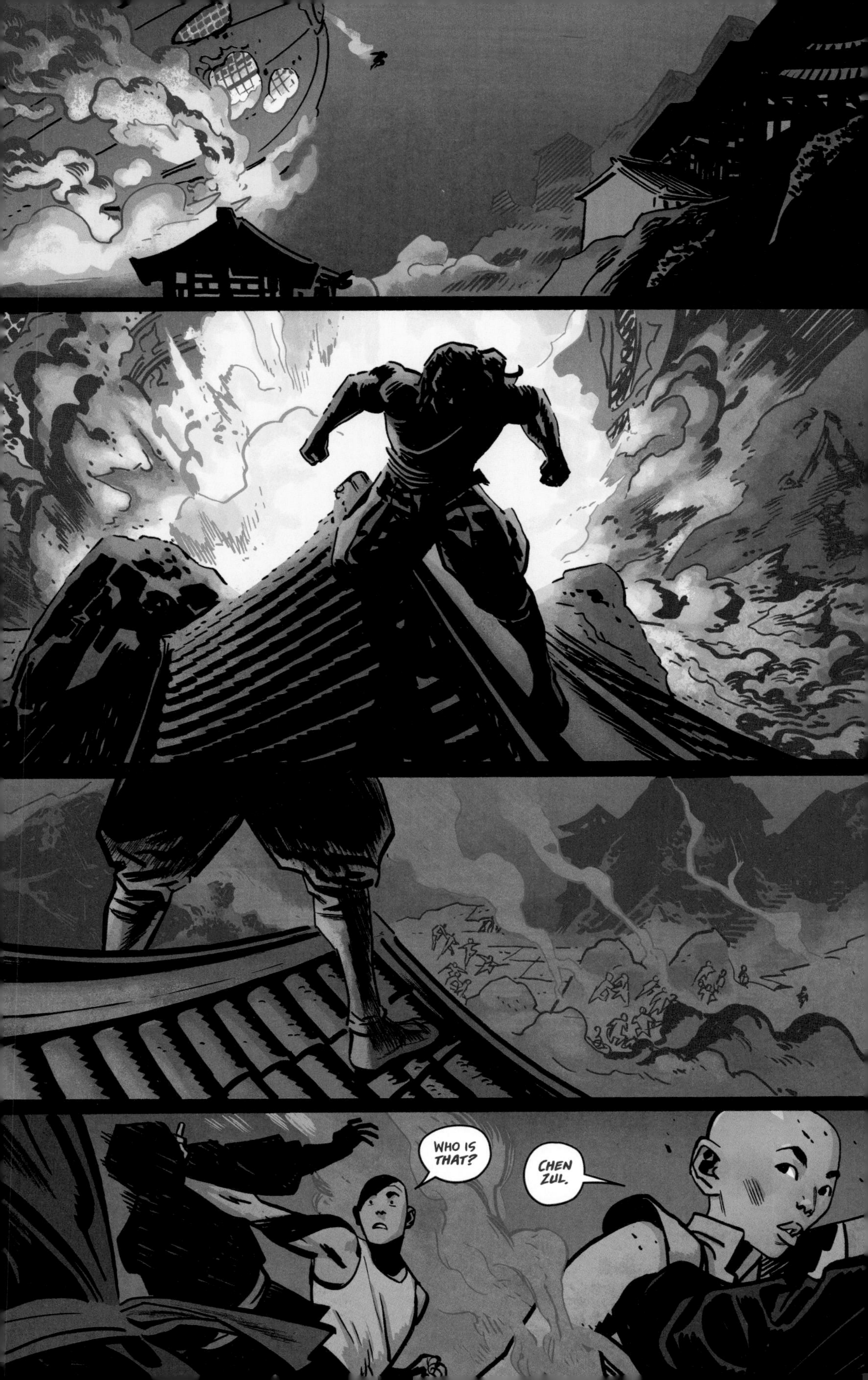
WHO IS THAT?
CHEN ZUL.

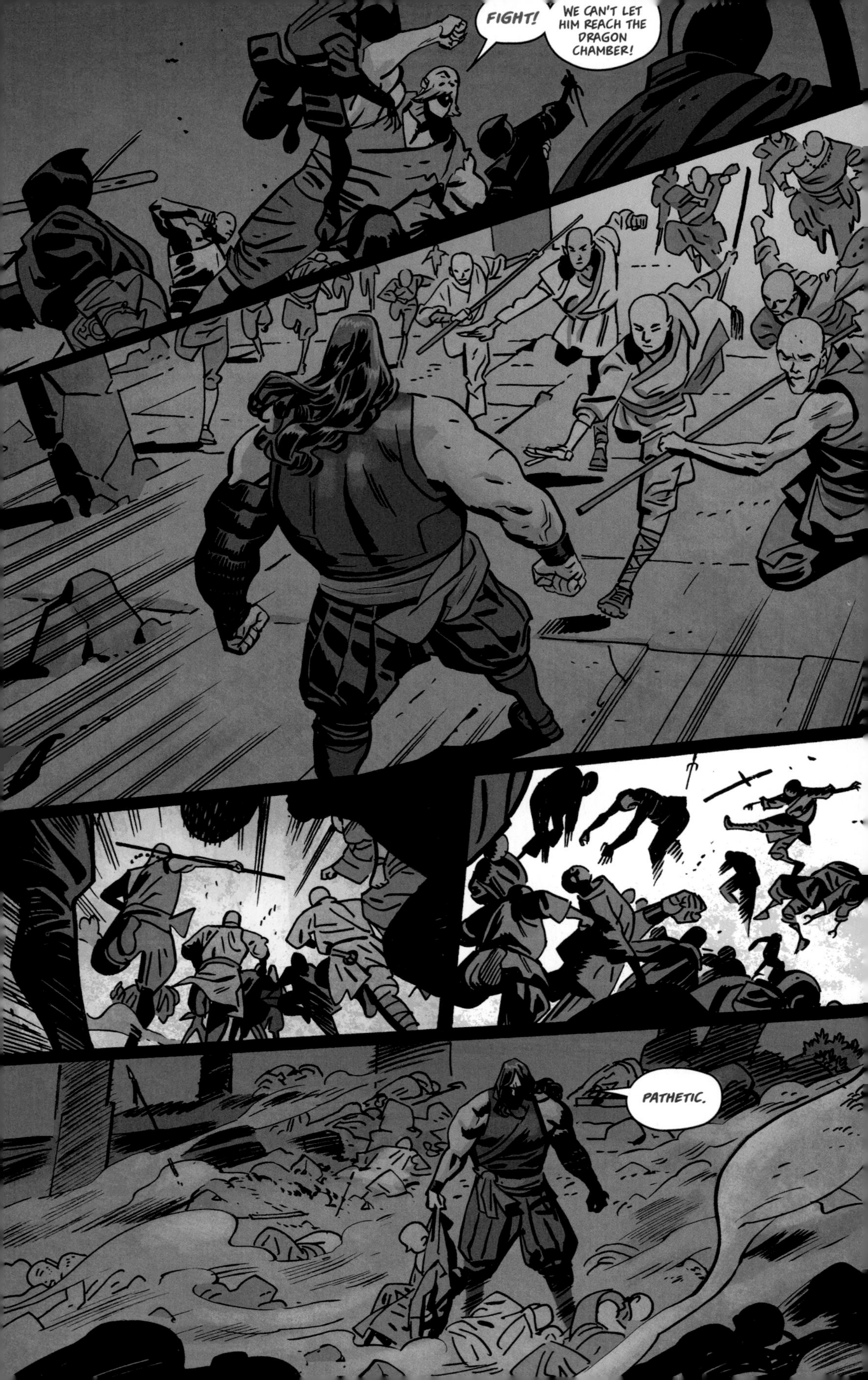
FIGHT!
WE CAN'T LET HIM REACH THE DRAGON CHAMBER!
PATHETIC.

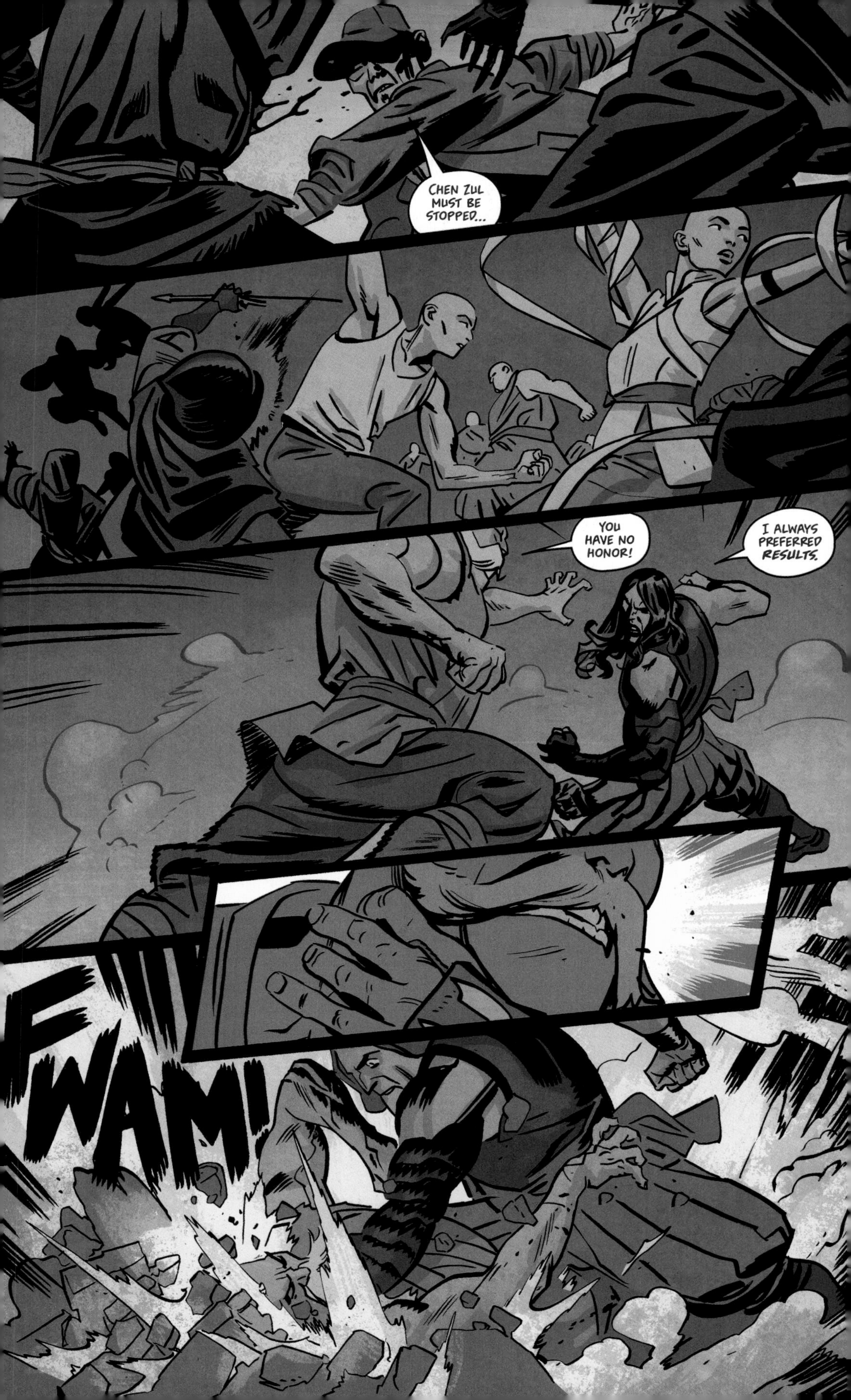
CHEN ZUL MUST BE STOPPED...
YOU HAVE NO HONOR!
I ALWAYS PREFERRED RESULTS.
FWAM!

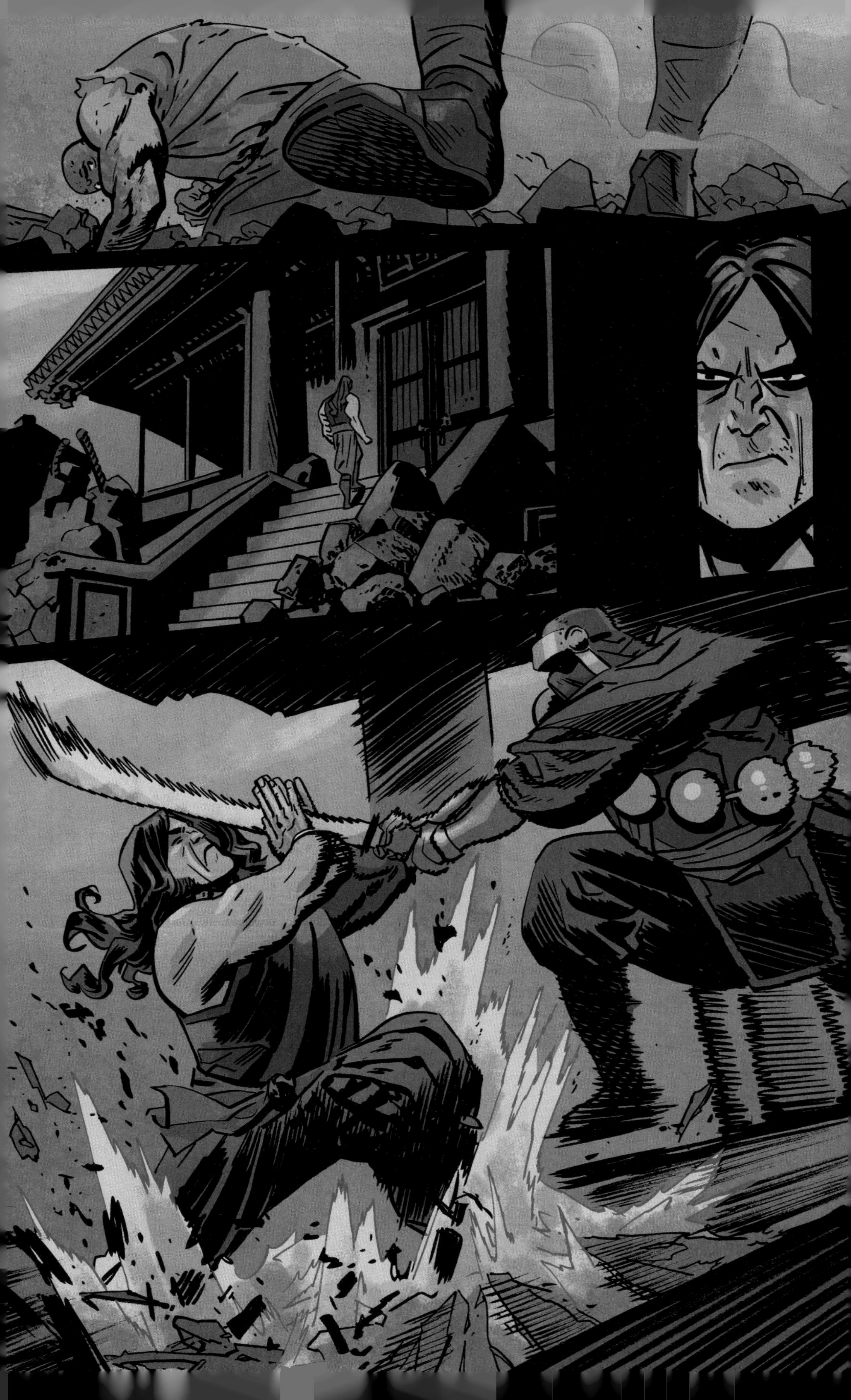

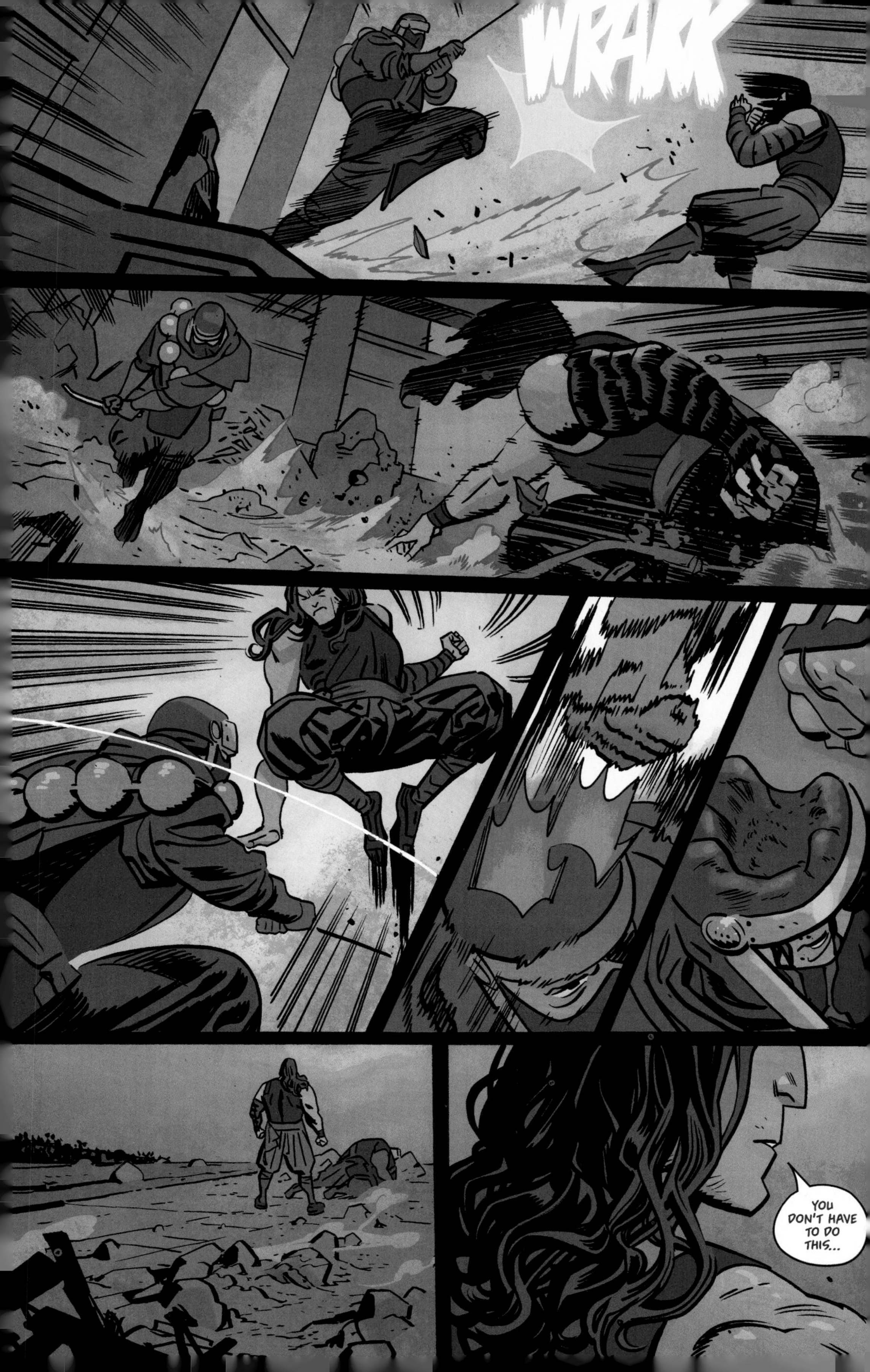
WRAKK
YOU DON'T HAVE TO DO THIS...

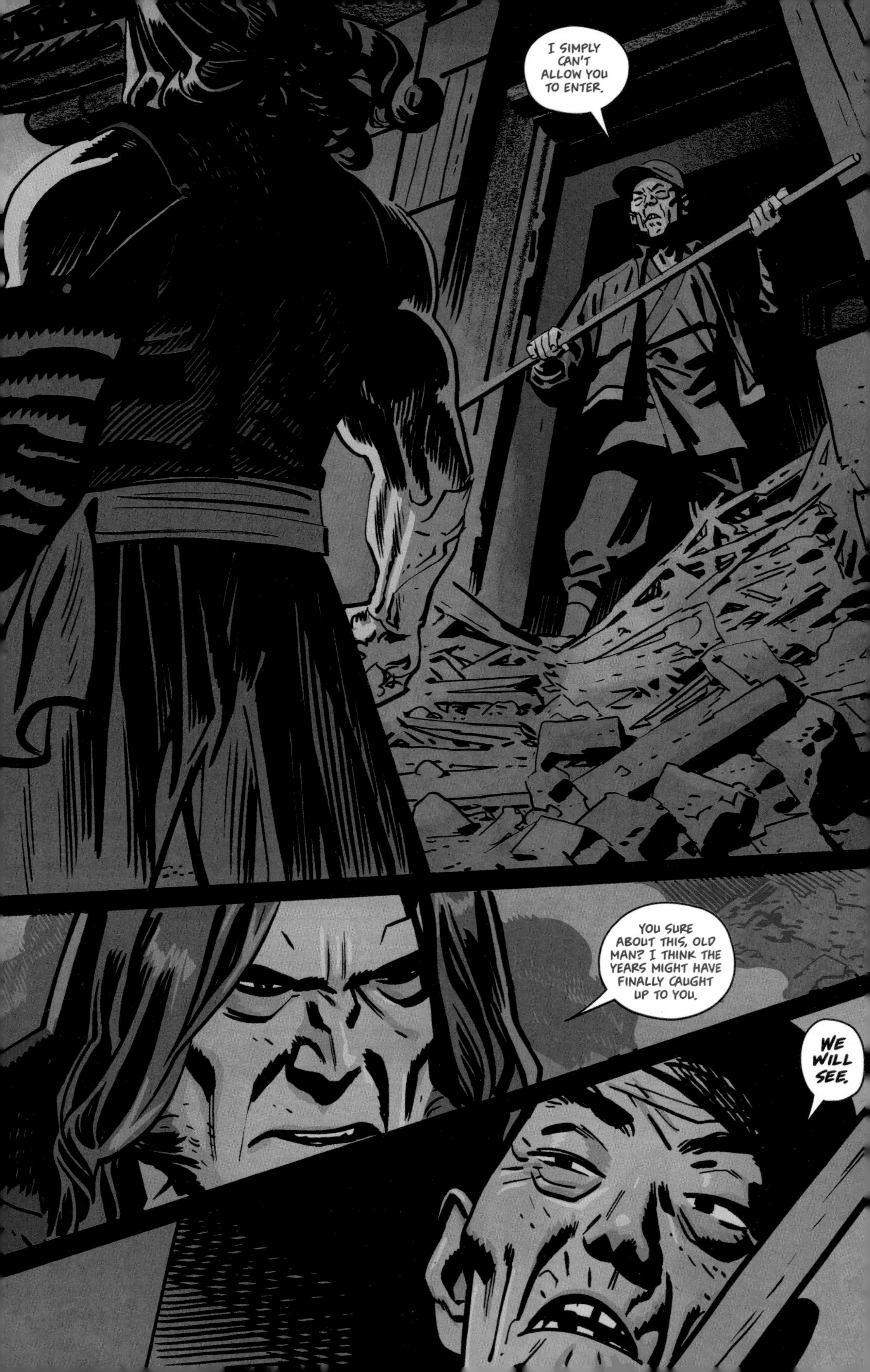
I SIMPLY CAN'T ALLOW YOU TO ENTER.
YOU SURE ABOUT THIS, OLD MAN? I THINK THE YEARS MIGHT HAVE FINALLY CAUGHT UP TO YOU.
WE WILL SEE.

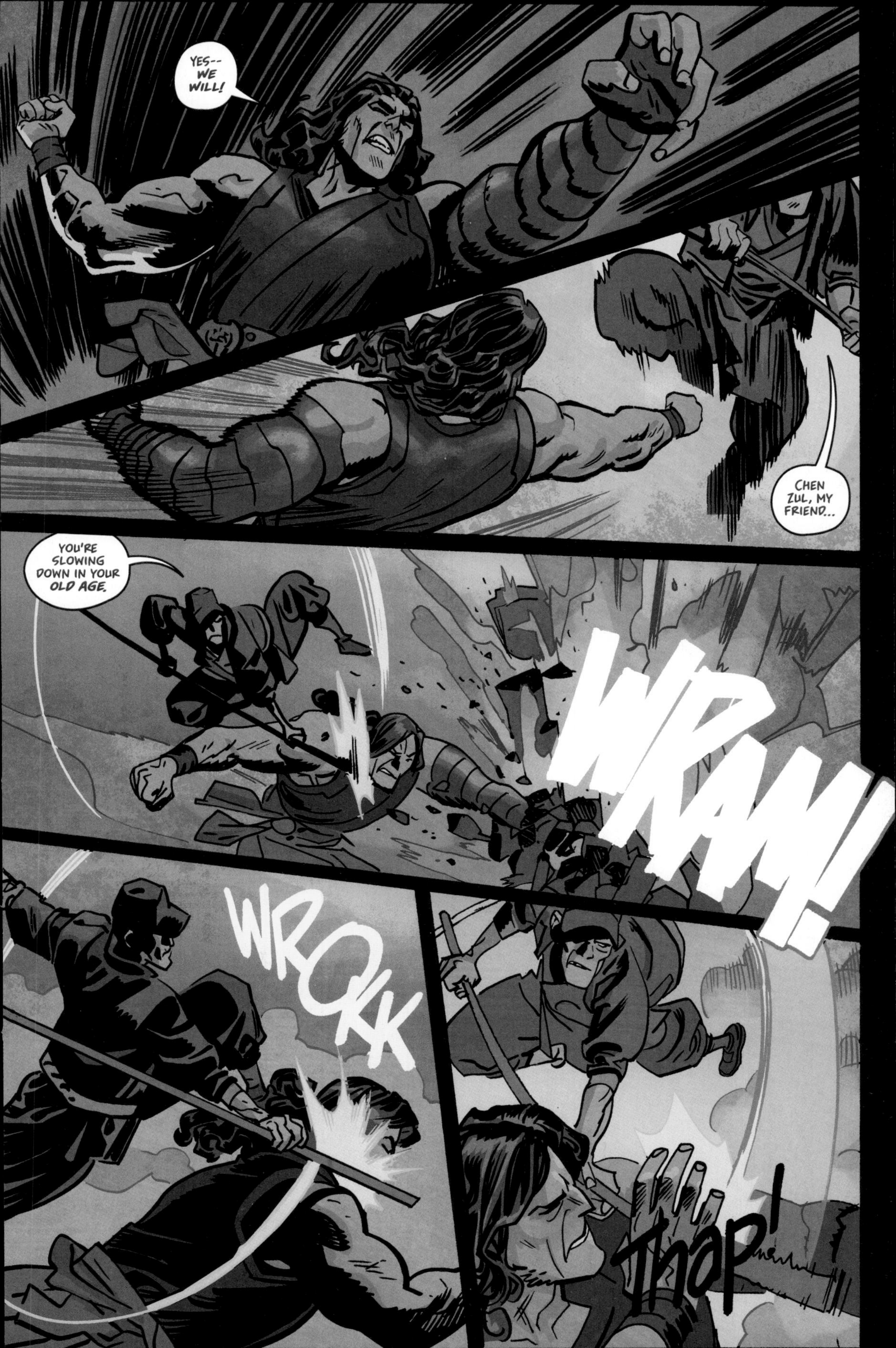
YES-- WE WILL!
CHEN ZUL, MY FRIEND...
YOU'RE SLOWING DOWN IN YOUR OLD AGE.
WRAM!
WROKK
THOP!

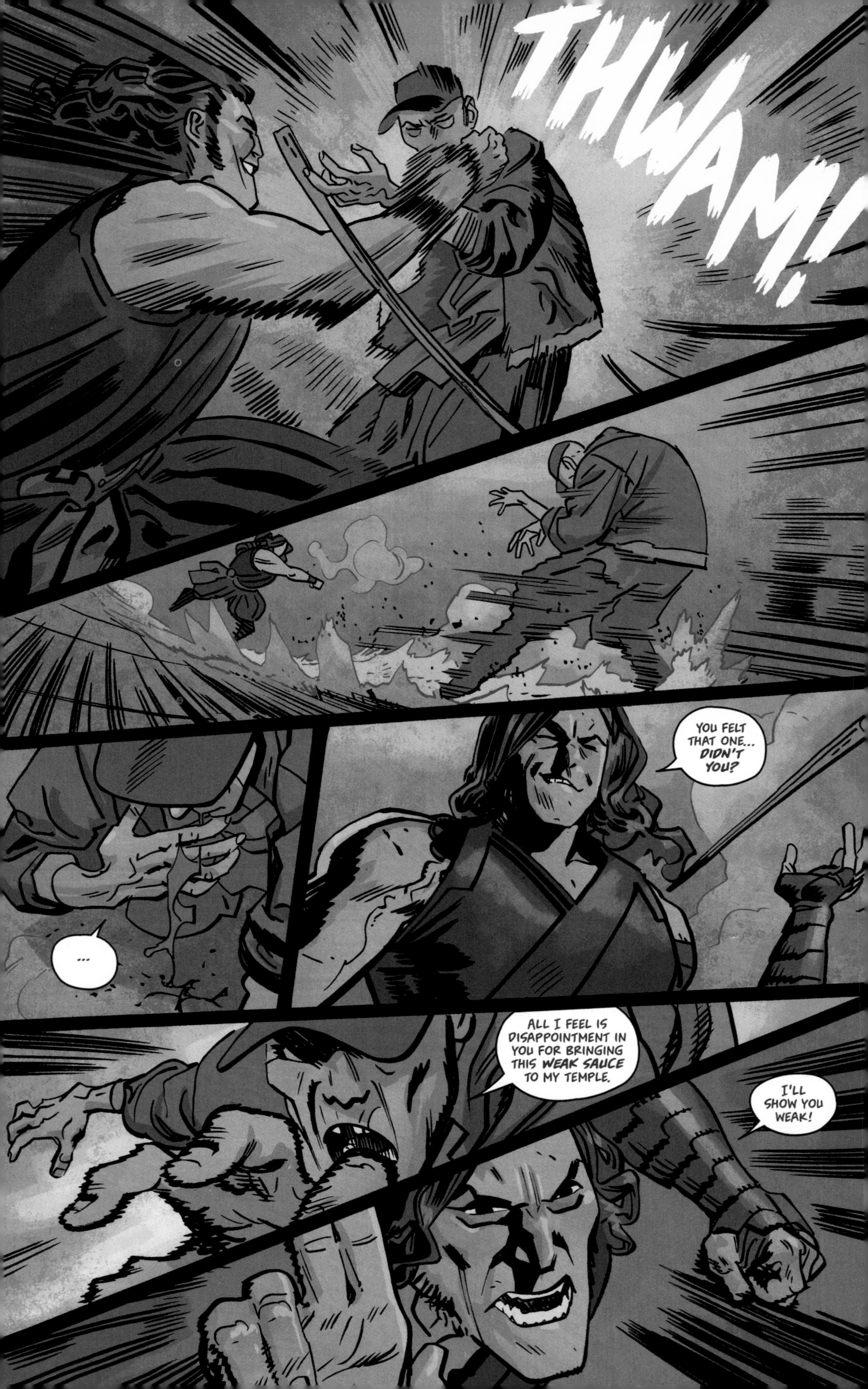
THWAM!
YOU FELT THAT ONE... DIDN'T YOU?
...
ALL I FEEL IS DISAPPOINTMENT IN YOU FOR BRINGING THIS WEAK SAUCE TO MY TEMPLE.
I'LL SHOW YOU WEAK!

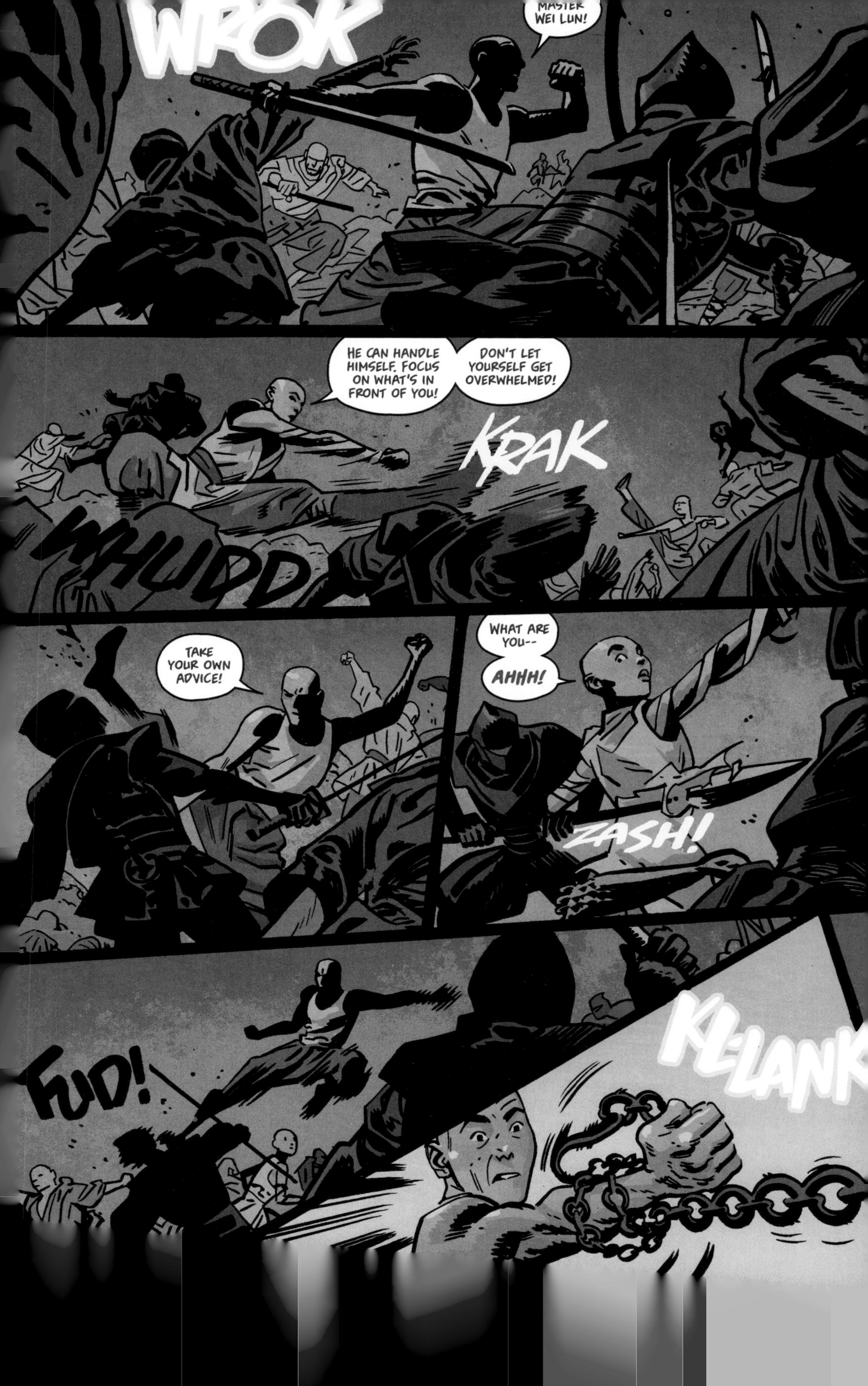
WROK
MASTER WEI LUN!
HE CAN HANDLE HIMSELF. FOCUS ON WHAT'S IN FRONT OF YOU!
DON'T LET YOURSELF GET OVERWHELMED!
KRAK
WHUDD
TAKE YOUR OWN ADVICE!
WHAT ARE YOU--
AHHH!
ZASH!
FUD!
KL-LANK

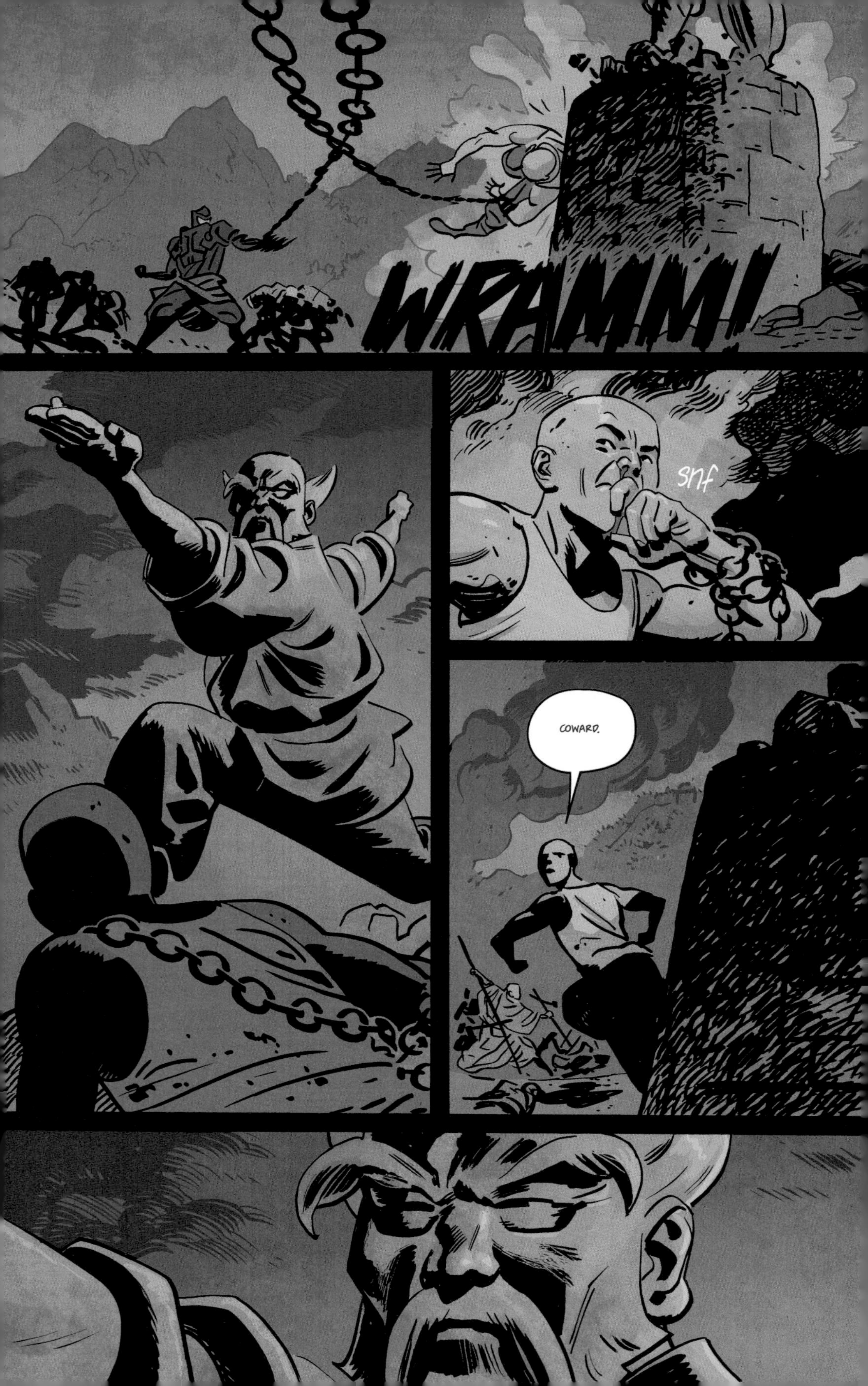
WRAMM!
snf
COWARD.

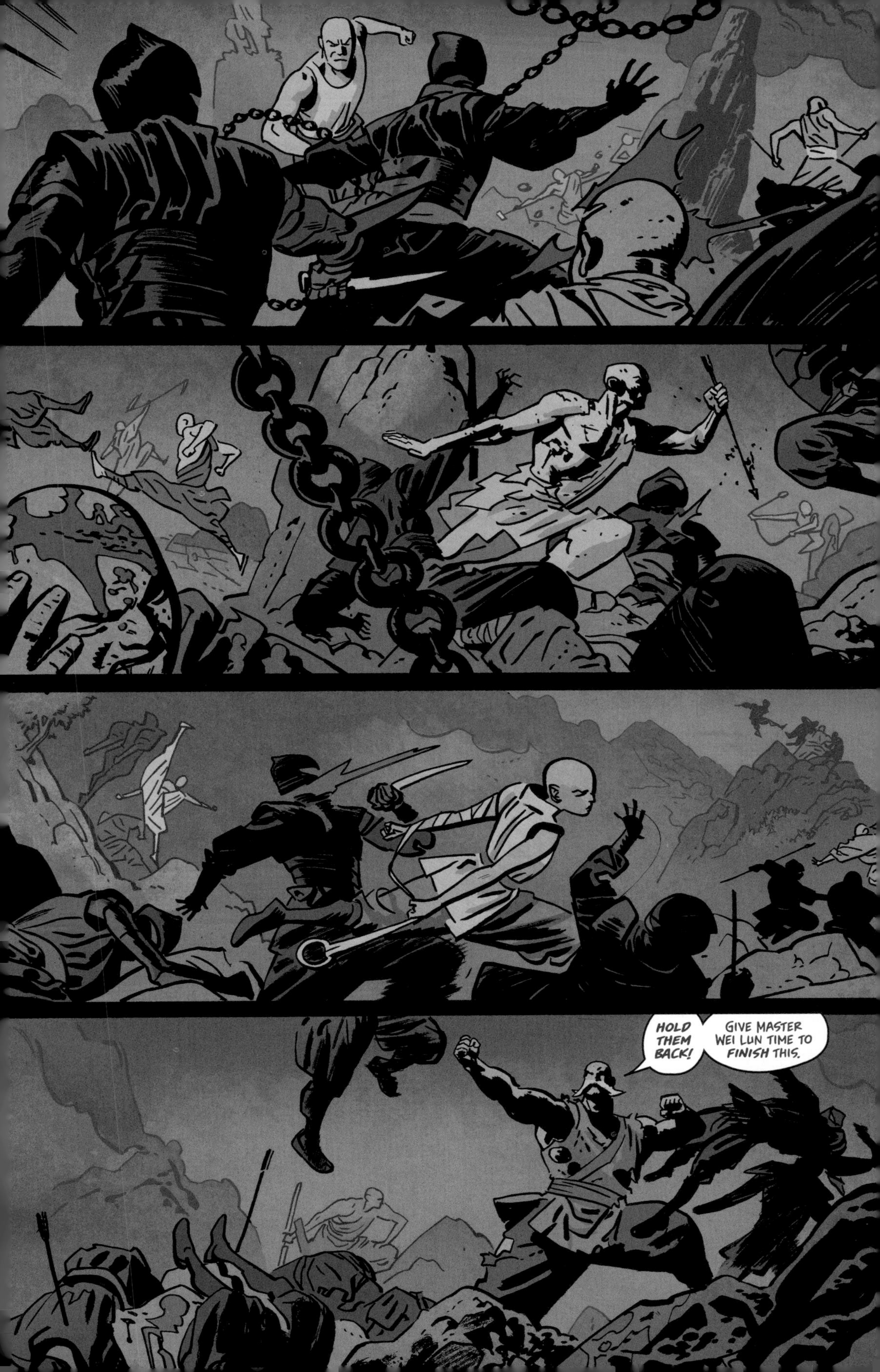
HOLD THEM BACK!
GIVE MASTER WEI LUN TIME TO FINISH THIS.

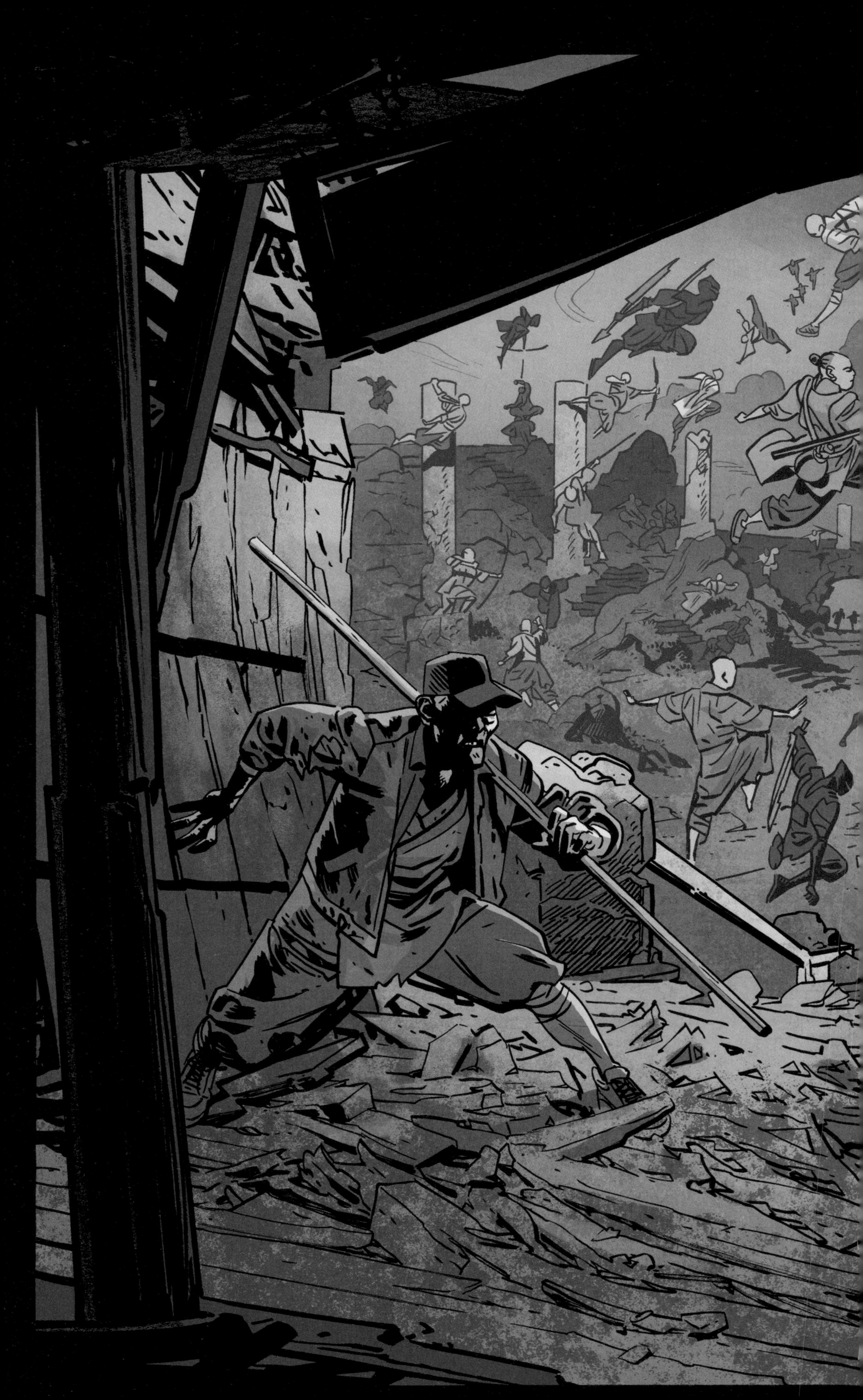

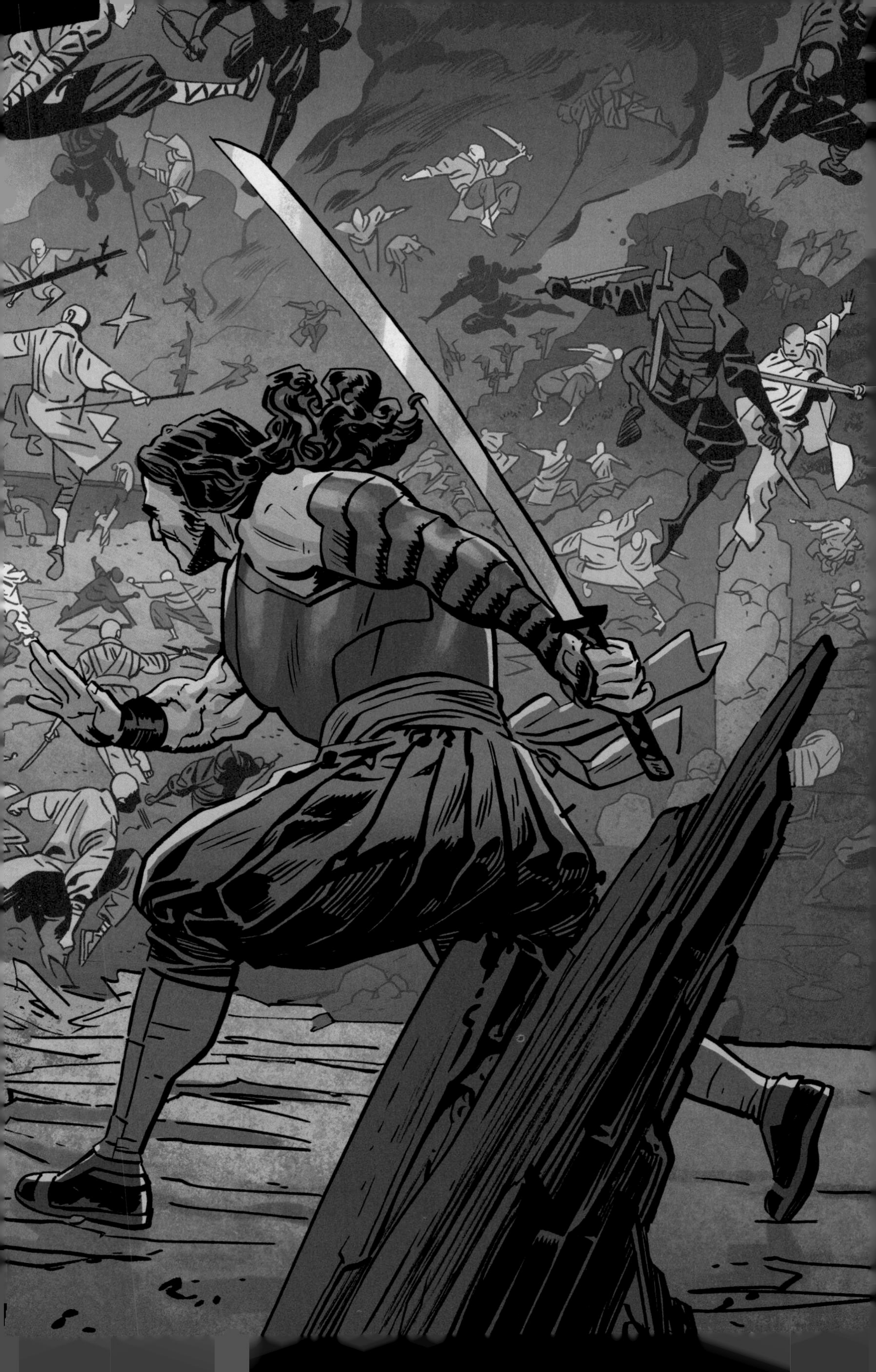

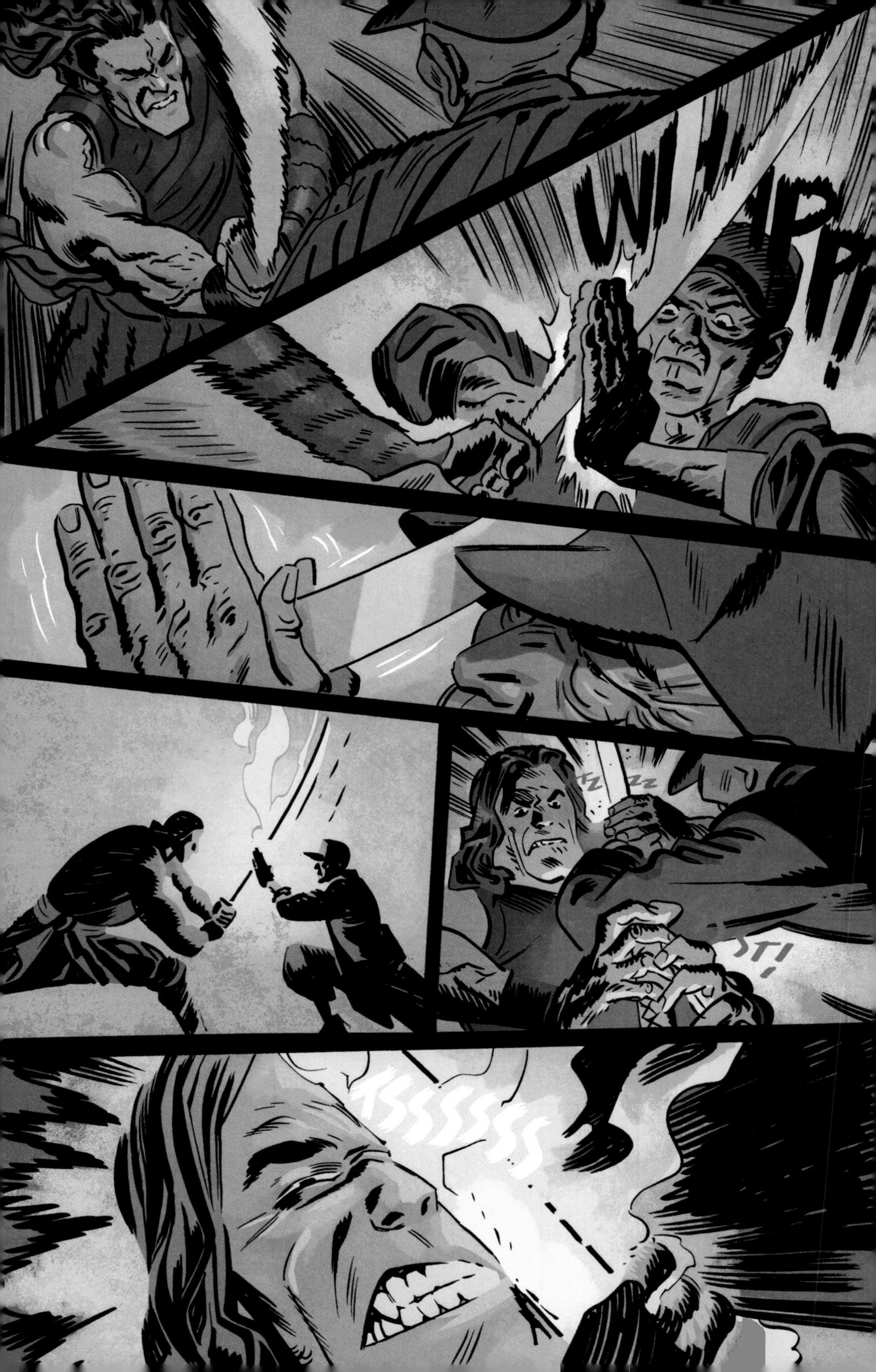

KSSSSSS

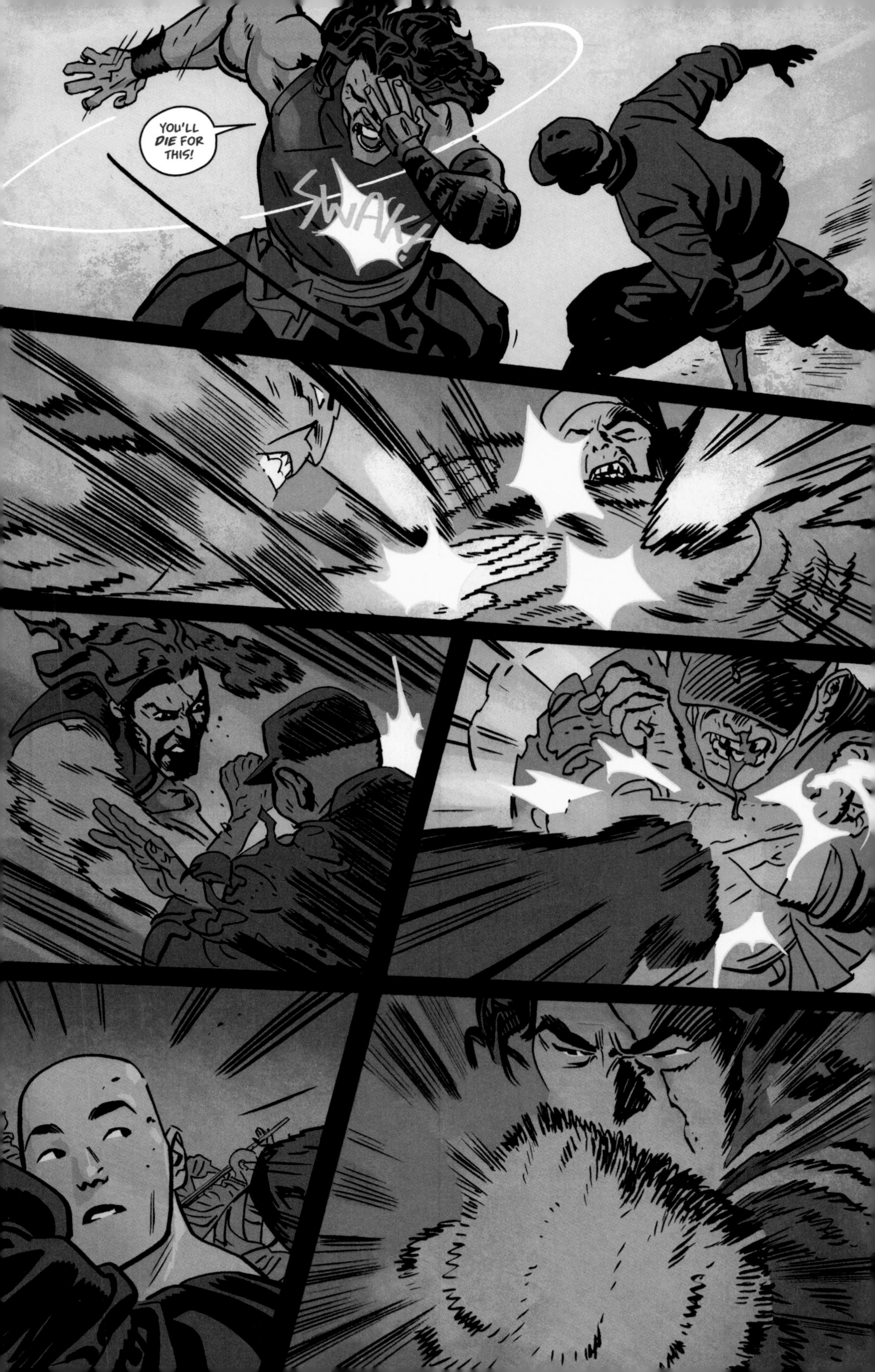
YOU'LL DIE FOR THIS!
SWAK!

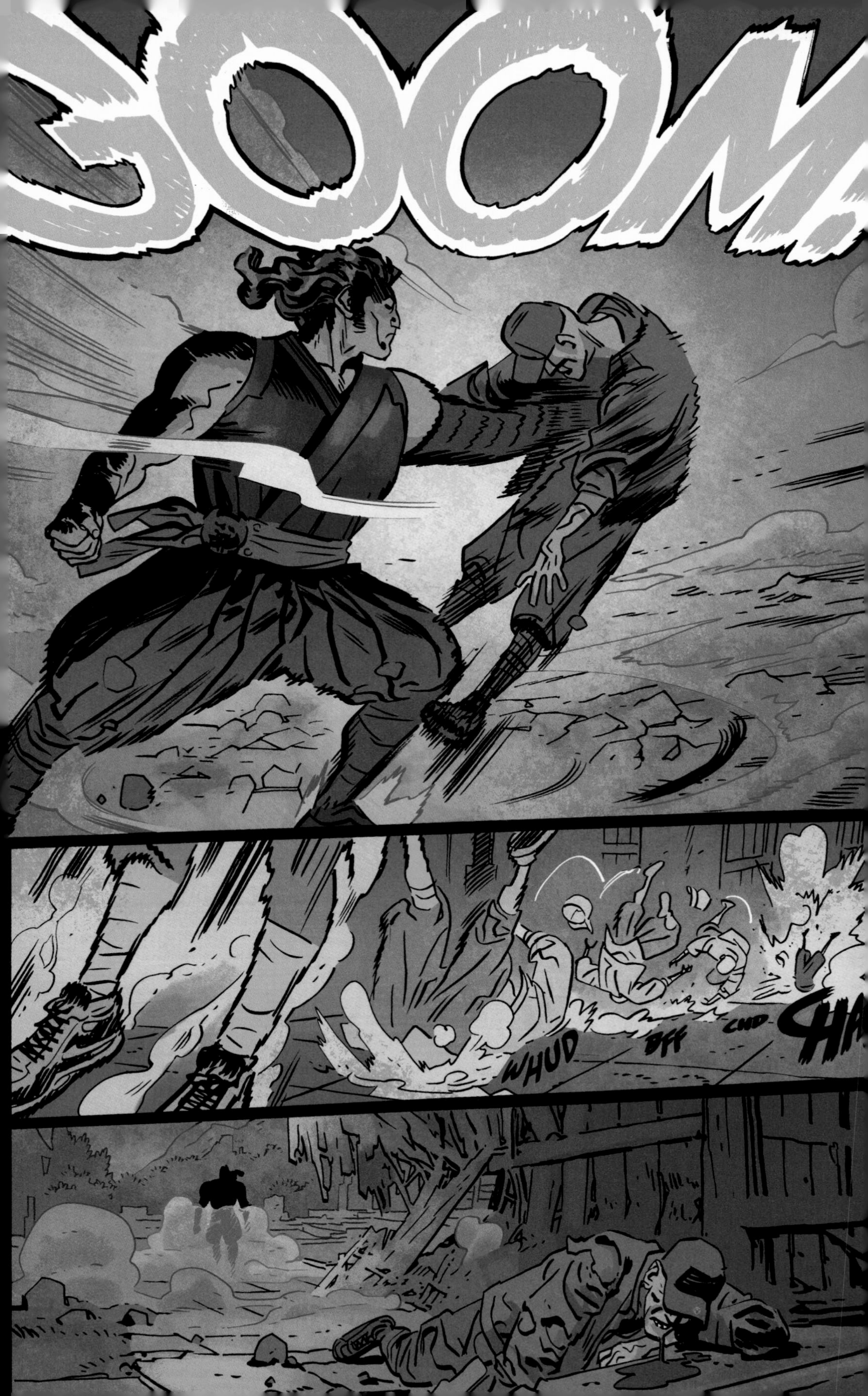
GOOM
WHUD
BFF
CHD
CHA

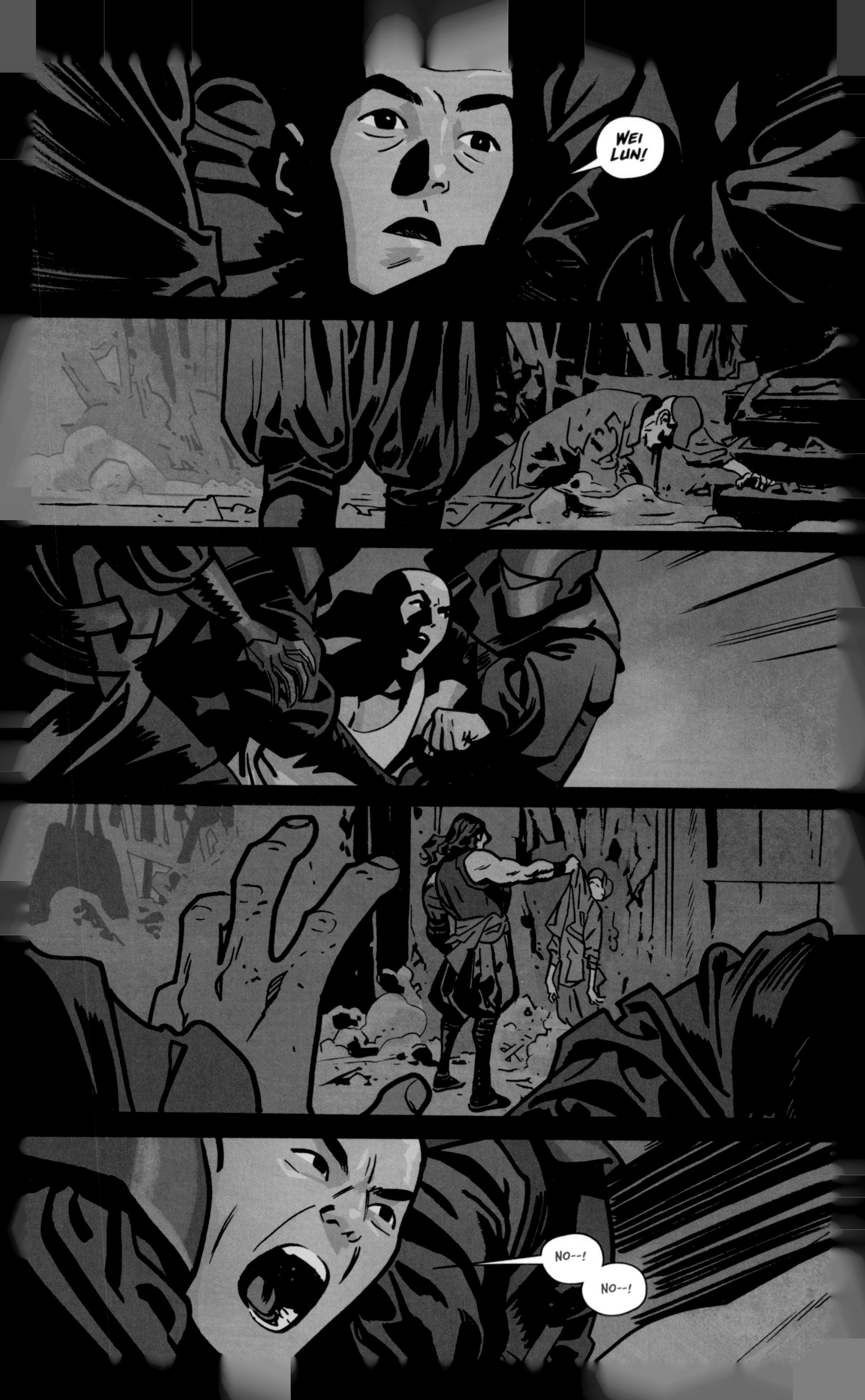
WEI LUN!
NO--!
NO--!

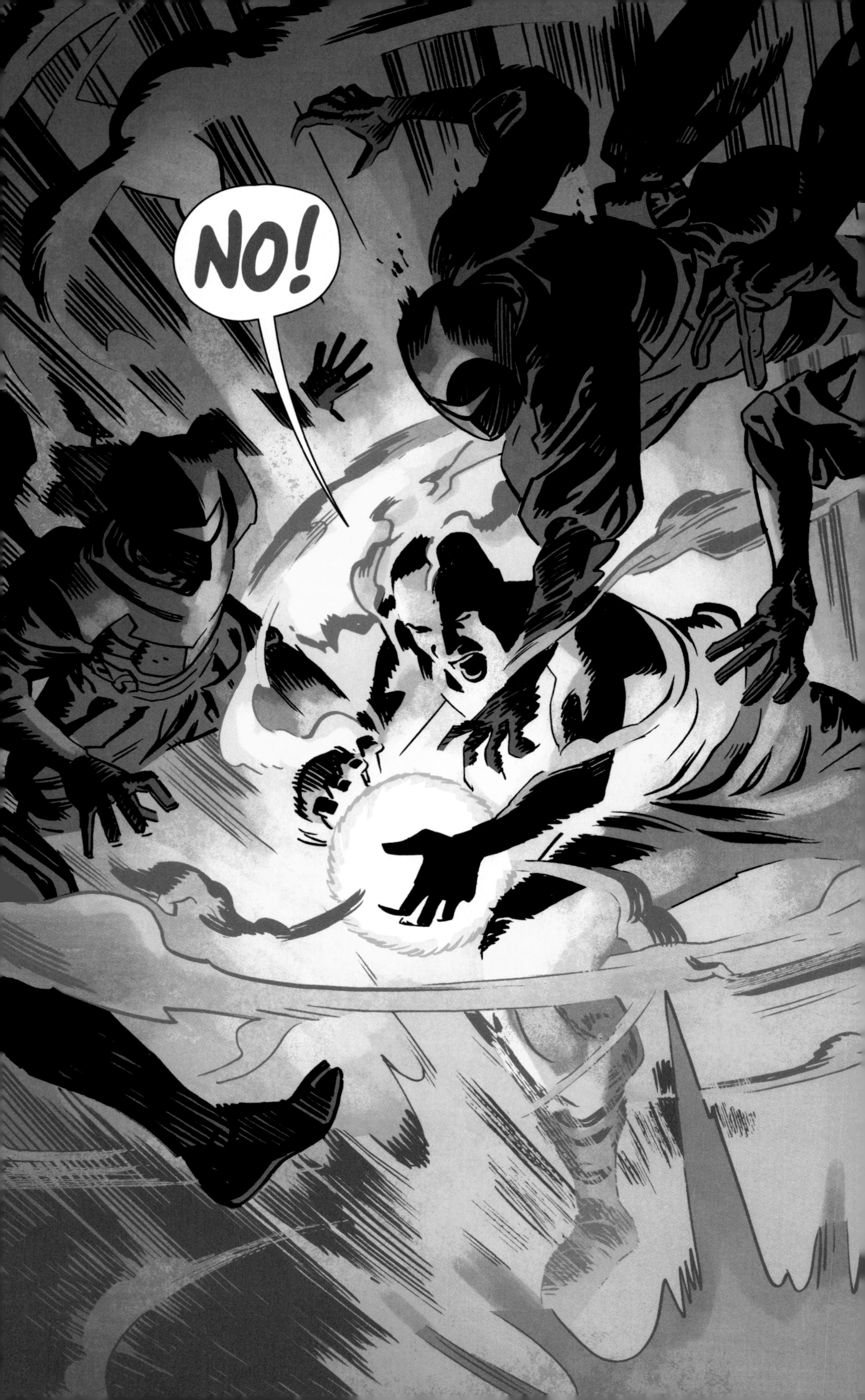
NO!

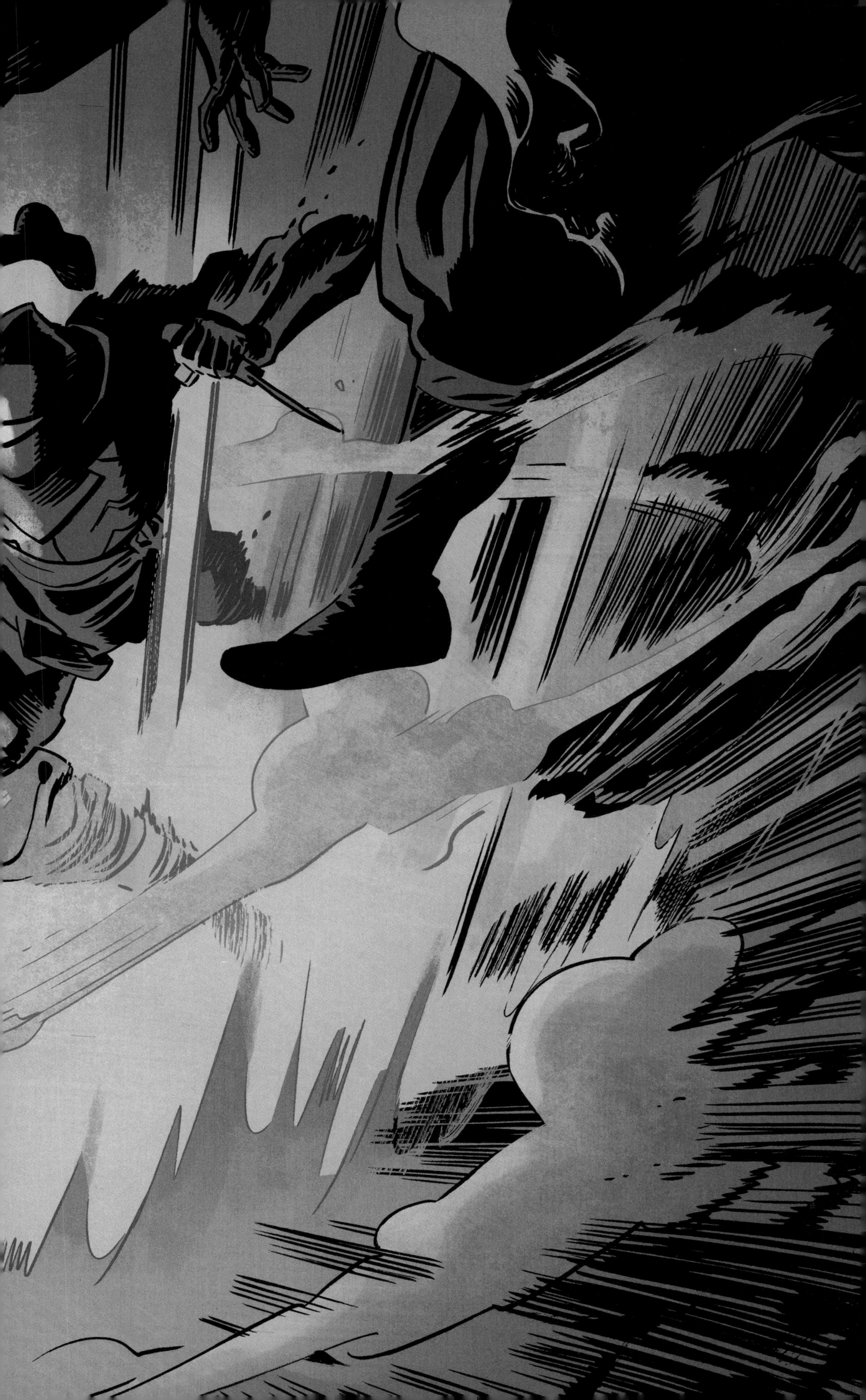

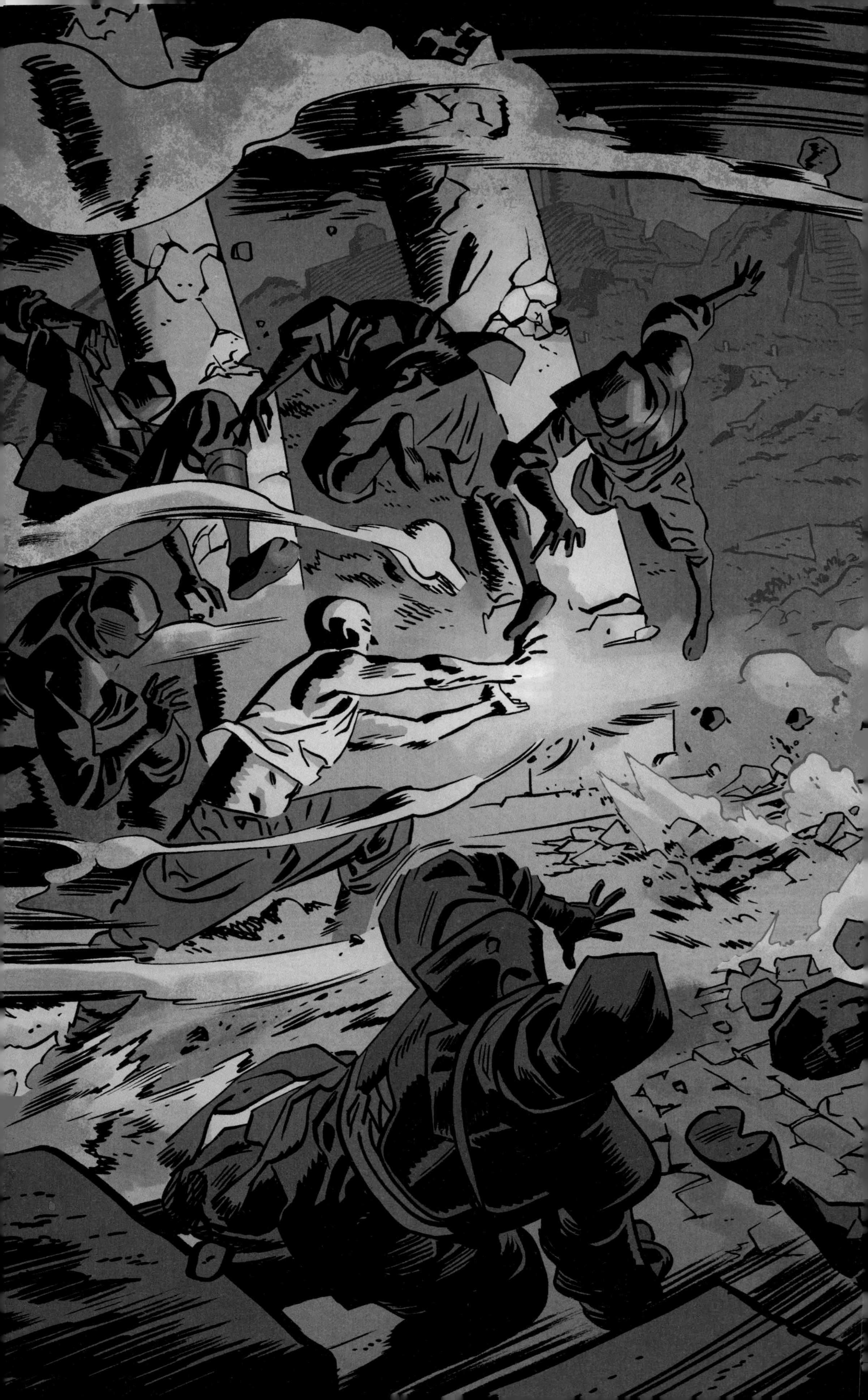

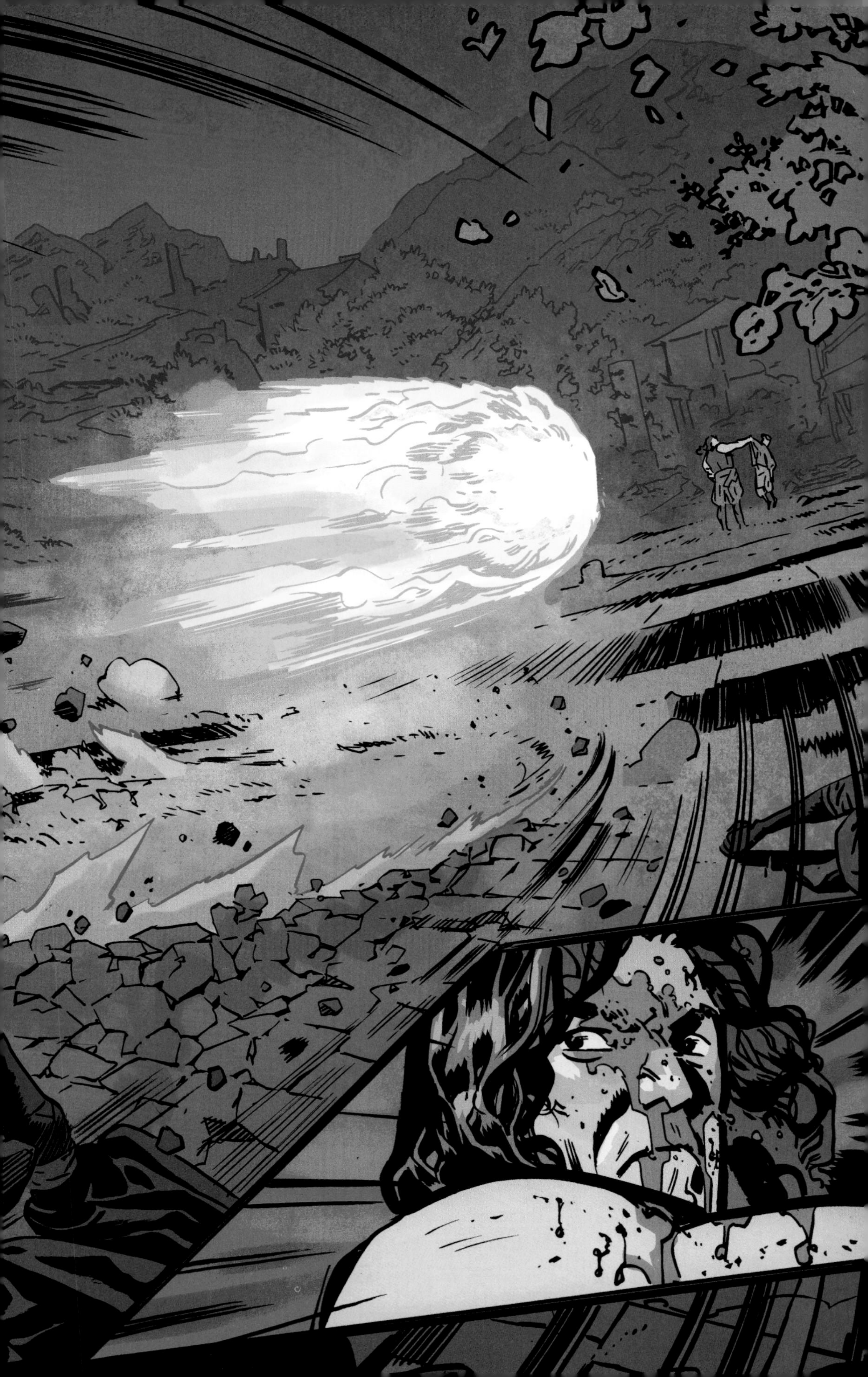

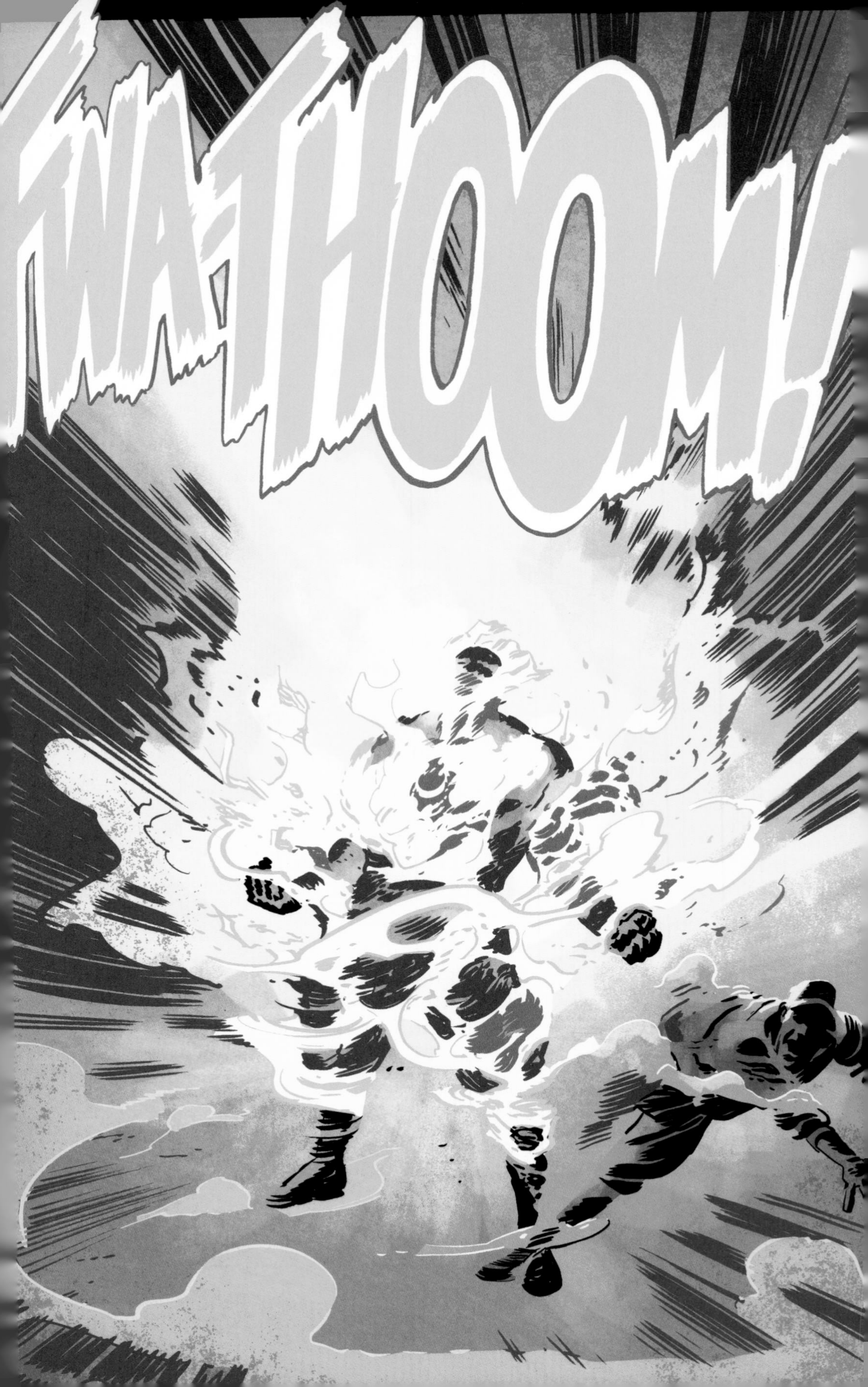

TWA-THOOM!

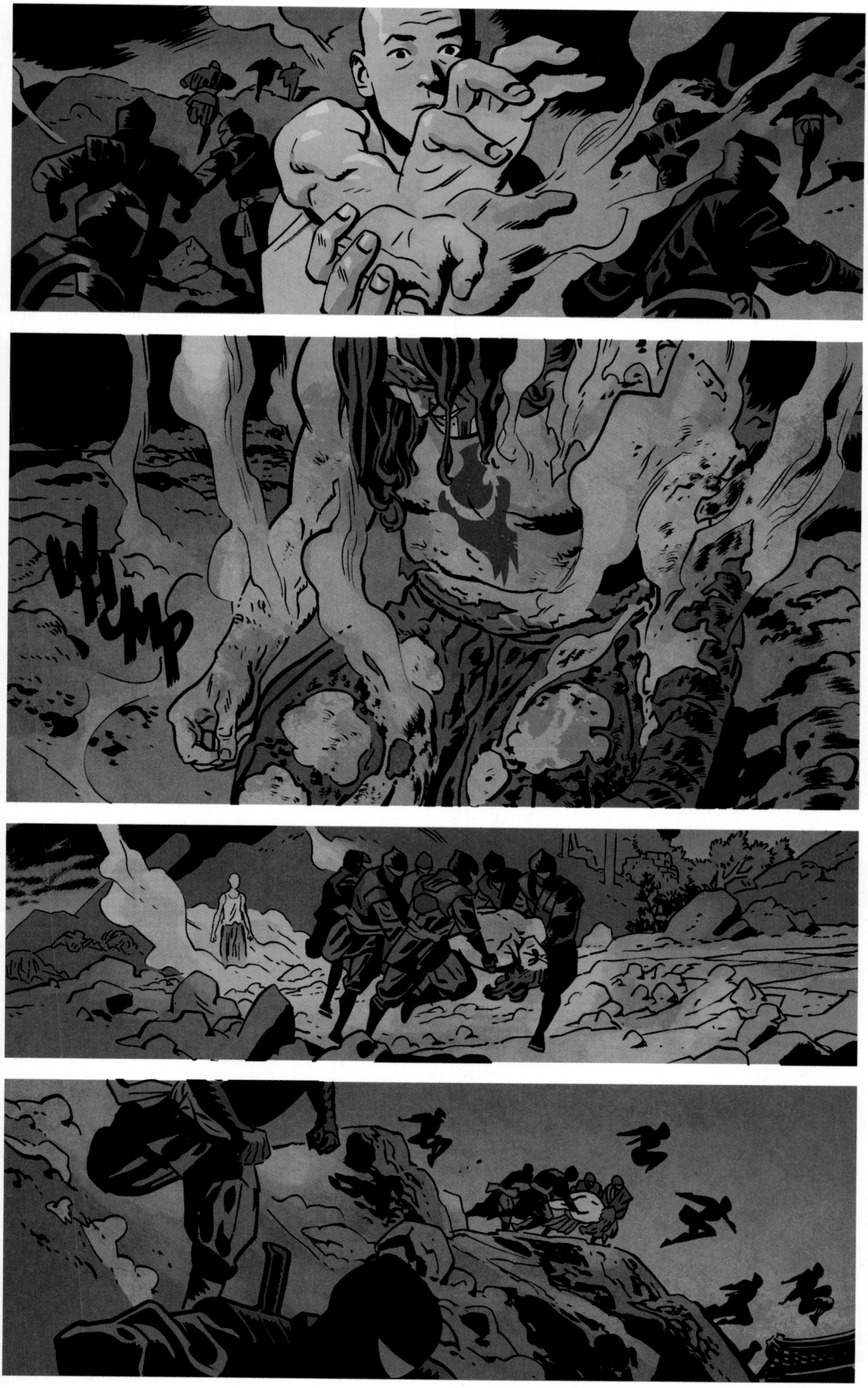
WHUMP

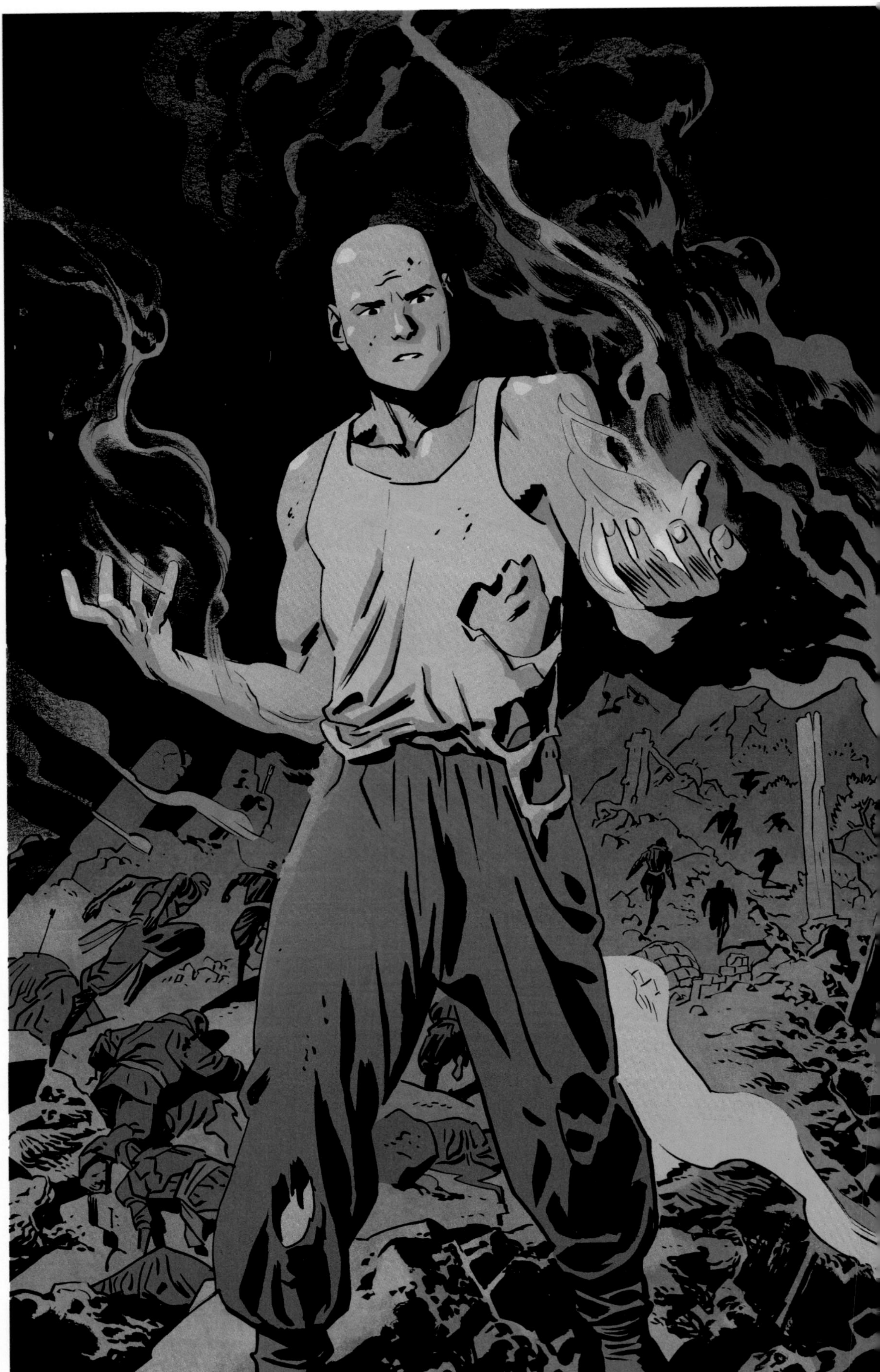

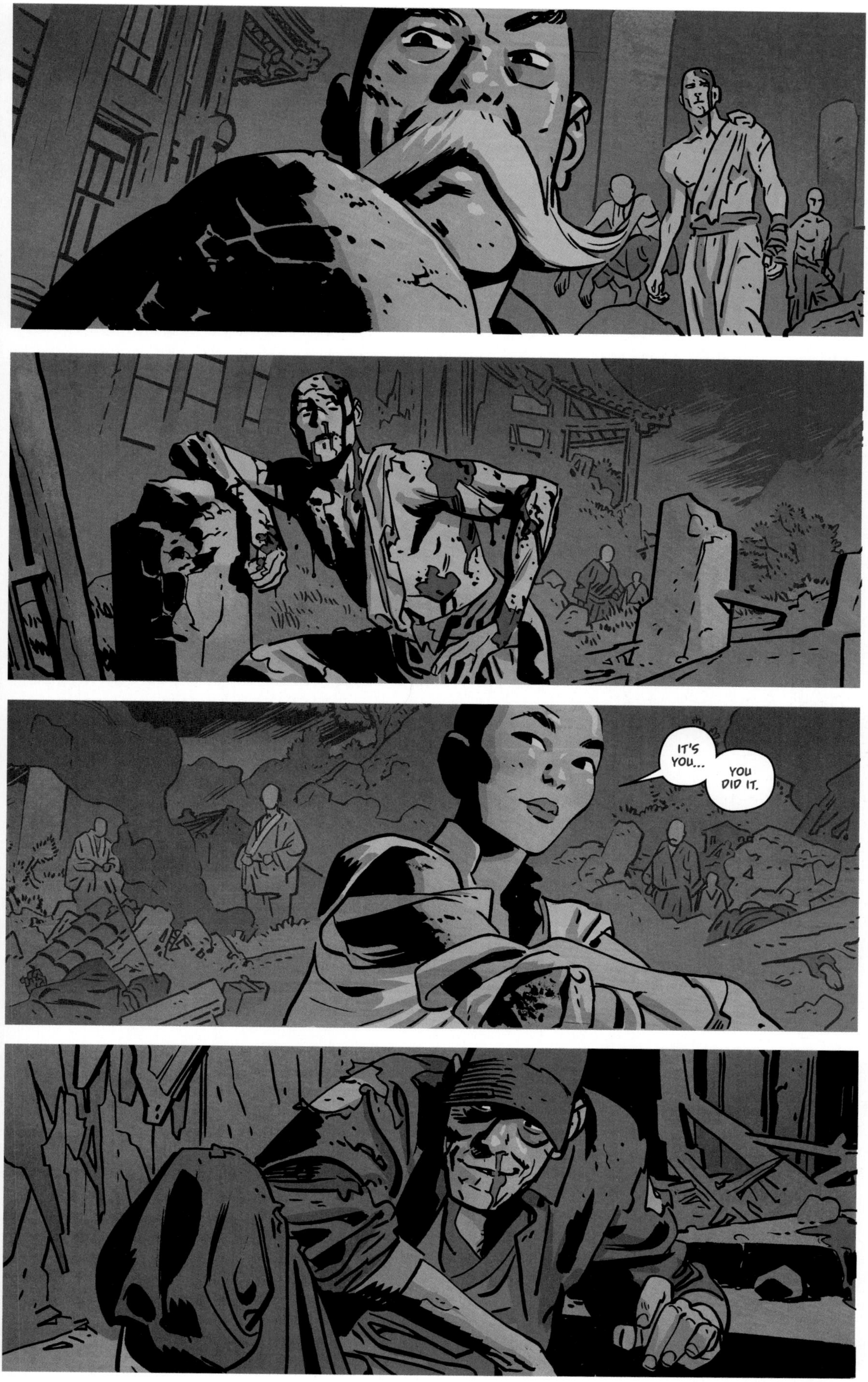
IT'S YOU...
YOU DID IT.

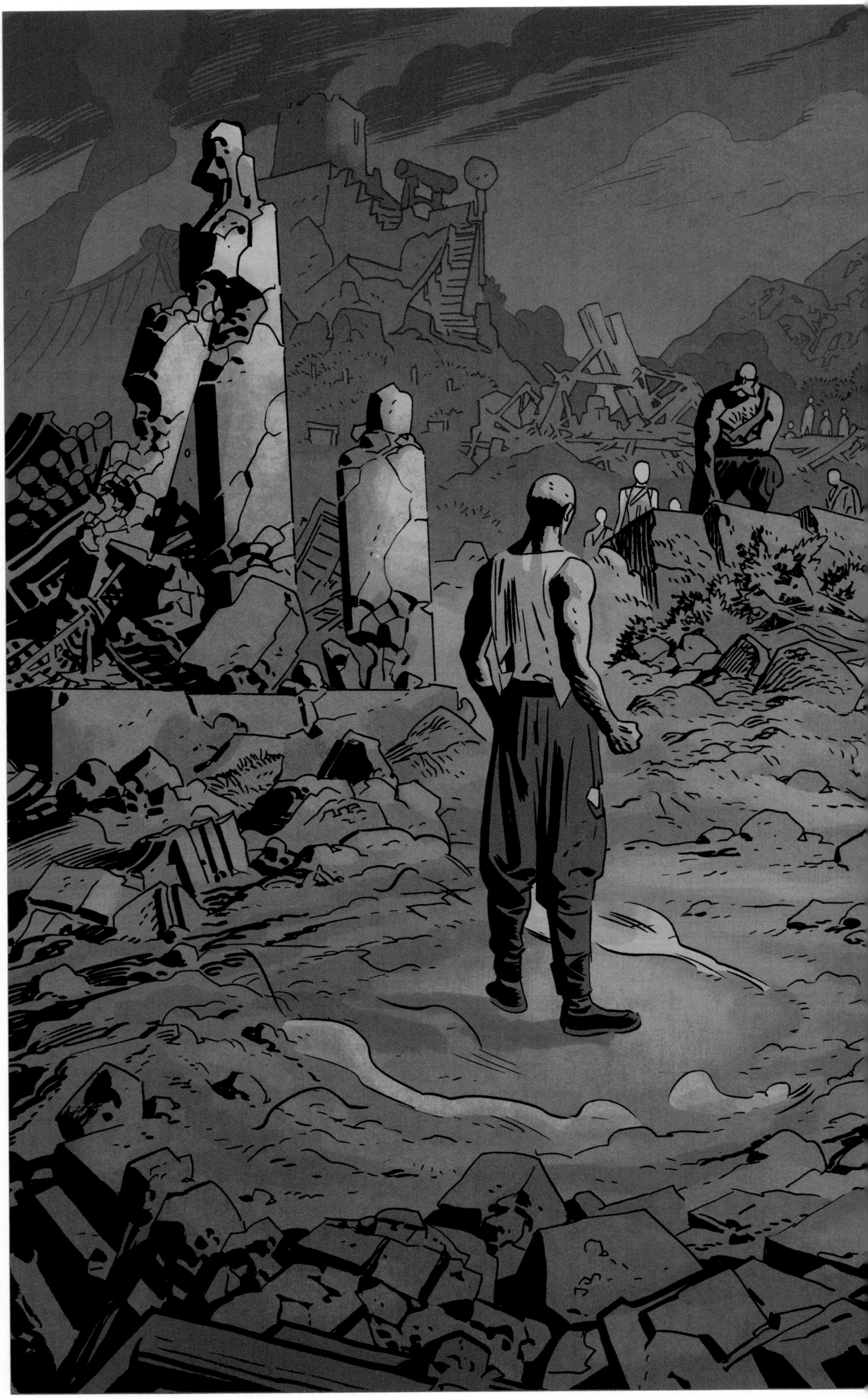

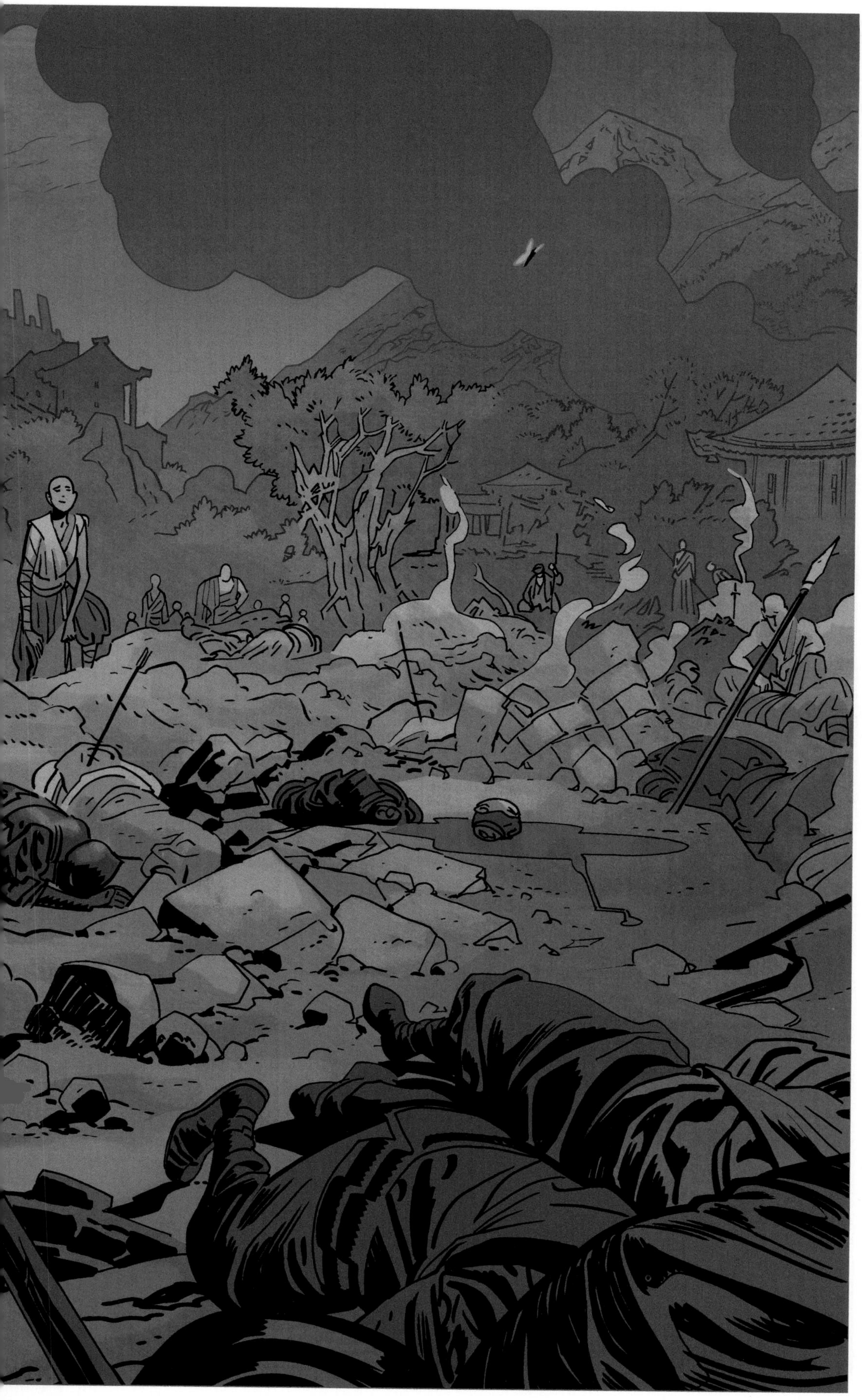

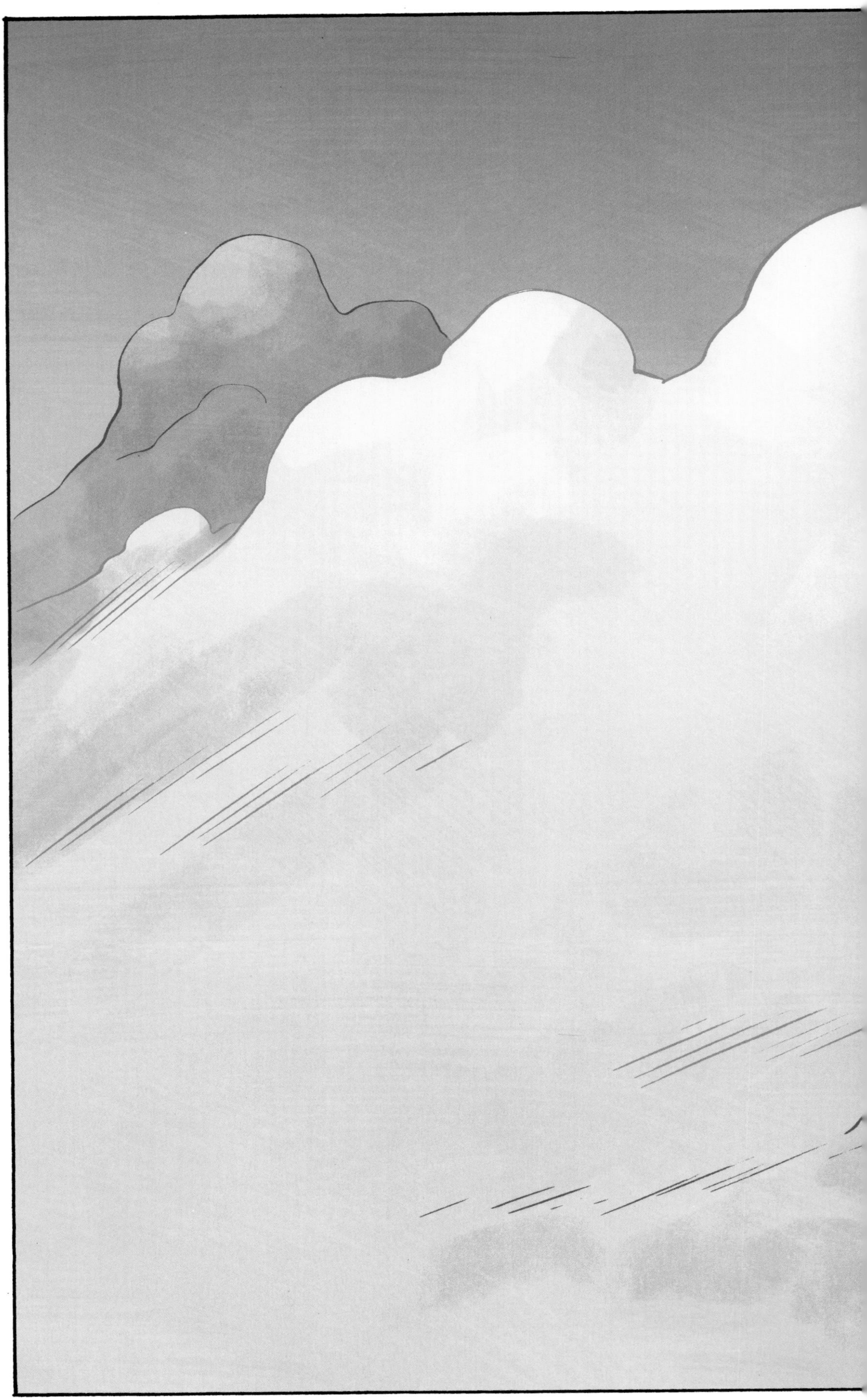

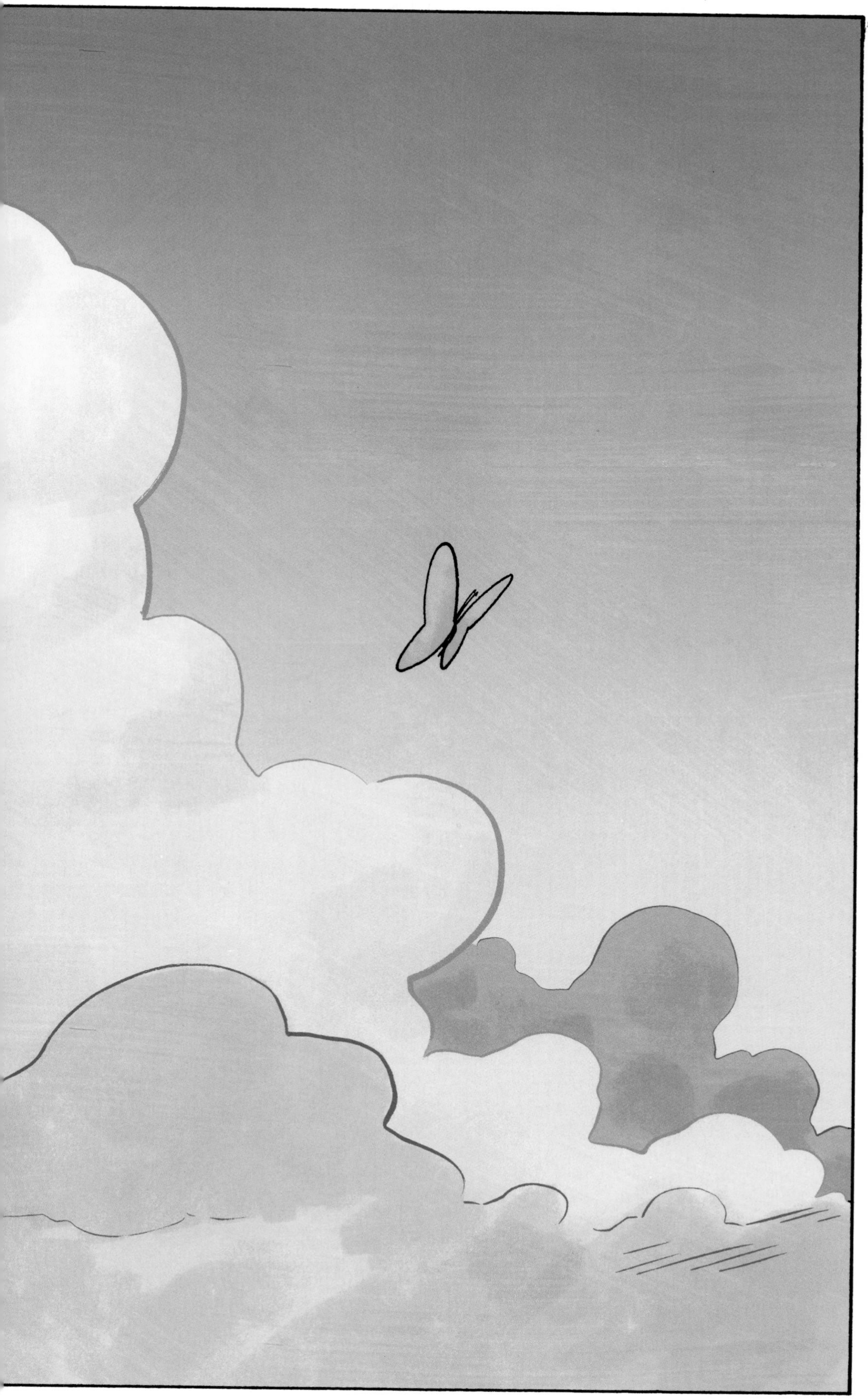

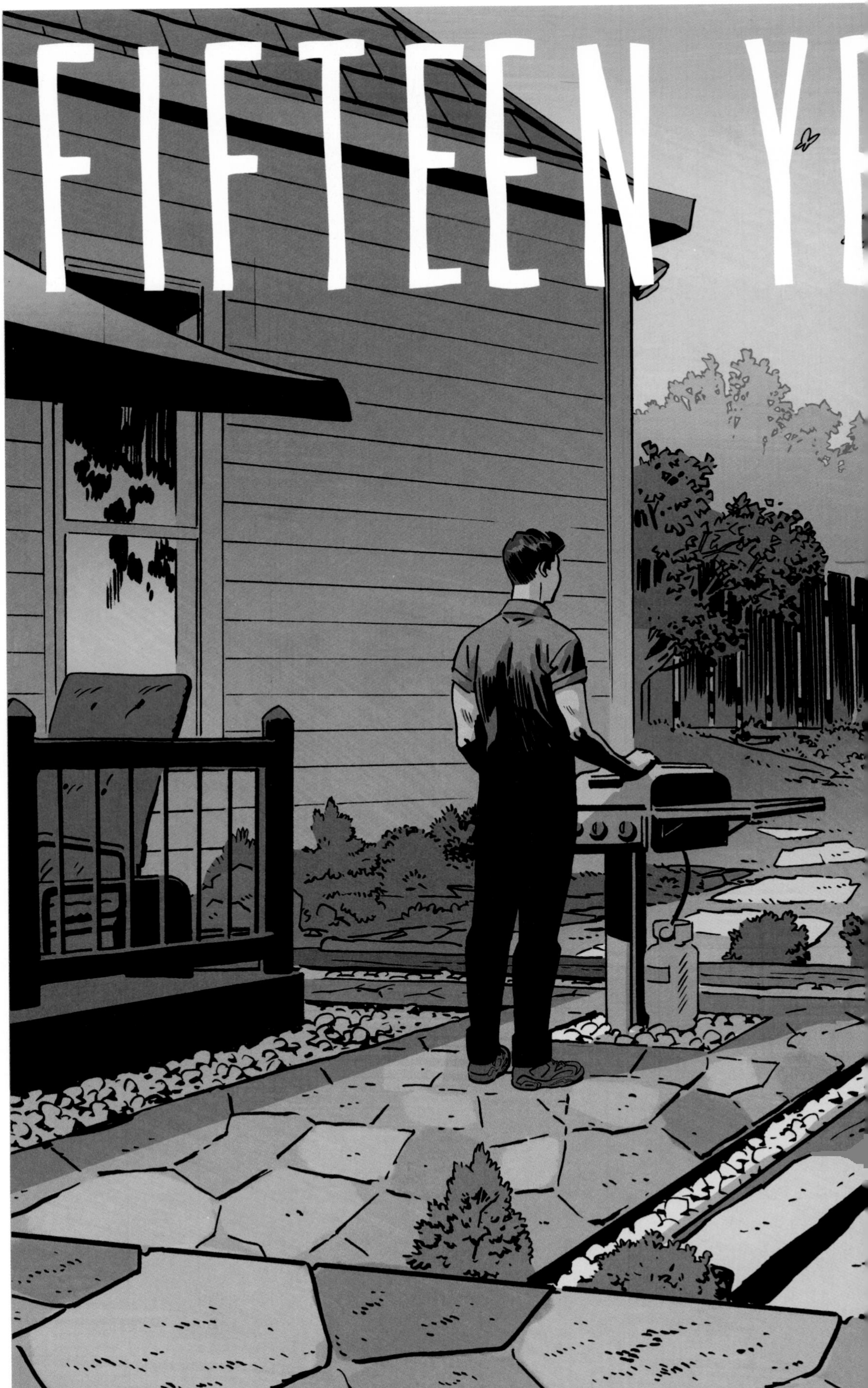
FIFTEEN YE

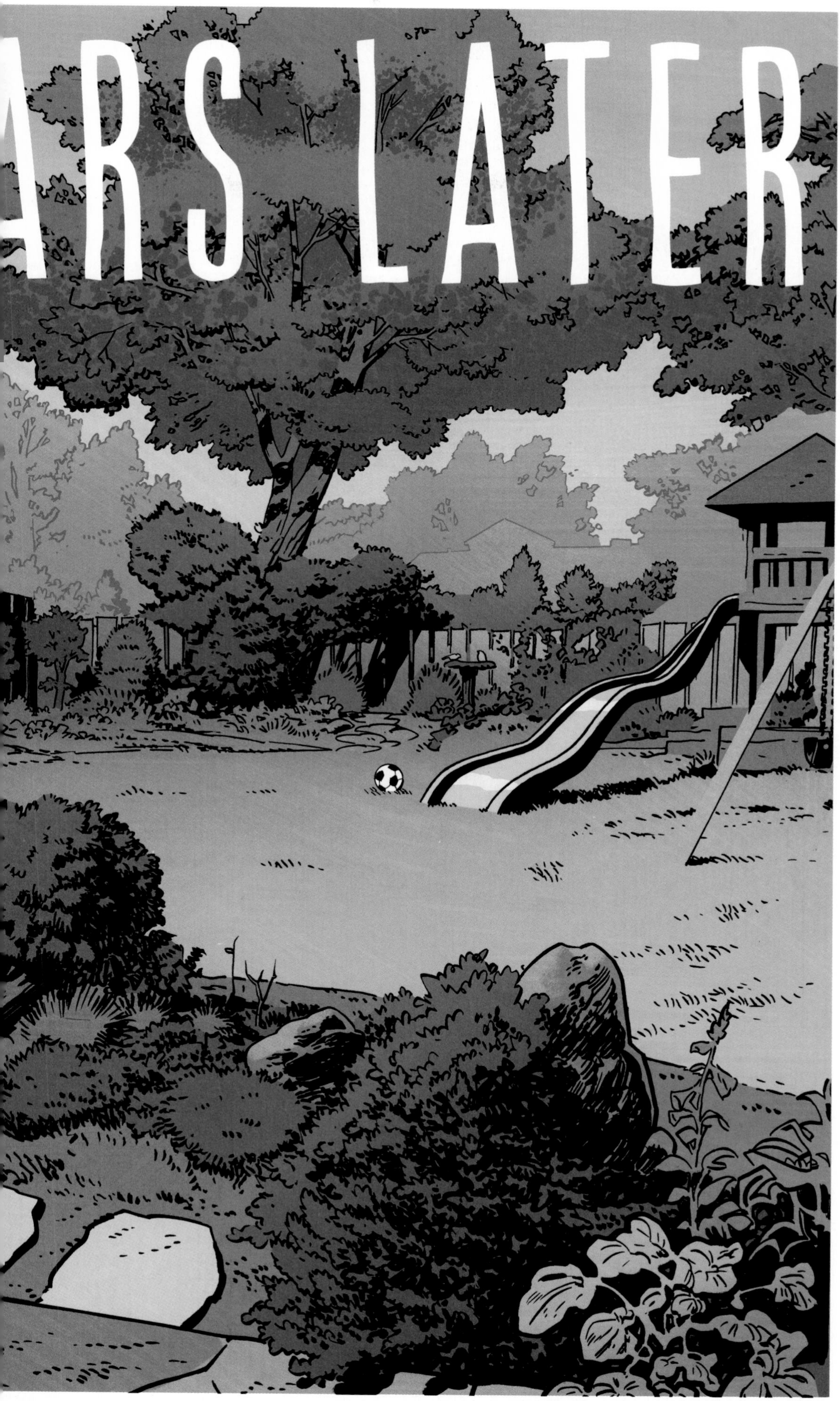
ARS LATER

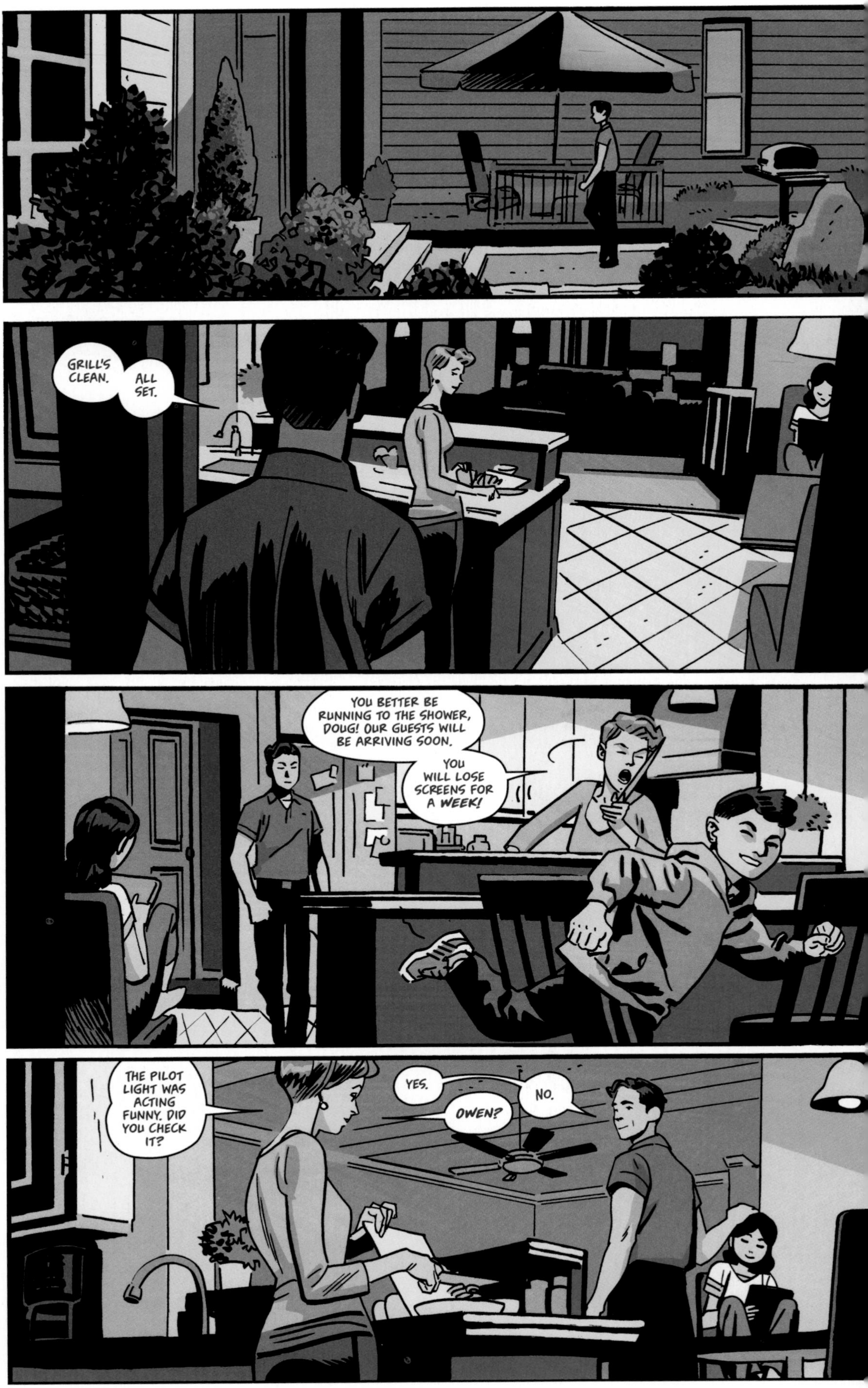
GRILL'S CLEAN.
ALL SET.
YOU BETTER BE RUNNING TO THE SHOWER, DOUG! OUR GUESTS WILL BE ARRIVING SOON.
YOU WILL LOSE SCREENS FOR A WEEK!
THE PILOT LIGHT WAS ACTING FUNNY. DID YOU CHECK IT?
YES.
NO.
OWEN?

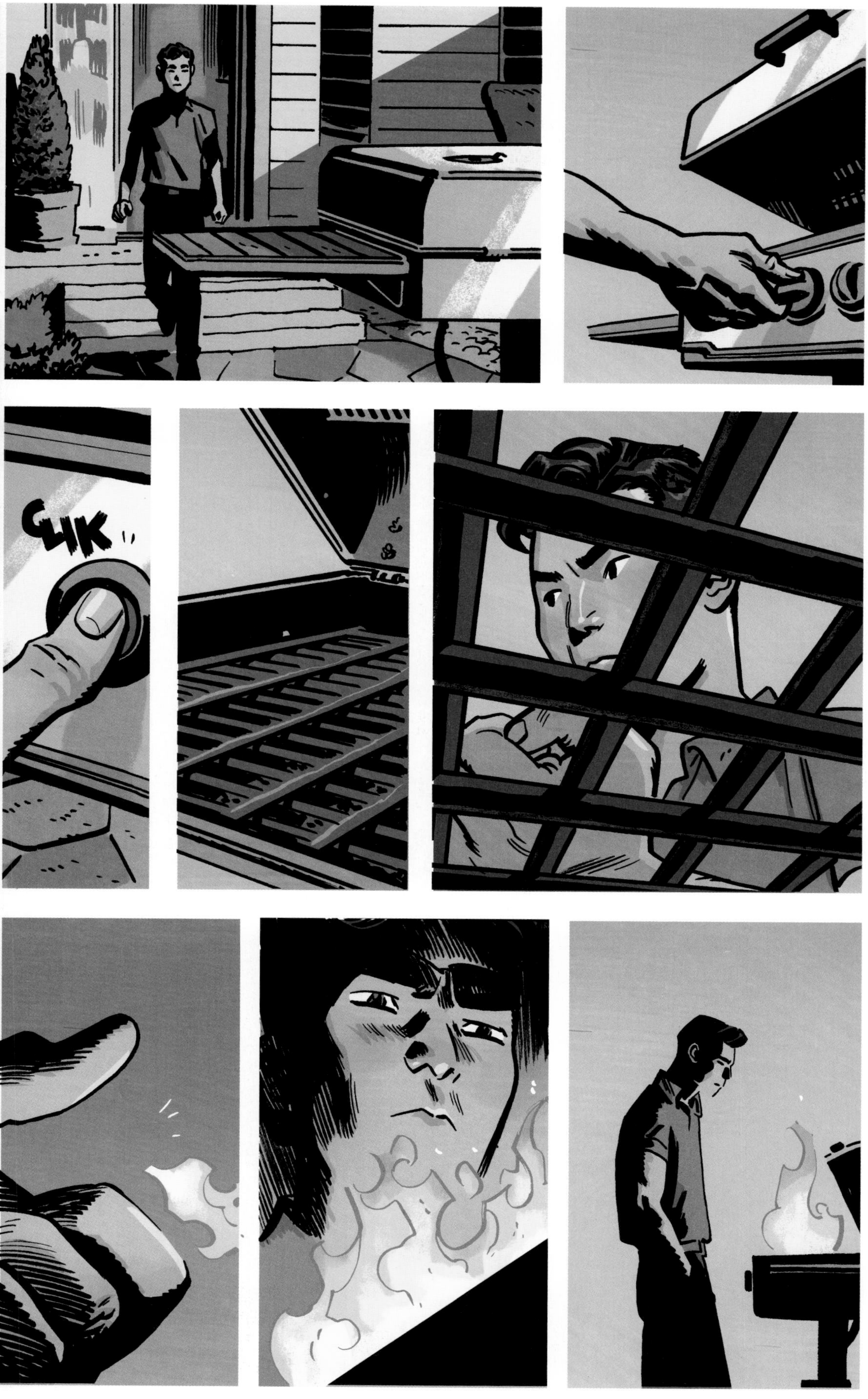
CLIK

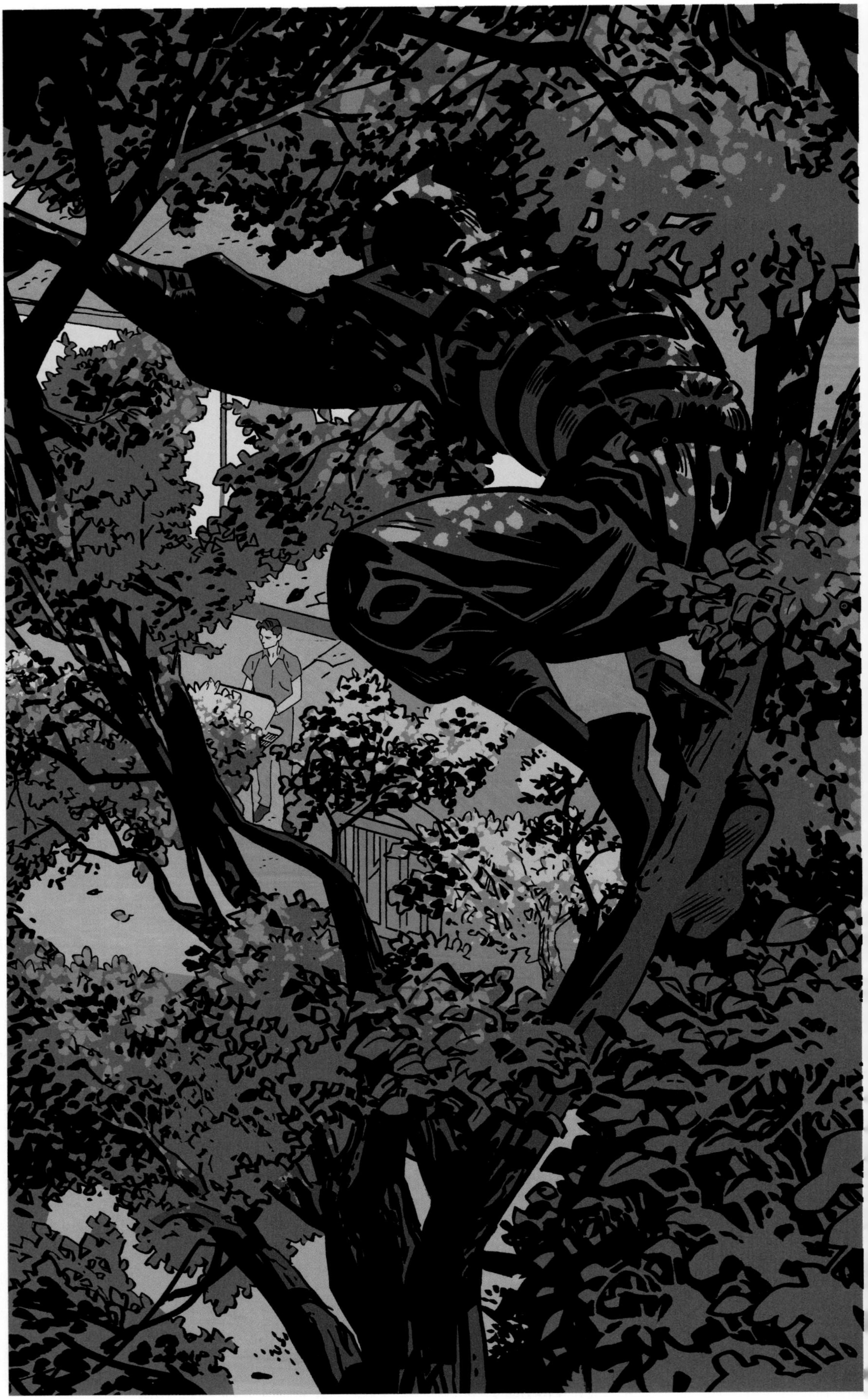

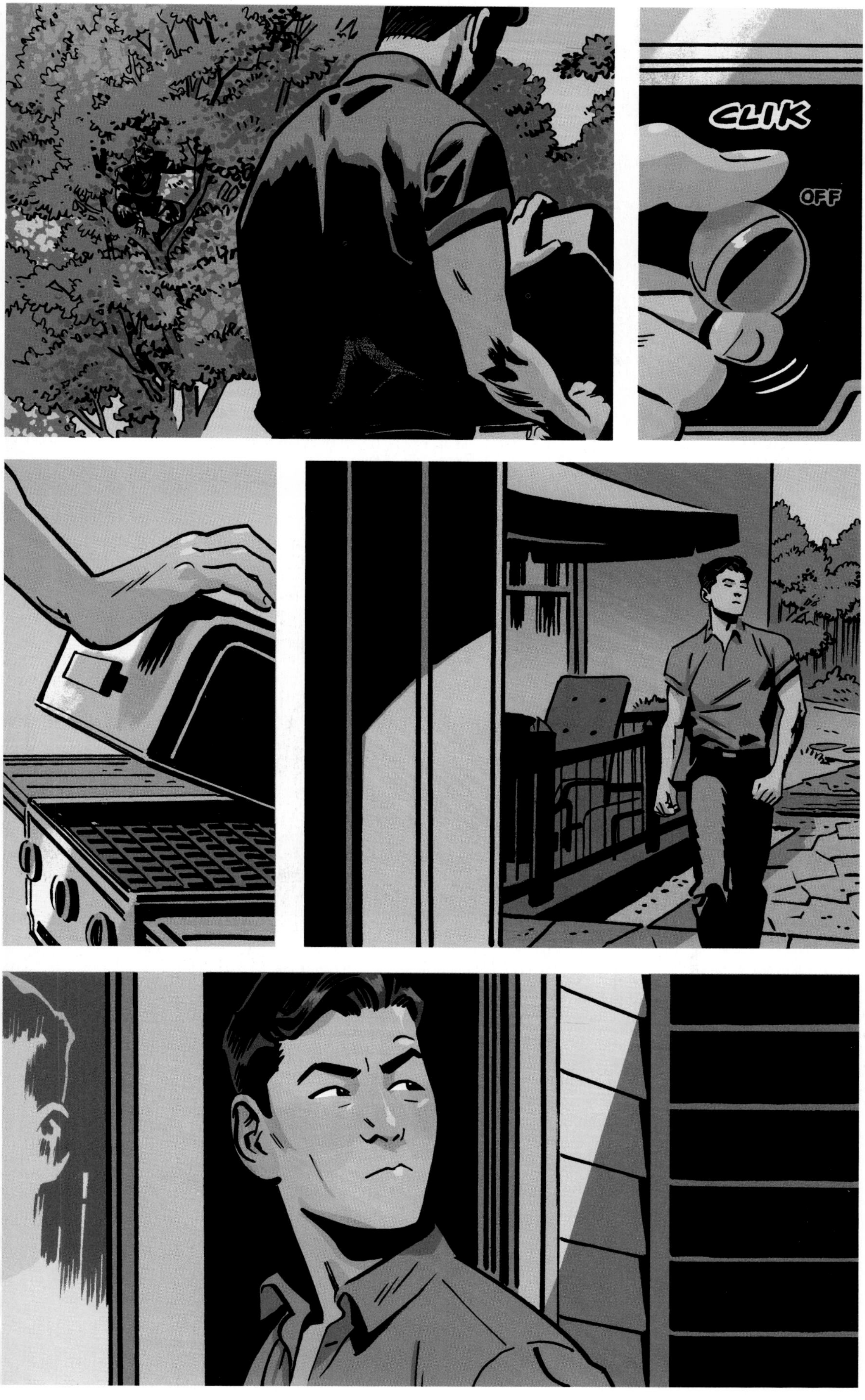
CLIK
OFF

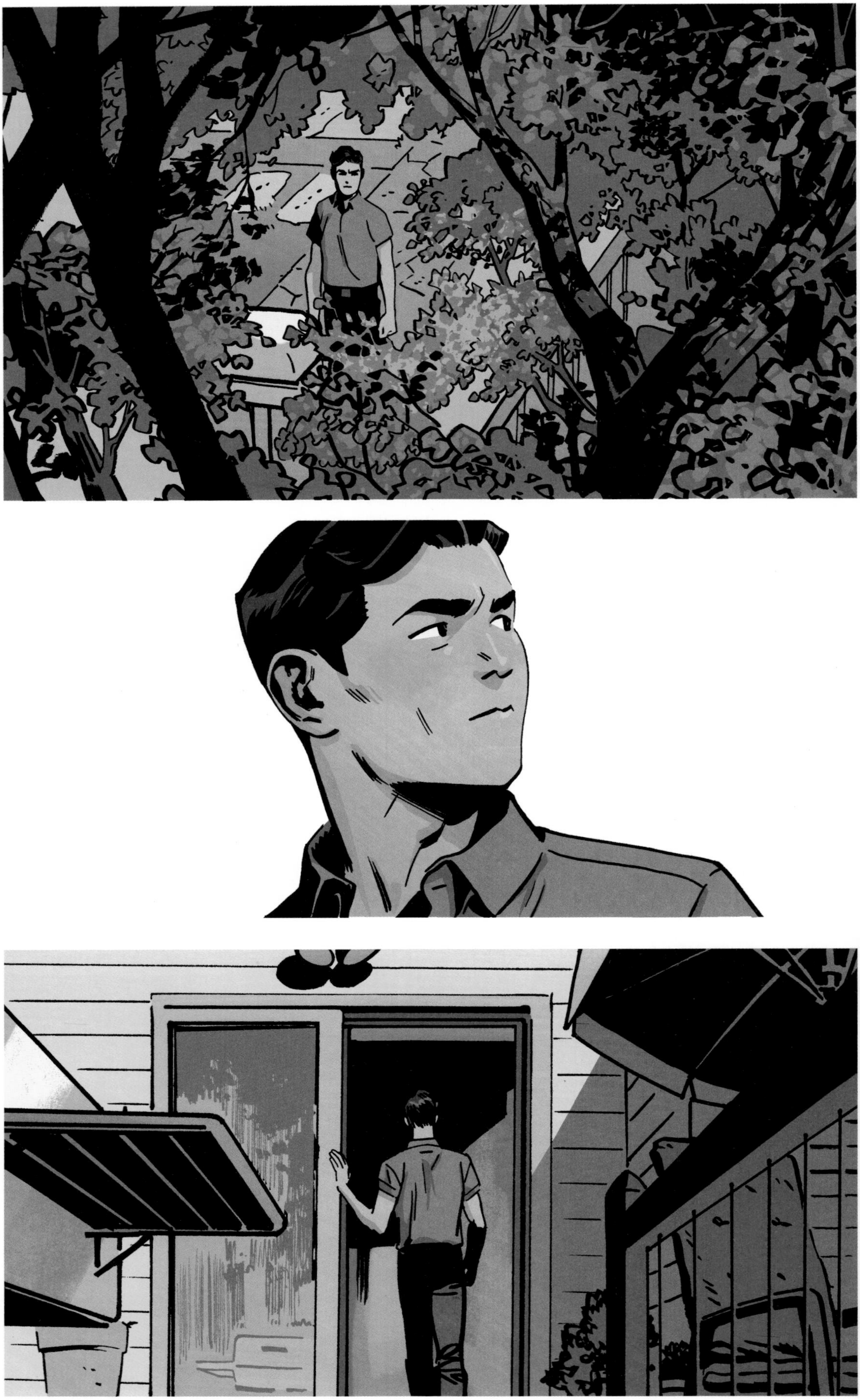

TO BE CONTINUED

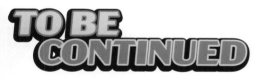

FOR MORE TALES FROM **ROBERT KIRKMAN** AND **SKYBOUND**

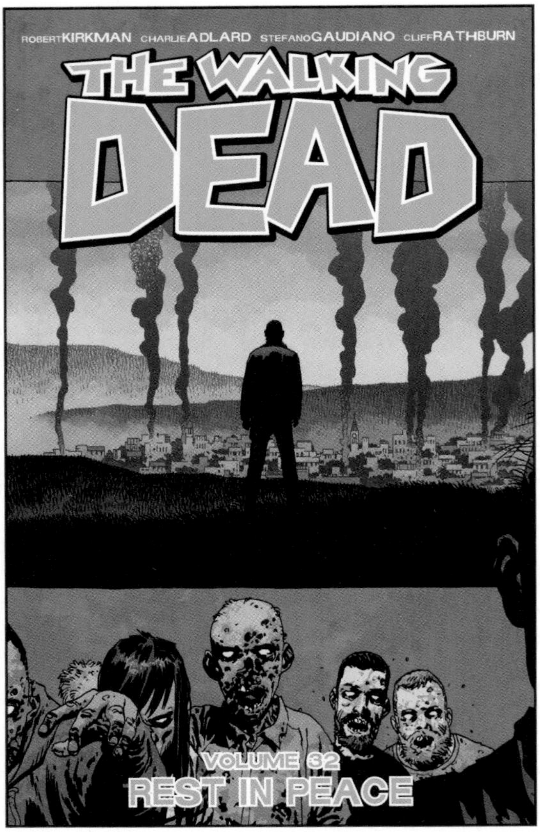
ROBERT KIRKMAN CHARLIE ADLARD STEFANO GAUDIANO CLIFF RATHBURN
THE WALKING DEAD
VOLUME 32
REST IN PEACE

VOL. 1: DAYS GONE BYE TP
ISBN: 978-1-58240-672-5
$14.99

VOL. 2: MILES BEHIND US TP
ISBN: 978-1-58240-775-3
$14.99

VOL. 3: SAFETY BEHIND BARS TP
ISBN: 978-1-58240-805-7
$14.99

VOL. 4: THE HEART'S DESIRE TP
ISBN: 978-1-58240-530-8
$14.99

VOL. 5: THE BEST DEFENSE TP
ISBN: 978-1-58240-612-1
$14.99

VOL. 6: THIS SORROWFUL LIFE TP
ISBN: 978-1-58240-684-8
$14.99

VOL. 7: THE CALM BEFORE TP
ISBN: 978-1-58240-828-6
$14.99

VOL. 8: MADE TO SUFFER TP
ISBN: 978-1-58240-883-5
$14.99

VOL. 9: HERE WE REMAIN TP
ISBN: 978-1-60706-022-2
$14.99

VOL. 10: WHAT WE BECOME TP
ISBN: 978-1-60706-075-8
$14.99

VOL. 11: FEAR THE HUNTERS TP
ISBN: 978-1-60706-181-6
$14.99

VOL. 12: LIFE AMONG THEM TP
ISBN: 978-1-60706-254-7
$14.99

VOL. 13: TOO FAR GONE TP
ISBN: 978-1-60706-329-2
$14.99

VOL. 14: NO WAY OUT TP
ISBN: 978-1-60706-392-6
$14.99

VOL. 15: WE FIND OURSELVES TP
ISBN: 978-1-60706-440-4
$14.99

VOL. 16: A LARGER WORLD TP
ISBN: 978-1-60706-559-3
$14.99

VOL. 17: SOMETHING TO FEAR TP
ISBN: 978-1-60706-615-6
$14.99

VOL. 18: WHAT COMES AFTER TP
ISBN: 978-1-60706-687-3
$14.99

VOL. 19: MARCH TO WAR TP
ISBN: 978-1-60706-818-1
$14.99

VOL. 20: ALL OUT WAR PART ONE TP
ISBN: 978-1-60706-882-2
$14.99

VOL. 21: ALL OUT WAR PART TWO TP
ISBN: 978-1-63215-030-1
$14.99

VOL. 22: A NEW BEGINNING TP
ISBN: 978-1-63215-041-7
$14.99

VOL. 23: WHISPERS INTO SCREAMS TP
ISBN: 978-1-63215-258-9
$14.99

VOL. 24: LIFE AND DEATH TP
ISBN: 978-1-63215-402-6
$14.99

VOL. 25: NO TURNING BACK TP
ISBN: 978-1-63215-659-4
$14.99

VOL. 26: CALL TO ARMS TP
ISBN: 978-1-63215-917-5
$14.99

VOL. 27: THE WHISPERER WAR TP
ISBN: 978-1-5343-0052-1
$14.99

VOL. 28: A CERTAIN DOOM TP
ISBN: 978-1-5343-0244-0
$14.99

VOL. 29: LINES WE CROSS TP
ISBN: 978-1-5343-0497-0
$16.99

VOL. 30: NEW WORLD ORDER TP
ISBN: 978-1-5343-0884-8
$16.99

VOL. 31: THE ROTTEN CORE TP
ISBN: 978-1-5343-1052-0
$16.99

VOL. 32: REST IN PEACE TP
ISBN: 978-1-5343-1241-8
$16.99

BOOK ONE HC
ISBN: 978-1-58240-619-0
$34.99

BOOK TWO HC
ISBN: 978-1-58240-698-5
$34.99

BOOK THREE HC
ISBN: 978-1-58240-825-5
$34.99

BOOK FOUR HC
ISBN: 978-1-60706-000-0
$34.99

BOOK FIVE HC
ISBN: 978-1-60706-171-7
$34.99

BOOK SIX HC
ISBN: 978-1-60706-327-8
$34.99

BOOK SEVEN HC
ISBN: 978-1-60706-439-8
$34.99

BOOK EIGHT HC
ISBN: 978-1-60706-593-7
$34.99

BOOK NINE HC
ISBN: 978-1-60706-798-6
$34.99

BOOK TEN HC
ISBN: 978-1-63215-034-9
$34.99

BOOK ELEVEN HC
ISBN: 978-1-63215-271-8
$34.99

BOOK TWELVE HC
ISBN: 978-1-63215-451-4
$34.99

BOOK THIRTEEN HC
ISBN: 978-1-63215-916-8
$34.99

BOOK FOURTEEN HC
ISBN: 978-1-5343-0329-4
$34.99

BOOK FIFTEEN HC
ISBN: 978-1-5343-0850-3
$34.99

BOOK SIXTEEN HC
ISBN: 978-1-5343-1325-5
$34.99

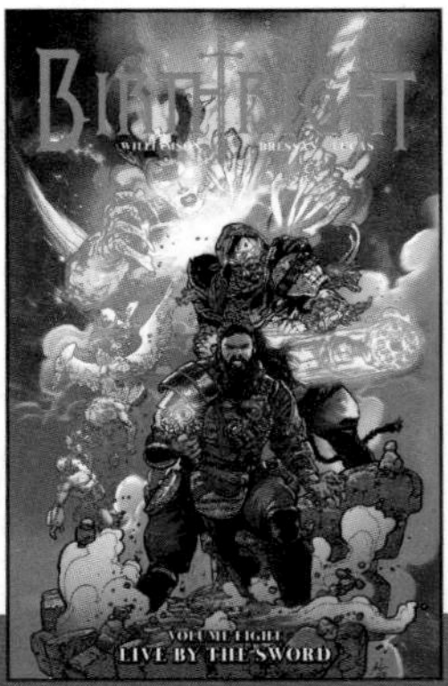
VOLUME EIGHT
LIVE BY THE SWORD

VOL. 1: HOMECOMING
ISBN: 978-1-63215-231-2
$9.99

VOL. 2: CALL TO ADVENTURE
ISBN: 978-1-63215-446-0
$12.99

VOL. 3: ALLIES AND ENEMIES
ISBN: 978-1-63215-683-9
$12.99

VOL. 4: FAMILY HISTORY
ISBN: 978-1-63215-871-0
$12.99

VOL. 5: BELLY OF THE BEAST
ISBN: 978-1-5343-0218-1
$12.99

VOL. 6: FATHERHOOD
ISBN: 978-1-53430-498-7
$14.99

VOL. 7: BLOOD BROTHERS
ISBN: 978-1-5343-1053-7
$14.99

VOL. 8: LIVE BY THE SWORD
ISBN: 978-1-5343-1368-2
$14.99

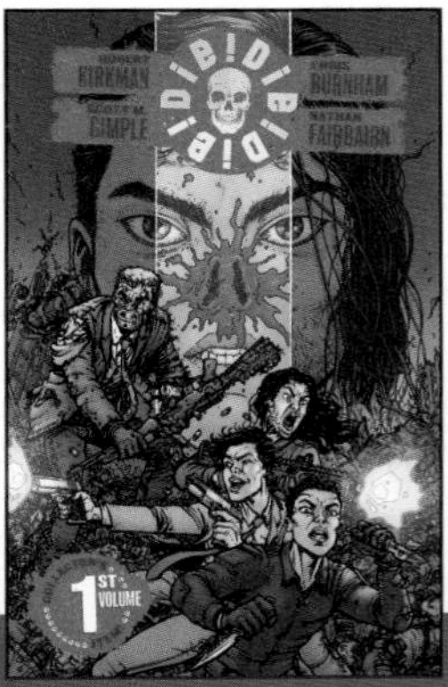
1ST VOLUME

VOL. 1
ISBN: 978-1-5343-1214-2
$19.99

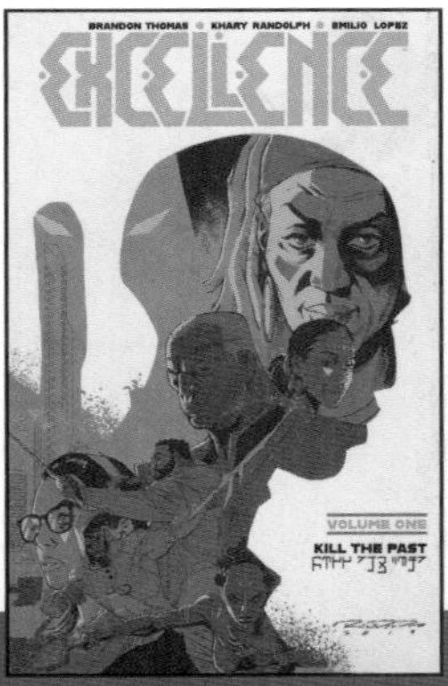
BRANDON THOMAS • KHARY RANDOLPH • EMILIO LOPEZ
EXCELLENCE
VOLUME ONE
KILL THE PAST

VOL. 1: KILL THE PAST
ISBN: 978-1-5343-1362-0
$16.99

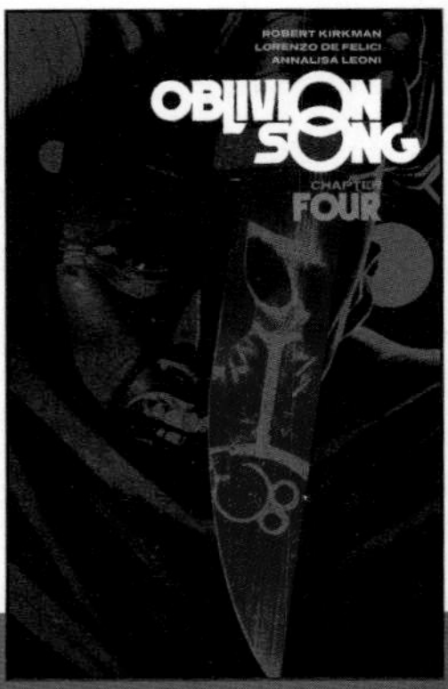
ROBERT KIRKMAN
LORENZO DE FELICI
ANNALISA LEONI
OBLIVION SONG
CHAPTER FOUR

CHAPTER ONE
ISBN: 978-1-5343-0642-4
$9.99

CHAPTER TWO
ISBN: 978-1-5343-1057-5
$16.99

CHAPTER THREE
ISBN: 978-1-5343-1326-2
$16.99

CHAPTER FOUR
ISBN: 978-1-5343-1517-4
$16.99